THE WINNING EDGE

THE WINNING EDGE

Maximizing Success in College

David E. Schmitt

Northeastern University

 HarperCollins*Publishers*

Photo Credits

Page 7, Kolvoord, TexaStock; 11, © 1989, Wachter, Focus on Sports; 15, © 1983, Siteman, Stock, Boston; 38, © Crews, Stock, Boston; 149, © 1983, Siteman, The Picture Cube; 198, Barnes, Stock, Boston.

Sponsoring Editor: Anne Harvey
Project Editor: Ellen MacElree
Design Supervisor: Mary Archondes
Cover Design: Zina Scarpulla
Photo Researcher: Mira Schachne
Production Manager/Assistant: Willie Lane/Sunaina Sehwani
Compositor: BookMasters, Inc.
Printer and Binder: R. R. Donnelley & Sons Company
Cover Printer: New England Book Components

The Winning Edge: Maximizing Success in College

Library of Congress Cataloging-in-Publication Data

Schmitt, David E.
    The winning edge : maximizing success in college / David E. Schmitt.
        p.   cm.
    Includes bibliographical references (p.) and index.
    ISBN 0-673-38825-5
    1. Study, Method of.   2. Reading (Higher Education)   3. College student orientation.   4. College students—Time management
    I. Title.
    LB2395.S363   1992
    378.1'71—dc20

91-15157
CIP

91 92 93 94 9 8 7 6 5 4 3 2 1

To Joan, with love

Contents

Preface

Several things inspired me to write this book. First, I've personally derived great benefit from reading and study skill techniques. An average student until nearly my senior year in high school, I took a short reading and study skills course and improved my grades to almost straight "A's" within a year. In college I read some of the literature on the subject, took another short course, and continued to achieve success in my courses. In undergraduate and graduate school, I began the process of modifying basic techniques and integrating a wide variety of ideas from other fields.

Second, as a manager, scholar, and a teacher of management techniques in public administration, I've been struck by the practical applicability of management success tactics to my own scholarship and the academic and personal success of my students. Over the years I've continued to read both the scholarly and practical literature in management and to develop and refine techniques of personal management and decision skills as they apply to productive scholarship, sharing them with my students whenever possible.

Third, having taught hundreds of full-time and part-time students over the past twenty years, I've been concerned that the great majority of college students lack basic skills in many areas needed for effective and efficient academic performance. Even the best students typically have much to learn about practical techniques and strategies of learning. In my classes I often discuss thinking along with study and writing skills, and have worked individually with many students. Given the pervasive lack of these abilities and having had to explain these techniques so often, I frequently considered sharing these ideas with a wider audience. Receipt of a Northeastern University Excellence in Teaching award in 1987 prompted me finally to write this book.

Fourth, I've been impressed by the need for a textbook that thoroughly covers such areas as thinking skills, practical research and writing techniques, values, personal success techniques, and other critical topics while at the same time inspiring students to try to achieve their own potentials. Although straightforward and lively in tone, this book attempts to provide an intellectual depth lacking in many sources. The discussion of thinking skills, for example, draws on a rich body of classic work in the philosophy of science and related areas.

Comprehensive in its treatment of study and academic success skills, *The Winning Edge* is distinctive in several important ways:

Provides highly readable text as well as cases students can identify with. Through a positive, motivating tone, this book encourages students to try as well as to believe in themselves. By providing dialogue and cases inspired by real students with whom readers can identify, topics become not only clearer but also more likely to produce an "I'll bet I can do it, too" response.

Appeals to students from a wide variety of backgrounds in both two- and four-year programs. I've been fortunate to have taught students in several full- and part-time programs at various levels of career development. Cases, examples, and techniques are included that make the book suitable to a wide variety of students and instructors. Traditional full-time, part-time, mid-career, and younger students will find the discussions and methods relevant to their needs and interests, whether they're attending two- or four-year institutions.

Emphasizes thinking skills. Because thinking skills are so central to academic and career success, their development is a central theme throughout. Chapter 4 provides a solid foundation of practical steps by which students can develop their ability to think critically and creatively. Subsequent chapters dealing with class attendance, reading and study skills, successful examinations, and writing all emphasize the application of thinking techniques. Unique to this book is a comprehensive and practical step-by-step presentation of techniques for developing creative ideas in courses (pp. 97–104).

Incorporates discussion of values and ethics from the standpoint of getting better grades as well as personal success. Values and ethical issues are an increasingly important concern of contemporary education. Knowing how to apply these issues as they think, write, study, and take exams provides college students with an important advantage by giving the work they present to their instructors added meaning and significance. Understanding the link between values and goal setting, motivation, physical energy, and other personal success attributes allows students to make choices more clearly directed toward their personal success and happiness.

Helps students develop and internalize an appreciation of knowledge and learning. The chapters on motivation, writing, choosing courses and majors, as well as other areas of the book show students the importance of acquiring a real interest in their studies and assignments. They're taught how to foster these attitudes and shown how an interest in their academic work will benefit not only their grade point average but also their careers and their enjoyment of life.

Emphasizes writing skills, including helpful techniques scholars use to conduct good research. The importance and techniques of good writing are presented in several places. Chapter 8 provides many practical means by which students can write better papers and reports. The methods for doing good research will save students time, help them learn and analyze more thoroughly, and also enable them to impress their instructors with their scholarship. Success Step One (pp. 239–240) at the end of the chapter provides a variety of ways to beat the common problem of writer's block.

Gives a thorough, clear presentation of personal management techniques necessary for success in college. This book offers a comprehensive, practical guide to time management and the problem of procrastination. It also gives students techniques for using the many resources provided by their colleges, with special attention to ways of getting help from their instructors. The treatment of course, major, and career choice as well as financial management and other areas includes practical techniques that are related in variety of ways to college as well as career success.

Provides Success Steps at the end of each chapter that are directly applicable to the improvement of academic performance. To maximize the rate at which they can improve, students need measures of where they stand and a way to tell how much they've improved. Grades are only one vehicle for providing this information. Many of the Success Steps at the end of chapters provide concrete measures by which students can determine their progress. Other Success Steps help them to establish measurable goals. Many Success Steps elicit their direct participation in applying the techniques presented in the chapters. These exercises are printed on perforated, removable pages to encourage regular use.

In sum, *The Winning Edge* provides students with an innovative and highly readable means of maximizing their performance in college.

D. E. S.

Acknowledgments

One of the pleasures of writing this book has been interacting with colleagues in a variety of specializations and programs. I greatly appreciate the advice of Patricia McDermott, who teaches reading and study skills at Northern Essex Community College; Gwen Rosemont, Associate Provost at Salem State College; and Ellen Kayser, Associate Director of Financial Aid at Salem State College. All of them read portions of the manuscript and made a number of valuable suggestions. Thanks also to Janet Lundstrom, Director of Financial Aid at Salem State College, for her advice and kind assistance.

Special thanks are due Dr. Judith Clementson, Dean of Counseling and Testing at Northeastern University, who made many useful comments on several chapters and read various draft versions of the material relating to psychological health and counseling. I am especially indebted also to Anthony Bajdek, Dean of Freshmen Affairs at Northeastern University, who read the entire manuscript and made many useful suggestions. Special thanks also go to Charles Devlin, Dean of Financial Aid, and Paul Pratt, Dean of Cooperative Education at Northeastern. These experts provided useful ideas for Chapters 9 and 10, and they graciously read drafts of these chapters, offering a number of helpful comments. I am particularly grateful also to Janet Carr, Department of English, who read two drafts of Chapter 8 and made numerous substantive and bibliographic suggestions.

The following colleagues from several departments at Northeastern University offered valuable comments regarding specific chapters: Joanne Hadlock and David Fischi, Counseling and Testing; Irene Fairly and Arthur Weitzman, Department of English; Chris Bosso and Eileen McDonagh, Department of Political Science; Edward Hacker and Carl Wolf, Department of Philosophy. Joseph Barbeau, Dean of Career Development and Placement, offered helpful advice, especially on the development of Success Steps, and Carol Lyons, Associate Dean of Career Development and Placement, was helpful in suggesting, among other things, numerous bibliographic sources. Harvey Vetstein, Associate Dean of Students at Northeastern University, and Ruth Karp, former Associate Dean of Students at Northeastern, read portions of the manuscript and made many suggestions.

I owe a particular debt to the reading and study skills specialists who served as reviewers for Scott, Foresman: Rochelle Mike, Tomkins-Cortland Community College; Jean Newcomb, Community College of Rhode Island; and Jane Rhoads, Whichita State University. In addition to recognizing the strengths of the book, these professionals provided many useful suggestions regarding organization, note taking, study skills, and other areas. I am very grateful for their detailed and helpful advice. After a corporate merger, the book came under the auspices of Harper-Collins. I wish also to thank the reviewers for HarperCollins who offered several helpful final suggestions: Ken Dulin, University of Wisconsin–Madison; Michael Radis, Pennsylvania State University; and Donna Wood, State Technical Institute at Memphis.

Many students offered practical suggestions and read portions of the manuscript. I am grateful to Chris Hood, Dennis Knudson, Rob Leaver, Nick Lehnertz, Michael Levin, Pat Maurer, Sharon Poulson, Bruce Skillin, and Jon Vickery. My research assistants over the past three years provided useful assistance as well as critical comments on the manuscript, and I am happy to thank Guillermo Cesear, Peter Casler, Pat DeSilva, Ben Nielsen, and Laura Routt for their good work.

I am particularly indebted to the following students who read major portions and in some cases all of the manuscript at various stages. Their evaluations of substance and style and their ideas were of major benefit: Mary Finn, Patrick Pirkl, John "Chip" Reilly, and my daughter, Alana, and son, Mike. My daughter Kara, a high school student, offered valuable suggestions on clarity as well as substance. All the above students have my special thanks for applying their excellent critical judgment and creative insight toward making this a much better book than it otherwise could be.

Staff members of the Northeastern University Library were most gracious, with particular thanks to Amy Breiting and Chris Zlatos, who read Chapter 8 and offered numerous helpful comments. The courtesy and assistance of the university libraries of the Boston Library Consortium as well as the Merrimack College Library and Ipswich Public Library are appreciated.

Joseph Carlin, a specialist on critical thinking, offered valuable suggestions concerning Chapter 4. Beth and Richard Cormier of Sussex, New Brunswick, offered helpful examples for the memory techniques section of Chapter 5. I am also indebted to John Wilbur of Beverly, Massachusetts, for his ideas on financial management. The bright and happy enthusiasm of Janelle Morse has been a continual source of inspiration.

Several editors at Scott, Foresman and HarperCollins offered encouragement, support, and helpful advice. I am especially grateful to Ellen MacElree, Scott Hardy, Anne Harvey, and Donald Hull for their gracious professional advice and support. Their assistance has meant much to the successful completion of this book. Also appreciated is the assistance of Jessica Hornstein. I am very grateful to Rosemary Mills for her excellent work as copy editor.

It is a pleasure to thank Mr. Alvin Zises, whose generosity to Northeastern University included the establishment of the Brooke Chair in Political Science in

1976. The research support provided by this chair has benefited many aspects of my research.

I am most grateful to Joan Morse, whose encouragement and helpful advice on several chapters were of great benefit in this undertaking, and I am very happy to dedicate this book to her.

D. E. S.

Introduction to Students

Why do some college students achieve academic success while others fail or stumble along with grades far below what they're capable of getting? Usually the key is the way they approach their studies. Techniques of study and strategies of personal development that reinforce academic progress can make the difference between failure or so-so performance on the one hand, and academic and career success on the other.

Brian came to me for help during his sophomore year. He had a record of mostly "C's," with couple of "B's" and "D's." He came from a disadvantaged background. His parents' fighting and subsequent divorce had created chaos at home; he was constantly worried about money problems.

But Brian's main difficulties were within himself. He managed his time poorly, frittering away countless hours watching television and reading popular magazines. He seemed to understand and remember little when he did study. And he believed that because he had an undistinguished record in high school, he could never become a good student. In short, he lacked motivation, direction, and confidence.

But Brian had vision. When he found that many others with records like his had gone on to distinguish themselves, he decided that he too could succeed. He worked hard on study and academic skills, and he developed a systematic approach to studying and time management.

His grades shifted to "A's" and "B's" and eventually to mostly "A's." Brian is now a senior. He has job offers from several excellent companies and plans to continue his studies in a Master of Business Administration program. Brian attributes much of his success to the study techniques and thinking skills he acquired—skills presented in this book. Not only did his academic performance skyrocket; he also began to enjoy life more.

The majority of students hamper themselves by the attitudes, strategies, and study techniques they bring to their college experience. It's amazing how ineffectively many students approach their studies. They waste time and energy with poor study habits and weak basic skills that prevent them from doing well. They fret about procrastination and other weaknesses without systematically attacking the difficulty. They fail to take advantage of the considerable sources of available help. But it's also amazing how students can alter their lives and become successful by making key adjustments in the way they go about their studies.

Whether you're just out of high school or in mid-career, this book can assist you greatly. It shows you how to get yourself motivated, how to set goals, and how to maximize the use of college resources. It gives numerous practical, sure-fire strategies for overcoming procrastination and taking charge of your time. In clear English, it shows you how to make a quantum leap in your analytical and thinking ability, which is one of the great secrets of good grades. It also covers such critical areas as successful studying, achieving excellence on exams and term papers, course selection, and other topics needed for achieving success in college.

As a college instructor, perhaps my greatest satisfaction has been working with students on the personal success aspect of their academic careers, often sharing my own experiences and those of other students when it can be of help. So I've written this book in an informal, personal style in the belief that this will communicate to you the enormous power of these principles and inspire you to work at them.

To encourage you to read and reread the book, I've avoided jargon and included real examples. Although I've changed names and some of the details, the basic events are authentic, and the dialogue is true to the spirit of conversations I've had with real students.

Success in college is important. This book is designed to help give you a winning edge, so that you can maximize your success in college and beyond.

D. E. S.

About the Author

David E. Schmitt is Brooke Professor of Political Science at Northeastern University in Boston, Massachusetts. He earned his Ph.D. at the University of Texas at Austin and has a B.A. from Miami University in Oxford, Ohio. He has written numerous scholarly articles and papers as well as the following books: *The Irony of Irish Democracy, Public Bureaucracy: Values and Perspectives* (coauthor), and *Dynamics of the Third World* (editor and coauthor).

In addition to his research in political science and public administration, he has a long-standing interest in biography, psychology, and the better self-help and success books as they apply to management, academic, and career success. Among Dave's pastimes are hiking, boating, camping, chess, playing the piano and guitar, as well as wide-ranging pleasure reading. Dave has a son and daughter in college and another daughter in high school. In 1987 he received a Northeastern University Excellence in Teaching Award.

THE WINNING EDGE

Chapter
1

Getting and Staying Motivated

Motivation is the energizing force that enables us to achieve complex and difficult goals. In a sense, this entire book is about motivation. It shows you techniques that get you involved and encourage you to do your best. Because these techniques can have such a high payoff in better grades and more interesting studies, you're motivated to keep trying.

Students are motivated by different things. Some work best when classes are organized into groups of students who work as a team. Some prefer the structure of formal lectures and perform best under close supervision by their instructors; others thrive in free-discussion classes, with few restrictions on assignments. Many students are motivated by a sense of competition, while others do better when they focus on their own performance.

It's important to employ motivational techniques that encourage us as individuals, yet it's also smart to develop new ways of encouraging ourselves to learn. Often there's little choice in how courses are structured. But college students can shape their own learning environment to a significant degree, and they can decide to develop new approaches to learning. One of the keys to using this book is an open-minded attitude in trying new techniques and adapting them to your own individual needs.

There are some basic principles of getting and staying motivated that can help you throughout your college career. This chapter discusses key principles of motivation and shows you specific steps for implementing them. Together with the techniques developed in the rest of the book, they can give you a decisive winning edge for succeeding in college.

RECOGNIZE THE MANY BENEFITS OF A COLLEGE EDUCATION

It's true that college isn't for everyone, and that there are other ways to attain a happy and productive life. But college can give you many advantages. It can provide the credentials to enter numerous interesting careers. It can produce dramatically higher lifetime earnings. It can enable you to discuss many subjects and help you interact with many different kinds of people. And, despite the work, the process of learning can become truly fascinating and give you interests that will provide pleasure all your life.

There's no question that college can also produce pressure and feelings of uncertainty. There are many assignments to be completed and exams to be taken. Unlike high school or most job settings, there's a lack of structure and supervision; this can produce indecision and procrastination. For some students there may be a feeling of insecurity from having some of their basic values challenged.

Instead of being held back by difficult requirements, financial pressures, and other problems, successful students see these same issues as challenges and opportunities. They develop a positive attitude toward college, and try to manage their circumstances and themselves rather than letting events dominate them. They manage their time, set goals, and monitor their progress. They make use of the considerable resources available to them and develop study, writing, and other skills that can help them succeed.

Sometimes students have unclear reasons for attending college. Maybe they feel pressured by their families, or have enrolled because everyone else seemed to be doing it or even just to mark time. If you've not yet developed a personal commitment to getting a college education, keep an open mind as you read this book and proceed through your courses. It's probable that you'll eventually regard your college education as one of the most valuable experiences of your life. In the meantime try to use your time effectively, and remember that college has been a fascinating, successful adventure to thousands of students who started out just like you.

Even older students who have had full-time careers may not fully realize all of the career and personal benefits to be gained from college. Among the many advantages of a college education is an increased ability to think effectively, leading to better decision making and greater career success. To maximize this potential merely requires the consistent application of some basic techniques in your courses (discussed in Chapter 4).

The opportunity to interact with many different people on career-related subjects is often identified as one of the most important benefits by people who complete college as mid-career, part-time students. There may also be opportunities for career development through networking with fellow students and instructors.

A college degree can give any student a greater degree of self-confidence and self-fulfillment. Undoubtedly there are benefits other than the ones already mentioned that can help motivate you to work effectively. Identifying these can help you develop and maintain your enthusiasm for your course work.

Whatever your current level of motivation or past level of academic performance, you can become a much more effective and successful student than you may ever have thought possible.

COLLEGE IS PART OF THE REAL WORLD

Eric began his freshman year with little sense of direction. On his own for the first time, he felt aimless. He began to party several nights a week, sometimes getting drunk or high on drugs. When I spoke with him he seemed thrilled with his newfound independence, and he talked as if wild partying was the sophisticated thing to do. His adjustment problems were more serious than those of most students, but his experience can help us understand the link between motivation and academic success.

Sometimes new students have a quite distorted belief about what college life is supposed to be like. "Nearly everyone gets drunk two or three times a week," Eric told me. He had just turned eighteen and seemed to be intelligent. I wasn't about to lecture him on the dangers of drinking and drugs. But I did ask him about his goals.

He'd not yet decided on a career, which is typical and of no great concern. He said he wanted to "do well" in college so he could get an interesting job that paid good money. When I asked him what kind of work he would find interesting he said, "I'd like to manage people and work my way up the ladder."

I asked him if he had any specific goals for his first semester and first year. He said, "No, but I hope to get a good job after I graduate." I asked him if his social life was contributing to his long-term goals.

"Not very much," he said. He laughed sheepishly about the hangovers that prevented him from concentrating in class and the lost sleep that made him sometimes miss classes. He'd gotten "C" and "D" grades on his quizzes, was behind in his studies, and was afraid of failing.

"Most of my friends love to party," he said, "and I really just sort of tag along."

I asked him if he'd like to develop some specific, measurable goals for his freshman year and stop back to see me later in the week. He readily agreed. We discussed techniques for setting goals and he left. (The next chapter discusses goal setting.)

When we met again he showed me a list of goals that correlated well with his general career plans. He told me he wanted to start getting serious but didn't quite know where to begin. "I don't want to give up my friends and be alone," he said.

Eric was right to be concerned that he have friends. It's important to feel connected to other people. Sometimes students can make useful adjustments that aren't as radical as they might think. Eric had been talking with a couple of his friends who also felt they were endangering a good opportunity at college. We talked about some study and time-management strategies that can help students get a grip on their efforts (these are discussed in Chapters 3 and 5). Over the next few weeks Eric began to implement strategies that would enable him to start becoming a successful student. He began to see improvement in his grades almost immediately, and by the next semester was performing at a level consistent with his goals.

Here are some of the specific steps he took:

- He substituted library time for some of the time he spent just hanging out, though he continued to allow time for having fun.
- He talked over his problems with a counselor in the Counseling Center.
- He persuaded several of his friends to work with him.
- When it became clear that two of his friends had no desire to begin working and tried to ridicule his efforts, he began to see them less frequently.
- He became acquainted with several good students in his classes and began to meet with them to discuss course projects.
- He looked into the extracurricular activities and clubs at his university and decided to get involved with the student radio station as well as intramural athletics. He gradually found himself substituting constructive fun for some of the partying he'd done.
- He continued to enjoy some partying, but developed a certain pleasure and pride in moderating his actions and behavior in accordance with his own goals and values. He found that this change alone helped him feel more secure and self-confident.
- He rewarded himself for his positive efforts in studying, and avoided belittling himself on those occasions when he didn't succeed.
- He developed a set of long-term and short-range goals.
- He established a system for managing his time.
- He began to see college as part of the real world rather than a place where responsibility could be ignored.

Eric found that a vague notion of wanting to be successful wasn't an adequate source of motivation. He had to harness his energies, and take specific steps in order to succeed. And he had to recognize that college is part of the "real world."

College is sometimes called an ivory tower, a place where real-world restraints and pressures don't apply. And it's true that college can provide an opportunity for you to freely try out new ideas and subjects in a supportive environment. It's a place where you can explore a variety of subjects and pursuits. Students can investigate possible career interests and make new friends from a wide variety of backgrounds.

For students just out of high school, college may sometimes present difficult problems of social adjustment. You're on your own far more than many self-employed professionals. There's no one to stand over you telling you to schedule your time, to study, or to be responsible. In short, you have to manage yourself more effectively than many people in the so-called real world. No one's going to hold your hand from one day to the next. There are many places in college where you can get help, but it's you who must take the initiative.

There's a competitive aspect to college just as there is on the "outside." You're regularly held accountable for your efforts through the grading system. The standards for independent thinking and competent, accurate work are high. To be successful you must manage yourself effectively.

It's these realities that help make college a great opportunity for preparing yourself for your career and for a successful life. To be successful you need to develop habits of self-management, effective thinking, and specific skills in such areas as studying and writing. These will assist you throughout your career. So college can be viewed as a challenging place where you can explore freely and develop self-management skills that will serve you well all your life.

RETURNING PART-TIME STUDENTS

Karen's problems were similar to those of many students returning to college after managing jobs or family responsibilities for a number of years. She had become a secretary right after graduating from high school. Divorced at twenty-seven, she had two young children to raise in addition to working a full-time job. Determined to earn an associate's degree and find a management position, she had a reasonably clear sense of direction. She managed her personal life effectively and had plenty of will power.

Karen found that knowing the direct financial and career benefits of college wasn't enough. Like many returning students, Karen feared that she'd have trouble competing in college given her long absence from the classroom. Her many responsibilities left her physically exhausted and mentally drained at the end of the day. It was almost impossible to study and do homework after getting her children to bed every night.

Today Karen has an associates degree and holds a responsible position in a mid-sized company. She's considering working toward a bachelor's degree in a year or two. Her accomplishments were in large part the result of applying consistently a number of effective strategies for college success. *The great majority of success techniques discussed in this book work equally well for returning mid-career students as for those just out of high school.*

These are some of the most important steps Karen took in her successful handling of the pressures of college:

- She took a study skills course and applied the techniques she learned in her other classes.
- She implemented an effective system of time management.
- She began to take a broader view of her college education, seeing many additional career and personal benefits.
- She established more specific goals, including learning goals for each of her courses.
- Occasionally she attended concerts, plays, and other activities sponsored by her college, recognizing that this would help broaden her horizons and provide indirect career and personal benefits.

- Although she had to cut back on some of her social activities, she continued to spend quality time with the important people in her life.
- She made use of the resources available to her at her college. She met with career counselors and began more seriously to implement career development techniques (these are discussed in Chapter 8).
- She developed a more positive attitude about her abilities and her capacity to succeed.
- She established friendships with other students in her classes, discussed assignments, worked together on projects and studied with them at exam time.

The cumulative effect of these steps helped Karen take command of her academic responsibilities and sustained her motivation to succeed in college.

WORK WITH OTHER STUDENTS

Our affiliation with other people and with organizations can be one of our most powerful sources of motivation. For the great majority of students, studying with others can be an important means of staying motivated and learning the material. Many students also find that participation in campus activities can be an important source of motivation and support. Feeling we're a part of worthy organizations can help give us a sense of identity, fulfillment, and purpose.

Studying with Other Students Can Motivate You to Work Harder and Help You to Learn More Easily

Acquaintances and friends who are willing to study can be an enormous asset. They become a source of inspiration and a vehicle for more effective learning. Many students have found that studying with friends and classmates gives them the early momentum they need to succeed academically.

Studying with friends and acquaintances who want to learn generates positive peer pressure. You're less likely to get up and wander around or let your eyes gaze about the room if you know your friends across the table will see you. You've got someone to give you moral support when you need encouragement. Because studying is more pleasurable, you begin to acquire a greater appreciation of your studies.

Many students find it helpful to study with one other student on a regular basis. Sticking with someone who helps you succeed in your studies can be a powerful vehicle for establishing good study habits. Especially during the first year of college. finding a regular study mate is one good way of getting started right.

Sometimes it's neither possible nor desirable to work with only one person. It may be that your friends are taking different courses, so there's little opportunity to help one another learn the material. Students who commute or attend college part-time may not have the opportunity to establish a relationship with only one other student with whom they can study regularly.

The idea is to be flexible and develop a system that works for you. If you can't study with other students on a regular basis you can still derive great benefit from

Figure 1.1 Studying together can contribute to motivation and learning.

weekly review sessions, or from study groups formed at exam time or for team projects. Occasionally students are so well-disciplined that they work better on their own, using group study only for special occasions.

Studying with others can facilitate learning. Explaining things to other students helps you see where your own understanding is weak. It reinforces what you already know and allows you to work out complex ideas and problems in a supportive environment. You can pool your intellectual resources in developing creative ideas, anticipating and practice-answering exam questions, and in many other ways.

Here are some practical suggestions:

- Get to know people in your classes, especially students committed to doing well.
- Don't let a study session turn into a social hour. After exchanging brief pleasantries, get on with the job.
- Establish clear goals for each group study session, just as you would when studying by yourself.
- Explain basic concepts to one another as a means of testing and reinforcing each student's understanding.
- Try to predict likely exam questions.
- Quiz one another and practice answering these questions together.

- Practice thinking critically about the material.
- Try generating creative ideas about the material.
- Share routine chores such as collecting books on a particular topic.
- Measure your progress. Make sure you're accomplishing specific goals and objectives (e.g., how many math, statistics, or physics problems you've learned how to do, how many new concepts you've learned, how many chapters you've reviewed, etc.). This will help keep you from wasting time and allow you to revise your goals as necessary.

Develop a Sense of Belonging

Try to develop a feeling of identity with your college or university and a sense of pride in being one of its students. Your particular institution provides countless people with the opportunity to enter or perform more successfully in many different careers. It supplies people with skills necessary to produce the many goods and services needed by a healthy economy and society. It serves to better the community and society in many ways, whether it be a two-year college or large university with post-graduate programs.

Joining campus groups whose activities reflect your interests provides recreation as well as a sense of community. Most colleges and universities have many organizations eager for members, including musical organizations and clubs devoted to particular hobbies and games, among many others. The dean of students office can give you a list and descriptions.

Attending concerts, plays, lectures and other activities helps you feel more a part of the college community, gives you a chance to meet people and also expands your horizons. Both two- and four-year institutions offer many such opportunities.

Feeling a part of the college community can help encourage a sense of responsibility—a desire not to let your school or your fellow students down. This can give an additional incentive to try harder.

DEVELOP MOTIVATING ATTITUDES TOWARD YOUR STUDIES

Among the most powerful motivators you'll ever possess are those that you develop within yourself. If you do something because you find it interesting and pleasurable, you're internally motivated. If you encourage yourself to value what you're learning, you'll make studying more enjoyable, and you'll understand and remember more. HIGHER GRADES WILL COME MUCH MORE EASILY.

The following attitudes are especially important: a sense of curiosity, a desire to be creative, a desire to achieve academically, and a desire for objectivity and truth.

Encourage a Sense of Curiosity

Curiosity and a desire for knowledge are powerful incentives for learning. You try harder because you want to learn. You understand and enjoy your courses more, and you're much more likely to earn good grades.

Here are a few tips for encouraging your sense of curiosity and appreciation of knowledge:

- Assume that you'll learn something of value in every course you take. In virtually every subject you can learn things that can help you better understand yourself and the world. You can never tell when some piece of knowledge or skill will pay high dividends in future courses, or in your career or personal life.
- If the general subject fails to inspire you at first, find some aspect of the course that holds meaning and interest.
- Try to figure out why tens of thousands of others have found the subject interesting.
- Try to relate your courses to your own life.
- Try to use every course as a means of developing some SKILL even if that skill is only indirectly related to the course (e.g., improved statistical and writing ability or insight that will help you manage people on the job).
- Try to look for the SIGNIFICANCE of the things you learn, for example the impact on human society, the environment, and so on.
- Look for MORAL AND ETHICAL MEANING of the topic. Often the struggle between good and bad or right and wrong adds drama to the subject, which makes understanding and remembering easier. Even when the issues are more complex, looking for the moral or ethical consequences can give a lot more meaning to your studies.

Try to Be Creative and Original

One of the most satisfying feelings a person can have is the idea that they've created something new. So attempting to be creative represents a powerful source of motivation. Being creative doesn't mean you must be a Madam Curie or Albert Einstein. It means simply that you try to develop interesting ideas in your courses and that you value the unique ideas you create.

Marie was an enthusiastic freshmen who asked to take one of my upper-level courses in political violence. Because of her unusual degree of interest and her good marks the first semester, I let her register for the course. Marie frequently raised her hand with a question or a comment, occasionally off-base because of her limited knowledge but also frequently interesting and insightful.

Marie's exam wasn't perfect. She missed a few points because she didn't have the background knowledge of the other students. But the exam was interesting reading. Marie related the questions to her other courses and to an experience at work that was directly relevant. I actually smiled as I read the exam, thinking to myself, "Hey, interesting point," and "Way to go." She got an "A−" on the exam and a "B−" on her term paper. Although she was a freshman in a class with more experienced students, she received a "B+" for the course. Instructors reward good creative ideas with higher grades.

Marie's appreciation for creativity did much more than help her get higher grades. HER CREATIVE ATTITUDE HELPED HER BECOME AN ACTIVE PARTICIPANT IN THE LEARNING PROCESS. This helped her concentrate and motivated her to try harder.

Most students greatly underestimate their capacity to be creative. Chapter 4 gives many excellent tips for developing creative ideas.

Stimulate Your Desire to Achieve Academically

The desire to do good work is a powerful motivator. Worthy achievement doesn't mean you have to be first in your class. If you try to perform well and to build on your accomplishments, you have every right to be proud of your efforts.

Marie was a great idea person, and she did get a "B+" in my course. But she tended to be too rushed and, well, a bit sloppy. Needless spelling and typographical errors marred her term paper. She hadn't bothered to let someone at the Writing Assistance Center look at her work. She didn't take time to check out some basic facts and so made several careless, simple mistakes. Had she spent two more hours on her term paper she would have received an "A−" instead of a "B−."

At first Marie didn't seem to realize that achievement involved many things, including attention to detail. But she seemed to respond well to my suggestion that spending a few extra minutes on projects to polish things up and correct minor errors was an essential part of doing a good job. "I really want to do good work," she said. She realized a little extra effort can produce dramatically higher scores.

Strive for Objectivity and Search for Truth

One of the things college instructors look for in evaluating students is their capacity for objective thought. Successful students take the viewpoint that our perception of truth should be tentative: what seems true today may be proven false tomorrow. They also try to be open-minded about their own opinions.

Marie took another course with me the following semester. She did a paper on Northern Ireland, focusing on cultural roots of the conflict. She'd grown up believing that just one side was to blame for the violence between the Protestant and Catholic communities. As she did research she began to view the conflict as more complex than she'd assumed and came to the conclusion that the other side had some legitimate viewpoints. Her paper demonstrated an ability to think objectively in an open-minded way. This time she also made sure there were no careless errors. She received a well-deserved "A" on her term paper.

Marie's work throughout the term showed an enthusiasm for learning, a sense of originality, and an attention to important details such as proofreading. Above all her work displayed a capacity to think for herself. She got an "A" for the course.

DEVELOP A POSITIVE OUTLOOK

One of the keys to being motivated is our attitude toward ourselves and our abilities. People who believe in themselves and their capacities are likely to perform at much higher levels than if they think poorly of themselves.

Larry Bird of the Boston Celtics is one of the most successful players in basketball's history. Bird practices his shots continuously and has faith in his abili-

Figure 1.2 Larry Bird is a classic example of the benefits of a positive attitude backed up by effort.

ties. But imagine how well he'd perform if he thought to himself, "I just don't have what it takes to be a great basketball player. I'm slow and I don't jump very well. Not much point overdoing it." Fortunately for basketball fans, Bird is enthusiastic and positive, and he's willing to work hard to achieve his goals.

It's true that people are sometimes motivated by negative attitudes such as the fear of failure. Working hard because you don't want to let down your parents or spouse illustrates this kind of motivation. The literature in psychology suggests that to some degree these kind of feelings can motivate you to work harder, though perhaps not to seek high levels of achievement. Like an excessive desire to win, these attitudes can limit your success if they produce excessive pressure or lead you to avoid challenging work.

There are some basic steps in developing a positive attitude, but this technique has limits. POSITIVE ATTITUDES CAN'T CHANGE REALITY, AND WE MUST DO THE WORK, NOT JUST THINK ABOUT IT. But a positive attitude makes the task easier and the outcome more likely to be successful. *It's a fascinating reality that what we believe we tend to accomplish.*

Don't Dwell on the Negative

For most people it's not enough simply to talk to themselves in a positive way. They must deal consciously with distorted perceptions and thinking. Examples of distorted, negative thinking include automatically blaming yourself when things go wrong, blowing things out of proportion, thinking you're worthless if you make a mistake, and emphasizing negative things about yourself while ignoring the positive.

The main tactic in dealing with negative thoughts is to confront them. Sometimes just saying "drop it" to yourself will work. Often a more systematic response is required. Suppose you didn't do well in high school math or avoided taking any meaningful mathematics course. Thoughts like "I'll never be able to understand math. I'm sure to flunk the required math course" can prevent you from mastering the subject.

Stop and analyze your negative thoughts rationally. You might say to yourself, "Ninety percent of the people in this class are as afraid of math as I am. Most other students get decent grades in this course, and I'll bet I can too."

You can often help motivate yourself by being more positive in your expectations. Try to visualize yourself as achieving your goals. Sometimes you may find it helpful to begin this gradually. "Perhaps I can pass the mid-term exam just fine. I'll just do the assignments, review regularly, and work with a study group." You can then shift to more positive statements such as "I'm going to get a 'B' on the history exam by keeping up with my assignments and reviewing before and after each study session."

Avoid Hostile Attitudes

There's little point getting in a stew about things beyond your control, such as a traffic jam that makes you late. Even our anger at other people is often misplaced. They probably see the situation from a different perspective or may be incapable of behaving otherwise.

Years ago I had a student who simply couldn't perform. He was hostile in class and in danger of failing out of school. Finally I persuaded him to come see me. Seldom have I met such an angry man. Bill sat down and put his feet up on my desk. I decided for the moment not to ask him to remove them.

When I inquired about his studies, he explained that I shouldn't expect students like him to be able to perform well and that the "system" owed him decent grades, a degree, and a good job. He said the system had cheated him and had stacked the deck against him.

Bill went on to explain what people from his background had to deal with. He told me about his own chaotic past. His father had been an alcoholic, he'd experienced financial distress, the tragic death of a sister, and another close relative who died a violent death. "How do you expect me to do as well as the others?" he asked.

Because I saw Bill as a fundamentally decent and capable man, I shared with him some similar experiences from my childhood and teenage years. I hoped that this might help inspire him and show that however difficult our backgrounds, we can usually overcome tremendous difficulties and lead good lives. I emphasized that despite some pretty bad events and circumstances, I had a number of advantages, like a mother who believed in teaching her kids fundamental values of decency and honesty. I ventured the guess that Bill probably had some advantages going for him, too.

He took his feet off my desk and slowly sat up in his chair. "Yeah, but the system's corrupt. It's not fair."

"Then why not work to change it?" I asked. "No country's perfect and there are undoubtedly things that could use changing." We went on to discuss the importance of education, knowledge, and skills and how many students had overcome obstacles similar to his. He seemed surprised to learn how many people with similar backgrounds had gone on to highly successful careers. I suggested that Bill talk to a counselor in the university's Counseling and Testing Center and to a colleague in the Dean of Students Office with whom I thought he could relate well.

Focus on Opportunities: Think About What You Have, Not What You Don't Have

I talked with Bill several times after our initial meeting. Eventually he compiled a quite respectable academic record, distinguishing himself in his last year. One question I almost always ask successful students, especially those who have shown dramatic improvement is: "What is the secret of your success?"

Bill answered, "I started to appreciate my opportunities and take responsibility for my life." He said he'd given up some destructive habits and had decided to get some real, wholesome fun out of life. To his surprise, he also found that most people really wanted him to succeed.

Bill's newfound motivation was largely the result of a more positive outlook. He began to believe that his instructors and textbooks had something important to say. He decided to work on the present, think about the future, and forget the past.

Focus on the Contribution You Can Make

In college and in a career, there's a danger of becoming too self-centered. This can result from real demands and pressures and from trying to achieve goals. The problem is that focusing exclusively on yourself can't lead to happiness and can even cause psychological difficulties. It can't produce success in any real sense.

One of the things that impressed me about Bill was his new interest in reaching out to others. He began to serve as a volunteer coach at his local YMCA, and took great pleasure in encouraging young people. This outreaching attitude seemed to help his disposition and soften his attitude toward other people.

A concern for others and for making a contribution to society can foster our sense of self-worth. It gives us a connection to the outside world and helps motivate us to try harder. It makes us appreciate our own achievements and reinforces our desire to keep trying. When you stop to think about it, we're repaying society and others for the advantages we've had.

Be Persistent

A determined attitude is a powerful source of motivation. Students with a positive attitude recognize that life is full of problems, but they see obstacles as challenges that test and build their character. Recognizing that we all face trouble sometimes, they take a certain pride in attempting to deal with difficulty as effectively as possible.

Any significant challenge such as getting a college education will inevitably produce some difficulties and setbacks. Successful students develop a persistent attitude that allows them to overcome the obstacles they face. They recognize that most worthwhile things require effort, and they are willing to persist toward their goals.

GIVE YOURSELF MOTIVATING CHALLENGES

Most people can be motivated by challenges. The trick is to generate challenges that work for you, whether they are specific grades for a course project or a specific learning goal, such as learning how to use computers. One of the keys to effective challenges is keeping them manageable. Setting unrealistically high goals or too many of them may produce inertia rather than enthusiastic effort.

The next chapter shows you how to make goals work for you. Keep in mind that any improvement may represent success, even if you do not fully realize your goal this time. Feeling positive about your accomplishments is one of the most important ways to stay motivated. You're reinforcing yourself to continue trying.

For most students it's probably best to see themselves primarily as competing with themselves rather than with others, trying to improve as they go along. STUDENTS FREQUENTLY OVERRATE THE COMPETITION AND UNDER-RATE THEMSELVES, leading to unrealistic pressure. Focusing on the task rather than other people is a realistic and powerful technique for achieving maximum performance.

Some students see their studies partly as a game, in which they compete with their classmates. Trying to write the best paper in the class may spur some students to their best effort. If this works for you, try to keep your sense of competition within reasonable limits. It's not necessary to have a killer instinct to compete successfully. A sustained sense of intense competition can produce exhaustion and block creativity. Cooperative work with others is usually far more important to long-term success than a sense of competition.

REWARD YOURSELF CONTINUALLY

One of the secrets of getting and staying motivated is to reward yourself as you go along. *By rewarding yourself you provide an ongoing incentive to work.* You can

Figure 1.3 Rewarding yourself with constructive activities you enjoy helps to keep you motivated.

reward yourself by any sensible activity that gives you pleasure and makes you happy. Chatting with friends, listening to a couple of songs from a favorite cassette, or playing a few minutes of hackey sack or frisbee will provide enjoyment and help give you the incentive to continue your studying.

Your own values and interests will determine which activities constitute the best rewards. *A word of caution*: avoid activities that are likely to seduce you into not going back to work. If you've scheduled a fifteen-minute break, it makes no sense to start watching a long television show.

Some chores can even be made pleasurable, allowing you to combine a change of pace and necessary work. Listening to music while answering a letter may enable you to accomplish a task while enjoying yourself. If you have the responsibility of minding children, doing something fun with them can be enjoyable and contribute to your sense of fulfillment. Rewards can even be tangible, such as buying a new blouse or sweater after completing your term paper or even having a refreshing soft drink.

One of the most important rewards is the positive self-praise you give yourself after completing a project or even a short study period. Reward yourself not just for completely meeting your goals but for *any improvement and for small steps forward*. This will help encourage you to keep trying.

RECOGNIZE THE RELATIONSHIP
BETWEEN MOTIVATION AND ACTION

Sometimes students make the mistake of not starting or of giving up too soon because they think they have to wait until they *feel* motivated. The trouble is that FEELING MOTIVATED OFTEN COMES ONLY FROM THE ACTUAL PROCESS OF WORKING.

A simple remedy for feeling unmotivated is to just begin at a set time and act as if you were motivated. *Start working on a part of the project that interests you most.* Most of the time you'll find that your level of interest and enthusiasm increases after fifteen minutes or so. Even if it sometimes doesn't, successful students recognize that they sometimes have to stick to the task at hand whether they feel inspired or not.

Any worthwhile accomplishment requires some sacrifice and effort. Although it's also important to build leisure and fun into your schedule, you've got to be willing to do the work. The techniques of motivation discussed in this chapter will go a long way toward stimulating you and keeping you going, but you do have to make the commitment to doing the job. You'll find that this sense of commitment itself is a powerful motivator.

USE THE TECHNIQUES DEVELOPED
THROUGHOUT THIS BOOK

Almost all the techniques presented in this book will directly or indirectly contribute to your sense of motivation. Goal setting, discussed in the next chapter, will provide clear targets and a way of measuring your progress. Time-management techniques will enable you to prioritize and stick to the task at hand.

The crucial chapters on thinking, attending class, and studying will help you get involved in your course work in a way that makes the actual processes of attending class and studying a significant source of motivation. By showing you how to succeed in exams and writing projects, Chapters 7 and 8 can inspire you to attack these challenges with much greater confidence. Subsequent chapters will explain how to tap your interests in choosing majors, courses, and a career, and give you incentives and techniques for managing your finances effectively.

SUMMARY

Human motivation is complex, with inherited, environmental, psychological, and other roots. We're all different in the things that motivate us, but we can improve our levels of motivation by emphasizing those motivators that help us most and by developing new sources of motivation.

There are many ways to motivate yourself. One of the most important is simply to appreciate the many benefits of a college education. If you've not yet developed a commitment to getting a college education, try to keep an open mind as you proceed through your courses. Later as you look back on your college years, you'll almost certainly feel that your college education was one of your most worthwhile and proudest accomplishments.

Working with fellow students gives many advantages that can result in higher grades and more effective learning. Establishing a sense of identity with your school also serves to encourage you to achieve academically.

The deepest sources of motivation come from within, and this kind of motivation can be stimulated by developing an appreciation for the subjects you study. Believing that all of your courses can teach you something useful and trying to think for yourself will greatly increase your incentive to learn.

No single technique can alone inspire us to achieve our potential. Nevertheless, a positive attitude, which includes dealing with our negative thoughts, can help alter our performance and our happiness. What we believe about ourselves and our abilities we're more likely to accomplish.

You needn't feel motivated in order to work. Getting started is probably necessary most of the time before you feel motivated. You'll often develop stronger feelings of motivation as you work. Letting challenges work for you will serve to inspire you while avoiding needless stress.

At the end of each chapter you'll find Success Steps that will help you measure your progress and set goals. These Success Steps can be an important source of motivation and give you many insights that can help you get better grades. Taking a few minutes to do them after completing each chapter is an easy way to help maximize the many benefits you'll gain from this book.

SUCCESS STEPS

TAKING THE TIME TO DO THESE SUCCESS STEPS CAN HELP YOU ACHIEVE YOUR GOALS IN COLLEGE. Success Step pages are perforated and removable so that you can keep them or post them where they'll serve as continual reminders.

STEP ONE: Identifying Ways of Increasing Your Motivation

The purpose of this Success Step is help you identify ways of boosting your motivation. Rate yourself on the following statements. Give yourself 1 to 5 points for each question; the more positive your response, the higher your number (1 = strongly disagree, 5 = strongly agree). If the question doesn't apply to you, write "N. A." for not applicable. Your answers can help you establish new goals. There are no passing or failing grades.

1. Do I recognize the benefits of a college education with respect to:

    a. Getting a good or better job that includes interesting work, good pay, good fringe benefits, prestige, self-fulfillment or other things I value.____

    _____

    b. Learning useful skills._____

    c. Being able to interact with many different people._____

    d. Becoming a more interesting person._____

    e. Acquiring new interests._____

    f. Having greater career mobility after graduation._____

    g. Acquiring more self-confidence._____

    i. Other benefits important to me (list)._____

    _____

    _____

2. Have I attempted to strike up acquaintances in class with students who seem serious about their studies in order to find people with whom to study?_____

_____

3. Do my social life and friends make a positive contribution to my success in college?_____

4. Have I attempted to become a part of the college community through organizations and sponsored activities?_____

5. Am I open to further developing my academic success attitudes and recognizing how they can help motivate me and lead to higher grades:

   a. My sense of curiosity._____

   b. My desire to be creative and original._____

   c. My appreciation and love of knowledge._____

   d. My desire for objectivity and truth._____

   e. My desire to achieve and do good work._____

6. Do I recognize that every course can teach me things of value?_____

_____

7. Do I try to think for myself?_____

8. Have I confronted negative thoughts?_____

9. Do I try not to dwell on hostile thoughts?_____

10. Have I focused on my opportunities rather than my limitations?_____

_____

11. Do I try to make a contribution, recognizing that even small positive acts are important?_____

12. Am I persistent and don't give up easily?_____

13. Do I keep my sense of competition within reasonable limits?_____

14. Do I try to create challenges that motivate me without undue pressure?_____

_____

15. Do I reward myself with self-praise and tangible rewards for my successes,

including my partial successes?_____

16. Do I realize that I don't need to feel motivated in order to begin working and
    that a feeling of motivation often comes only after beginning the task at hand?

_____

STEP TWO: Techniques for Motivating Yourself More Effectively

Based on your answers to the questions in Step One, list five or more specific ways that you can motivate yourself more effectively. Keep the list where it can serve as a helpful reminder.

1. _____

_____

2. _____

_____

3. _____

_____

4. _____

_____

5. _____

_____

6. _____

_____

7. _____

_____

8. _____

_____

9. _____

_____

10. _____

_____

STEP THREE: Challenging Your Negative Thoughts

Part I. Pay special attention to your thoughts for one day. Write down the most negative of these thoughts below (the first two are examples):

"I can't get these math problems. I'm just not good at math."

"I really screwed up talking to my instructor. She must think I'm a real jerk. I'll never be any good at dealing with people."

1. _____

   _____

2. _____

   _____

3. _____

   _____

4. _____

   _____

5. _____

   _____

Part II. Now systematically analyze those thoughts, noting exaggerations and more realistic views (the first two refer to the examples above).

There has to be a way for me to do these problems. Thousands of students have done it. It's just a matter of finding the right approach. I'll try comparing them to similar problems in the book and take it step by step. If that doesn't work I'll stop by the math center. I'll also try to work on these with Jim. He seems serious about learning this stuff. Most people underrate themselves at math. If so many others can get it, I can too, so I'll just be patient and persistent.

Why should my instructor expect me to be smooth and polished? Most people aren't, including most instructors. I can learn to relax with people and to quit expecting myself to be perfect. I'm not really so bad. I like most people; I try to be kind. Maybe I can try accepting myself a little more.

1. _____

_____

_____

2. _____

_____

_____

3. _____

_____

_____

4. _____

_____

_____

5. _____

_____

_____

STEP FOUR: Getting a Positive Perspective

Part I.   List five (or more) things that make you happy. Include little things and big things. Here are ideas of the range of items you might want to include: sunsets, talking to a friend, people who love me, the chance to make something of myself, Ms. Henderson's witty comments in her lectures, dancing, and so on.

1. _____

2. _____

3. _____

4. _____

5. _____

6. _____

7. _____

8. _____

9. _____

10. _____

Part II.   Now list five (or more) advantages you have. Think globally: things like the availability of modern medicine, the chance to go to college, people you know who can help you. Consider experiences, background, hobbies, interests, positive traits about yourself.

1. _____

2. _____

3. _____

4. _____

5. _____

STEP FIVE: Considering What Worked Before

What things motivated you most in the past? How might these motivators contribute to your success in handling the course assignments you have during the upcoming week? Be imaginative and as specific as possible. Keep this list where it will serve as a reminder.

_____

_____

_____

_____

_____

_____

_____

_____

_____

Chapter
2

Setting Goals and Tapping Your Resources

*I*magine a sailor about to cross the Pacific Ocean in a fifteen-foot sailboat. Further picture that our sailor hops into the boat in his or her street clothes, with nothing more than a small knapsack containing a lightweight blanket, six-pack of beer, sandwiches, and some fishing gear. Imagine that our sailor has only the general aim of crossing the Pacific with no specific goals, just a vague plan to follow the setting sun and arrive somewhere in Asia.

You know the fate of our sailor. The Pacific has claimed thousands of lives. The men and women who have successfully navigated this giant have employed enormous resources. They've analyzed charts, studied case histories of earlier attempts, used the latest, most sophisticated equipment, and relied on a host of experts to guide and advise them on weather, supplies, and rescue procedures. And they've set a precise course and goal for each step of the journey.

Tens of thousands of college students are like our slap-dash sailor. They attempt a complex and sometimes difficult journey without clear goals to guide them along the way. They fail to tap the many resources available to them. They wander aimlessly through a thicket of requirements, courses and assignments. The amazing thing is that the necessary resources are right at their fingertips. The techniques for setting winning goals are likewise readily available to anyone taking the trouble to apply them.

In this chapter you'll learn how to set goals that give clear directions and precise targets to guide you along the way. You'll also learn how to mobilize the considerable resources available to you.

HOW TO SET WINNING GOALS

One of the most important components of success in college and success in life is the establishment of specific goals. It's not enough to have a general feeling that you'd like to succeed, do well, or accomplish a great deal. If you lack clear goals you'll tend to dissipate your efforts, like a hockey team that tries to move the puck in all directions rather than toward the opposing net.

This doesn't mean that early in your college career you need to have clear career goals or even be sure of what major to choose. Instead, it means that to be successful you need direction. You must have targets at which to take aim. The most important goals are the short-term objectives you set on a weekly, daily, and especially hourly basis.

Establish Specific, Measurable Goals

Effective goals must be quite specific to lead to academic or any other kind of success. Deciding to "take my studies more seriously," for example, is not a very useful goal. It's so vague that it can actually produce frustration. Studying chemistry one hour more each day is a specific goal that will give you a clear target. PRECISE GOALS SHOW YOU WHERE YOU'RE GOING AND PROVIDE A WAY TO MEASURE YOUR PROGRESS.

One of the most common mistakes people make in setting goals is failing to state them in measurable form. Stating goals in a measurable way makes them specific and gives you a precise target. Even more important, *it lets you know how you're doing.* Almost any goal can be phrased in a measurable form.

Deciding to write more effectively is a fine initial feeling, and it's good that you realize the importance of writing skill. But it's better to be more precise: "I'll revise my papers at least three times; I'll let the Writing Assistance Center critique my draft; and I'll write three pages per day" are examples of clear, precise goals that are more likely to lead you to a successful outcome.

Establish Long-range, Middle-range, and Short-range Goals

Long-range goals are those with a completion date more than one semester away. Earning an associate's or bachelor's degree, deciding on a tentative major by your sophomore year, getting a job with the U.S. Customs Service, or making lieutenant on the police force are examples of long-term goals.

Middle-range goals fall between one week to one semester long. These are especially helpful in enabling you to complete projects successfully. The main goal might be to finish a report for a nursing course by November 20. This report could further be broken down into phases, say, two weeks for research and interviews, then two weeks for writing, followed by one week for details such as typing and proofreading.

Breaking down middle- and long-range goals into segments is one of the secrets of successfully completing these goals. It makes the task seem more manageable and gives you more precise targets at which to aim. The next chapter will show you how to do this with a simple bar graph system that can save you much worry and indecision and help you complete your goal on time.

Short-range goals have a deadline anywhere from a few minutes to one week. SETTING SPECIFIC GOALS FOR EACH STUDY OR LAB SESSION WILL HELP YOU TO CONCENTRATE AND ACCOMPLISH SOME REAL WORK. It will help you prioritize since you have to think about what you want to do. Setting a goal of reviewing one chapter of your sociology text each night for ten minutes is a means of accomplishing a longer range goal of getting a "B+" on the sociology final exam.

It's usually not enough simply to decide that you'll work for one hour on a particular topic; you should also set a precise goal of what you want to achieve, such as completing Chapter 20 of your history textbook. Naturally, you'll often have to modify these goals as you go along; you may find that the history chapter takes two hours. But the goal helps motivate and orient your efforts and allows you to get more done.

Set a Time Limit on All Your Goals

It's crucial to put a time limit on your goals. Tasks and projects tend to extend themselves indefinitely unless you establish a cutoff point by which time you will be completed. This helps make your goal specific. If you're starting a project for your geology course, you might logically plan to complete it five days before its due date to allow for unforeseen delays. You should also set time limits on all short-term objectives.

Emphasize Short-Term Goals and Objectives

Getting a degree and starting your own company are important, but you can get your teeth more easily into goals that are immediate, like reading Chapter 20 or doing five accounting problems. It's the ability to work at short-term goals that determines your success in the long run.

If we focus on short-term, narrow objectives, we make it easier to believe in the success of our undertaking. We're motivated to continue because we can see these short-term goals being achieved. And we ease the pressure because the task we face is far simpler than most long-term and middle-range goals.

Be Flexible

Having specific, precise goals doesn't mean that you have to be a slave to them. It may be that you'll decide to change or modify even a major long-term goal to another specific objective.

In my sophomore year I broke up with a girl I was very much in love with. My grades plummeted for a semester and I failed a course in my major. In addition to the perhaps excessive sadness I felt about splitting up with my girl friend, I began to realize that my heart wasn't in my major field. I'd previously gotten good grades and in the abstract I liked it, but the actual work bored me. I realized that the field would make a poor career choice, and that it wasn't consistent with my real values.

During the semester break I did some serious thinking, and when I returned to school I talked with professionals in the career counseling office as well as with some instructors and others I respected. I implemented many of the steps outlined in Chapter 8. It became clear that I shouldn't spend my college career and my life doing something I was not fully committed to. I changed my major to political science. It's been one of the most important decisions I ever made, because it enabled me to enter a field and a career I really enjoy.

Changing goals can sometimes help you stay motivated. Of course, every major and every career has some tedious and negative aspects, and we shouldn't easily give up something we really value. My experience helped me to understand both the wisdom of flexibility as well as the benefits that can sometimes be found even in failure.

Make Your Goals Believable

You can't work effectively toward goals that you don't believe are achievable. If you weigh 130 pounds and are of average athletic ability, all the goal setting in the world won't make you a star lineman for the varsity football team. It's good to aim high, but it's also necessary to face reality.

Visualize the Achievement of Your Goals

When we visualize the achievement of our goals, we help program our minds to achieve them. The trick is to visualize in as much detail as possible and involve as many senses as you can.

If your goal is the achievement of an associate's or bachelor's degree, picture the president or dean handing you the diploma at graduation ceremonies. See the diploma with your name on it, perhaps on your wall at home or work. Hear the music playing. Feel the grip of the handshake as you receive the diploma. Notice the smiles on the faces of the school officials and faculty on this happy occasion. Imagine the congratulations of your family, friends, and fellow employees.

Use the same technique for shorter range goals. It is extremely important to *visualize yourself performing the tasks* that lead to the achievement of your goals. See yourself successfully completing your math assignment. Notice your patience and confidence as you proceed systematically and neatly through each step. Observe yourself as you go to the math assistance center for help. See yourself handing in your assignment on time.

On a regular basis think about your assignments and goals as quite manageable. Picture yourself as believing deep in your heart and soul that you can study or work diligently for the next hour, week, and semester.

What If You Haven't Yet Decided on a Major and a Career?

You can still have specific goals even if you haven't yet chosen a major or a career. One of your goals should be to acquire information on your skills and values as well as on careers and possible majors. It's quite common for people to change their majors and career interests as they go along.

The main thing is to not worry; there's no rush. Even is you have no major or specific career path, you can set precise targets for grades, assignments, and skills you want to acquire. The process of choosing a major and a career are discussed in Chapter 8.

TYPES OF GOALS TO ESTABLISH

This entire book presents techniques that will enable you to set precise goals that can dramatically improve your grades. But the following areas are particularly critical in considering specific goals to establish.

Aim for Good Grades

You should set a specific grade as a target for each course as well as for each assignment and exam. You can always modify your goal for course grade up or down once you're into a course, but aiming for specific goals motivates and helps you see a clear direction.

Good grades are important. They show that you're learning and that you understand. They bolster your self-esteem and give you motivation to set and reach still higher goals. They're also a reward for good work and a source of motivation to students who work toward these goals.

High grades open up the possibility of scholarships and membership in honorary societies. Dean's lists, honorary society membership, and other indications of good performance increase the power of your resume when you apply for jobs or graduate or professional school.

Future employers will look at your grades and consider them as one indication of your abilities and self-discipline. *Some employers consider grade point average in determining starting salary.* You may also begin in a higher position if you've got the grades to demonstrate your command of the subject.

Even if you have no plans for graduate or professional school now, you may someday want to go back for an advanced degree. Teachers, government workers, law enforcement personnel, business people, and many others may find that their opportunity for promotion depends on graduate education. So striving for high grades now may pay off handsomely after you graduate and are out on the job.

But grades aren't everything. SUCCESS IS INDICATED MUCH MORE BY WHAT YOU LEARN. Sometimes getting "B's" and "C's" is a real achievement. The men or women working full-time, raising a family, and taking college courses in the evening may be succeeding even if their grade point average is below a 3.0. Students with a poor academic background can often succeed even if they don't do well initially, providing they're working hard and getting the skills they need to achieve academically. Everybody has different backgrounds, abilities, and circumstances.

Sometimes a "C+" or "B" can be a fine goal because of the difficulty of the course or because you've not yet developed skills in the subject. Don't be deterred from taking courses important to your future academic performance or your general knowledge just because you feel you can't get an "A" or "B." *The goal of high grades shouldn't displace even more important goals, such as taking solid, useful courses with good instructors.* Employers and admission officers typically consider the quality of courses taken as well as improvement in grades over time.

Set Precise Learning Goals in Each Course

Most instructors will tell you specifically their goals for the course at the beginning of the term. Some will even include them right on the course outline. It's a good idea to make their goals part of your own learning goals for the course. Exam questions will often be based on them, and they usually reflect the most important aspects of the subject.

Also, figure out what interests you most about the course and construct some measurable goals concerning your interest. Suppose you're taking a course in Spanish and have always wanted to travel in Spain. Pay special attention to those parts of the course that touch on Spain. Consult an atlas and encyclopedia at the library and get to know the country's geography. Decide specifically to learn the location and characteristics of major cities, rivers, mountain ranges, and regions. Ask your instructor to recommend a couple of books about contemporary Spain. The course will be more interesting, and you'll be more motivated to learn the vocabulary and grammar.

Develop Specific Skills

One of the most important goals is to develop as many skills as possible that will aid you in your courses and your career. Skills that help you get better grades can also aid you in your career. Thinking skills, study skills that allow you to read and learn more effectively, and listening skills developed by good note taking are examples.

Try to apply the techniques developed in this book in all of your courses, and you'll greatly facilitate the development of these abilities. Taking a study skills course is also an excellent investment of time.

Mathematical and statistical capabilities are increasingly important in most fields. The social sciences and even the humanities often require statistical know-how for performing and reading some advanced research. Whatever your field, facility in these areas may give you a competitive edge when you're applying for a job and on the job. The ability to write well will help you not only in your classes but also in your career.

Some courses will give you specific skills such as the ability to operate computers, the ability to use various computer programs, and the ability to perform accounting procedures. But many of these skills can also be developed in courses dealing with other subjects. For example, you can gain experience with Lotus and other computer programs while working on a course project.

At age thirty-two Tony held a secure but uninspiring civil service job in his city's public works department. He decided to study evenings for a degree in engineering. With family and job commitments, Tony had little free time. He viewed college as a vehicle to a more interesting and financially rewarding life.

A colleague introduced me to him when we met in the cafeteria. As we ate our sandwiches I asked, "How do you like your courses this semester?"

He said, "Calculus is tough, but I've found a couple of people in the class to work with. I find most of the course work pretty interesting, but I can't stand Engineering Economics. I'll do all right, but it's torture."

"How do you get yourself to work in the course?"I asked

"Well, I've decided to master Lotus [a computer program] as I do course projects. *That's* something that will really help me, and I'll probably find I can use some of the other course material later on."

I met Tony a couple of years later. He had one more year until graduation. He'd quit his old job and now worked with computers for a large engineering company at higher salary than his old job.

"I've got my foot in the door for a permanent position as an engineer when I graduate," he said. "And I really enjoy the work."

"How did you get the job?" I asked.

"I got it through an employment agency. They gave me a test to see if I really knew the computer programs I put on my application. Got an 86 on a tough test. The office manager has me in charge of several projects, and I'm beginning to get involved more in engineering."

Become Well-Rounded

Being well-rounded pays off in personal pleasure and in career success. A well-rounded person has knowledge and interests in a variety of fields. A scientifically trained geologist with a background in the humanities and social sciences, who appreciates classical music and art, is well-rounded.

The most successful people in your career field and the top leaders in most organizations typically are well-rounded. So you'll probably fit in better and may have more influence if you develop broader interests. You'll have more things that give you pleasure in life. Well-rounded people have a decided edge in social situations because they can talk about many subjects.

Even though some majors and programs leave few options for elective courses, these courses can be carefully selected for their ability to round out a student's background. Courses in western civilization, great literature, philosophy, and macro- and micro-economics illustrate the types of course that can be taken. It's also important to try to understand the non-western world. Courses in third-world politics and religions of the world illustrate the kind of offerings that can make you more literate about the increasingly important non-western world.

If you're in a program that doesn't allow the selection of such courses, there are people on campus who can suggest books as part of a lifetime reading program.

Other opportunities such as college-sponsored concerts and guest speakers can also be a part of the successful student's education. The effort to broaden yourself will not only enrich your life; it will undoubtedly make you a more effective person in many subtle ways.

Establish Goals Connected with Your Primary Values

Values are simply things or ideals that are important to us. They can be lofty and philosophical, such as religious and humanitarian concerns: helping the poor, or contemplating theological questions. They can also be down to earth: athletics, our families or children, nature, or whatever. Many college courses can help you clarify your values and enable you to get to know what's really important in your life.

It's sometimes tempting to ignore primary values in college because of the pressures of studies and the many distractions that exist. But it's smart to think about your values in establishing goals for yourself. For example, family is usually a central value, and a student might decide to write one letter every Saturday morning to a relative. If music is important to you and you play the guitar, it may be sensible to play the guitar least a few minutes every day.

Setting goals linked to values contributes to our happiness and energy. It helps us feel good about ourselves, and motivates us to work. In fact, these activities can be rewards for work. Our guitar player might strum a few tunes during study breaks, providing an incentive to keep studying. Of course, avoiding behavior that conflicts with our personal values, even in the face of peer pressure, is another means of enhancing our self-esteem and our success in life.

Naturally we shouldn't plan everything in our lives. We're not machines, and there has to be room for spontaneity. But setting goals around important values is one way to keep us from forgetting those things that matter most to us.

Don't Let Your Goals Press You Down

High and worthy goals are fine—just as long as they don't pressure you into unhappiness or inaction. Goals become self-defeating if they load so much pressure on you that they weaken your performance or make life miserable. Setting perfectionist goals and dwelling on unrealistically lofty expectations can cause you to freeze up.

Here's how to prevent your goals from pressuring you into inaction:

- *Don't make achievement of your goals a life-and-death issue.* Just do the best you can and chances are things will turn out fine. But nobody achieves all of their goals. Sometimes an unsuccessful outcome may be partly due to circumstances beyond our control. Even when failure to achieve a goal isn't caused by external circumstances, successful people come back swinging and eventually become winners.

   Failure to achieve a goal may even have positive benefits. It can be a source of good information and even motivation. It can show people they're on the wrong track. Successful people continue to have faith in themselves despite the inevitable failures and foul-ups that are experienced by every human being. They relax and get on with the task at hand.

- *Focus on the process, not the outcome.* Once you've fixed a goal in your mind and begun to work, let your mind concentrate on the task at hand. LET THE PROCESS OF WORKING ON A SPECIFIC TASK BE A WAY OF EASING PRESSURE.

  See yourself as becoming calm when you sit down to work, becoming isolated from personal and academic pressures. Visualize the work as a source of pleasure and imagine the feeling of satisfaction you'll have when the specific task is done.

  Forget the outcome as you work. Your responsibility is only to complete the brief little segment you're working on. Breaking the achievement of goals into segments helps prevent freeze-ups and liberates creative energy.
- *Don't base your self-esteem and self-worth on the achievement of specific goals.* Your goals are there to serve you, not immobilize you. The purpose of doing well in college is to help you fulfill some of YOUR values. So ease up on the pressure. If success in terms of achievement becomes your measure of personal success and self-worth, you'll never be happy because everyone experiences some failures and because there'll always be something loftier to achieve.
- *Concentrate on a few major goals.* It's a good idea to have three or four goals for each of your courses (not just grades but what you hope to learn and the skills and attributes you want to develop). Try not to overload yourself.
- *Get beyond yourself.* Dwelling constantly on our own needs, including our worthy personal goals, creates a kind of self-centeredness that cannot produce long-term happiness or satisfaction. It can lead to frustration and a vague feeling of unworthiness, partly because such self-absorption is in a way selfish. Taking time to show interest and concern for others and for worthy causes is a fundamental part of long-term successful living.
- *Laugh and have fun.* Pleasure, leisure, and fun are an important part of your ability to work effectively and creatively. But having fun is worthy in its own right provided you're not hurting others or yourself. You're going to work hard and you deserve to enjoy life.

Our goals give us direction and help motivate us to succeed. But getting a college education is a complex and sometimes difficult process. Like sailors crossing the Pacific, most students would greatly simplify the journey and perform much more successfully if they took advantage of the many resources available to them.

CAMPUS RESOURCES

There are scores of people on campus who can help you succeed. The trick is to know where to go and then to follow through and seek their advice or help. The sheer size and complexity of some colleges and universities can be frightening.

There are three excellent reasons to learn the system at your institution. First, you'll save enormous amounts of time and avoid much frustration. Second, you can get better grades and achieve them more easily. Third, by learning the organizational ropes at your school you'll be developing a talent that will serve you throughout your life. The fact is that all modern nations are organizational societies. Most people work in large, bureaucratic organizations, and everyone has to deal with them.

At first the maze of offices and departments may seem confusing, but if you try you'll soon learn to let the bureaucracy work for you. Don't expect miracles. Sometimes you'll just have to be patient. In any organization there are going to be delays and a certain amount of waiting in line. But these inconveniences can be minimized by employing the following simple techniques.

Take Time to Learn the Formal Organization of Your School

Read the material that's provided or made available by your college. Freshmen orientation books, course catalogues, and the college catalogue all describe the major offices you will need to know. Success Step Four at the end of this chapter helps you develop a list of relevant names, office locations, and numbers as well as an organization chart for your school.

Learn the Informal Network of Power, Information, and Help

It's knowledge of the informal networks of information and influence that often enables people to succeed. Maybe a particular assistant dean or instructor is supposed to advise students on course selection but doesn't know answers to basic questions either through incompetence or inexperience. There will be many instructors and administrators who are terrific, caring about students, and giving friendly, efficient advice. Possibly a secretary or assistant understands the requirements or can tell you where to go.

Successful students keep their eyes and ears open. They listen to other students and to faculty and staff when they talk about where help lies. They ask pertinent questions. Some students are naturally adept at this and seem to learn the informal organization without trying. Most have to remind themselves consciously to do so.

See Your Academic Adviser Regularly

At most schools your adviser is assigned to you by your department or program. Particularly during your first year these advisers are crucial. They help ensure that you enroll for the right courses and can answer a wide variety of questions. They also know where you should go to get help with special problems. You can save yourself many hassles by knowing and consulting your academic adviser. THROUGHOUT YOUR COLLEGE CAREER MAKE IT A HABIT TO MEET WITH AN ADVISER AT LEAST ONCE EACH SEMESTER TO DISCUSS COURSE SELECTIONS AND OTHER MATTERS.

Let Your Instructors Help You Succeed

Your instructors are your most important college resource. They're the ones best positioned to help you succeed academically. Like everyone else, they're often pressed for time, but most will be glad to see you if you need help. They can also discuss ideas from the course that you'd like to explore further. Some will enjoy just chatting with you if they have the time. Try to be reasonable in your demands on their time, but don't be timid about seeing them.

Instructors can help you when you're having problems understanding the material. You can ask a question after class, or, better yet, see them during their conference hours. First try to solve the problem yourself, by a more careful reading of the book or alternative approaches to the problem.

Although most instructors write comments on exams, projects, and papers, they can often give you extremely helpful advice if you see them personally. You should always get an explanation for any written comments that you don't understand. The most important questions you can ask your instructor are: HOW CAN I IMPROVE? and HOW CAN I DO BETTER NEXT TIME?

Instructors Can Give Advice on Many Subjects

Your instructors can advise you about going on to graduate or professional school, the job market, and the advantages of their subject as a major or career. Just remember that they can be biased like anyone else, so you need to get other sources of advice when deciding whether or not to specialize in their field.

Most instructors really enjoy helping students. They can be a great source of help when you're having problems with the college bureaucracy. If they don't know the answer themselves, they usually know whom to call or where to send you. Of course the knowledge and interest of instructors varies just as it does with any group. If your adviser or instructor can't help you with a particular problem, find another who can.

Instructors can assist you in obtaining scholarships and jobs, even after you graduate. One of the most satisfying aspects of my profession is writing letters of recommendation for present and former students when they apply for jobs or professional or graduate school. Like other college teachers I sometimes call people I know, frequently former students, to let them know about a promising student. To write useful letters, instructors must know you personally.

Interacting with your instructors also helps you develop social poise and the ability to handle yourself professionally. Meeting with instructors gives you experience that can help you do much better in job interviews and in your dealings with superiors on the job. It's a great way to get practice.

How to Meet with Your Instructors

The first step is to relax. The great majority of instructors genuinely like students and don't expect them to be perfect. Instructors are people, too.

Try to be courteous. A smile and a friendly hello are as appropriate in college as in business, as is a thank you when you're done. If you have an appointment,

Figure 2.1 Meeting with instructors is a good way to improve your academic performance.

show up on time. If you're late, apologize. Knock on the instructor's door before entering and sit down when asked. The right demeanor is friendly respectfulness. But don't worry about doing something wrong; instructors know that students may be a little nervous. Instructors aren't perfect either.

Come prepared. IF YOU HAVE A QUESTION ON THE LECTURE OR ASSIGNMENT, MAKE SURE YOU'VE DONE THE READING OR REVIEWED THE NOTES. Indicate that you've tried to figure it out for yourself. Bring a notebook and pen, as well as any text about which you want to ask a question; have the pertinent sections marked.

If you see that your instructor is rushed or pressured, or if there's a long line of students waiting, try to be brief and efficient. It's usually best to approach instructors when they're not so busy.

Call during conference hours unless your instructor has announced an open-door policy. If you can't make it during conference hours, ask for an appointment at a mutually convenient time. Look for signals that the instructor would like to end the discussion. "Well, thanks for stopping by" or "it's been good talking to you" or similar phrases indicate that it's time to end the meeting.

Courtesy works both ways. You have every right to expect friendly and courteous treatment from your instructors. And you certainly have every right to expect your instructors to keep their posted conference hours. Nor should instructors be chronically late for class. Two or three minutes may allow for a more settled, quieter class, but instructors who are typically ten or fifteen minutes late are cheating students. Even worse is the occasional instructor who misses classes without good reason and then fails to schedule makeup classes.

If you have a problem with the teaching assistant in a large lecture section and can't resolve it at that level, you should speak with the instructor in charge of the course. For instance, if you believe that you've been assigned a grade less than you deserve and the teaching assistant is unresponsive, it may be worth seeing the instructor. Most teaching assistants are competent, but they usually lack experience. Instructors don't like to change grades, but most will want to rectify a real injustice.

If you have a serious problem with a full-time faculty member that you can't resolve directly with the instructor, you can see the person's department chairperson. Most schools have grievance procedures, usually found in the Student Handbook, if you can't resolve the problem at that level. The Dean of Students office may be of help as may special offices such as Affirmative Action. Many schools have special personnel or mediation teams to deal with problems.

One example of behavior that should not be tolerated is sexual harassment, including improper sexual comments addressed to you or pressure for sexual favors. Your school may have special procedures for this serious problem. Chronic nonperformance of duty (e.g., missing frequent classes or skipping conference hours) by college faculty is also unacceptable. But realize that instructors can have understandable human problems such as a divorce, death in the family, or illness that may temporarily reduce their effectiveness.

Disagreements on grades should be taken up directly with your instructor. Before complaining about a grade you should courteously ask for an explanation of the marking. In the overwhelming majority of cases the experienced instructor will be correct, and the best approach is to try to learn how you can do better next time.

If you attend evening classes or a program where instructors don't hold conference hours, you may have to meet with your instructor before or after class. Even when not required to do so, some instructors may be willing to meet with you at some other prearranged time.

It's worth keeping in touch with instructors who have had a particularly significant impact on your studies or with whom you have done well. Even after graduation, students who have valued a special instructor will often send holiday greeting cards or an occasional letter telling about their career or further education. Not only will instructors appreciate your remembering them; they will more easily remember you should you ever need a letter of recommendation.

The Office of Freshman Affairs and/or Dean of Students Office

The people in these offices can be an enormous source of assistance for everything from information on special study skills courses to helping deal with a family or personal emergency. Most people who work full-time in these positions like students and enjoy helping them. They typically have connections all over the university and can often quickly cut through red tape. If you are getting a run-around from some other university office, and your adviser or course professors are unable to help, these people are often a great source of assistance. On major administrative matters they may be a good first bet.

Academic Support Services

Using academic support services can dramatically improve your grades and help you learn. This is one way that learning the school's organizational setup can pay great dividends. Most schools have tutors. The Dean of Students Office can tell you which ones you may be able to use and how to find them. Relevant departmental offices such as the Mathematics Department can often give you assistance.

Writing labs, math labs, and computer labs are especially important. These will actually assist you with your homework assignments and projects. Using them is one of the smartest things you can do to improve your academic performance. Why struggle with a math problem you can't get when help is literally just around the corner? Why get lower grades on a writing assignment when the writing assistance center will show you how to improve your paper? Why be frustrated trying to figure out how to do a procedure on the computer, when people are being paid with your tuition money to help you out?

Religious Life Offices and College Chaplains

Religious conviction is a personal matter. If you do have a religious faith, you'll find that the college chaplains can be a source of emotional support and help with personal problems. Social groups of these organizations offer continuity to those brought up in a religious tradition, and they often offer interesting social activities and a way to meet people in a supportive setting. (Many writers have observed, in contrast, that some cults have exploited students and have been the source of emotional distress, health problems, and poor grades.)

Campus Police and Security

It's important to protect both yourself and your possessions. Students often become the victims of theft and occasionally of violence, many times because they're unaware of basic safety requirements. If you're living on campus or in a nearby apartment, you'll probably have to be more careful about leaving valuables lying around or your door unlocked.

Some areas on or near your particular campus may be unsafe, particularly at night. Walking in groups or getting a security escort may sometimes be essential. Learn the emergency numbers of the campus and local police. Read and heed any safety brochures passed out by your school. College should be a rewarding and enjoyable experience, but ignoring basic safety precautions can lead to needless tragedy.

Other Offices Offering Important Services to Students

For academic matters not handled by your adviser, you can often consult with counselors in the colleges of your university or divisions of your college (e.g., the Division of Fine Arts, College of Business, and so on).

Numerous specialized offices such as Veteran's Affairs, Handicapped Services, Women's Service's, International Students, Transfer Students, and others can offer invaluable assistance. Your review of the school's organization will show you which offices will be of direct benefit.

Financial aid and assistance will be discussed in Chapter 10, and libraries will be examined in Chapter 8. The Financial Aid office is an important resource for many students, and the library is a major resource in many ways.

Don't Forget Other Students

Learning the ropes can be greatly facilitated by the insights of experienced students. They can be a source of valuable information about faculty, majors, and many other matters. You should balance student input against official publications and advice from professors and staff. The informal student grapevine may sometimes be wrong, but it can also be very helpful.

Here's what a junior-year business major wrote on the margins of the manuscript when he reviewed the third draft of this chapter: "Other students have been there before. They know how to get things done, who to see and what to do. I can often get what I need at this university by asking the *right* student how to get it done." Of course, this successful student also made regular use of the official resources available to him.

Participate in Appropriate Extracurricular Activities

Students who participate in extracurricular activities are frequently among the top academic achievers. These activities can provide an opportunity to meet people, a chance to develop new interests, and even a means of gaining career skills. Pre-law students, for instance, can get valuable experience in the debating club.

Even if you're commuting to a junior college and attending classes after work, you'll find opportunities to attend concerts, plays, lectures, and sporting activities. The Student Activities Office or Dean of Students can provide a list or description of possible activities.

Provided you don't overdo it, extracurricular activities can be a powerful source of motivation. You can view them as a reward for studying, and the interest and enthusiasm you generate can spill over into your course work.

MAXIMIZING YOUR HEALTH

Maximizing your health is one of the best ways to give yourself the energy you need to be successful in college.

The First Principle in Maximizing Your Health Is to Avoid Needless and Foolish Risk

Driving drunk or with drunk drivers illustrates this danger. Abuse of drugs such as alcohol and marijuana can deplete energy, impair memory, and destroy the ability to concentrate effectively. Other drugs such as cocaine pose even greater dangers.

Intelligent students are also conscientious about protecting themselves from sexually transmitted diseases. Decisions about sexual morality and conduct are a personal matter. Responsible people are concerned about themselves and care about the well-being of their partners. Intelligent people who engage in sexual relations perceive reality. They practice safe sex and learn the techniques and practices that will protect them. Most colleges and universities have health centers and offices that offer free booklets, advice, and contraceptive devices.

Date rape is a tragic problem. Smart, decent people stop *anytime* a partner says "no." They do not risk an increasingly likely felony conviction and long prison sentence for rape. Students can help protect themselves by trying to avoid obviously risky situations and by figuring out—in advance—what decisive words and actions they will use to protect themselves and get away, should it ever be necessary. Many schools have seminars or brochures on this subject. Advice may also be available from the counseling or health centers.

Tobacco is a major factor in heart and lung disease as well as a central culprit in many other illnesses. Increasingly, educated people, and the culture generally, look down on smoking as a dangerous and unpleasant habit. The Student Health Center or your personal physician can give you specific advice on available seminars and other techniques that can help you quit.

Watch Your Diet

What we eat and drink helps determine our capacity to work effectively in many ways. Excessive sugar and caffeine, for example, can make us jittery, tired, and depressed. A reasonable, balanced diet will stimulate our energy and contribute to our emotional health. It's sometimes difficult to eat well while attending college, but most of us can make significant improvements if we're conscious of the importance of healthful food. If you plan to go on a weight loss or other specific diet, be sure to consult a physician first.

Exercise

Healthy exercise contributes to our energy level and our self-esteem. Most colleges and universities have programs ranging from aerobics classes to intramural sports. It's important to get a physician's approval before beginning a rigorous sport or activity such as jogging. Avoid obvious dangers such as running on busy roads. Swimming and walking are particularly good exercises.

Numerous studies have shown that exercise can alter brain chemistry in positive ways that contribute to feelings of well-being. From a variety of standpoints, exercise can be an important part of a successful college career, and it can make life a lot more fun.

The Counseling Center

This office may also be called "Counseling and Testing" or a similar name, and it may be combined with other offices such as career planning. At many schools, licensed psychologists familiar with a wide range of emotional difficulties have the primary duty of helping students with adjustment and other personal problems. Other professionals may assist them in this effort. These professionals also sometimes do career testing and counseling.

Among the problems dealt with by counselors are stress and anxiety, intense loneliness caused by leaving home, alcohol and drug abuse, and the severe psychological pain sometimes associated with the breakup of romantic relationships. If a personal problem remains unresolved despite your best efforts to deal with it and is interfering with your academic work or personal life, you would be well advised to discuss the matter with a counselor in the Counseling Center. IF YOU HAVE FEELINGS OF SERIOUS DISORIENTATION OR THOUGHTS OF SUICIDE YOU SHOULD SEEK PROMPT HELP. The Student Health Center or Counseling Center can help you get through your difficulties. Be sure to tell them it's urgent that you need to see someone right away. Sometimes emotional difficulties are caused by physical problems. If this is a possibility in your situation, counselors should refer you to a physician.

The Student Health Center

If you attend a school with a health center, you will find that the nurses and physicians may be a good source of advice and help on numerous issues such as drugs, including alcohol, assistance on protection from sexually transmitted disease, and problems of stress or depression. As noted above, the Counseling Center also deals with these matters.

If you have physical symptoms such as a chronic cough or sore throat or knee injury, don't just hope they'll eventually to away. Strep throat, for example, can cause permanent difficulties such as injury to the heart. Walking or using an injured joint can create permanent injury. If you're sick or have an injury, be smart rather that brave. Go to your campus health center. If you're in a program that doesn't give you access to a student health center, see your doctor, or go to a public health clinic or hospital emergency room.

SUMMARY

Establishing specific, realistic, measurable goals with time limits contributes to your motivation in several ways. It gives you clear targets to work toward, and it encourages you as you measure your progress and see positive results. A precise goal also helps you to concentrate on the task at hand.

The most important goals are short term. Focusing on your goals for the next hour and the rest of the day will help ensure your success and ease pressure.

Most students seriously let themselves down by failing to tap the many college resources and services designed to help them in their studies and personal lives.

There are many people at your college or university who want you to succeed and who will take pleasure in helping you.

Our emotional health and ability to study is effected to a significant degree by our physical condition. Diet, exercise, and the avoidance of dangerous drugs are fundamental to good health. The abuse of alcohol can lead to tragedy in many ways. Responsibility in matters of sexual conduct is not only smart, it can save your life. The Counseling Center and Student Health Center are resources that should be used when needed. Counseling for emotional problems is provided by many schools and can help with adjustment difficulties and a host of other issues that can interfere with your academic success and your happiness.

SUCCESS STEPS

STEP ONE: Identifying Your Values and Interests

Our values and interests should determine our most important goals, so it makes sense to try to identify them. The purpose of this Success Step is to help you think about this important matter and assist you in clarifying your values. Naturally, developing and clarifying our values can be a lifelong process, and college courses can be an important part of this endeavor. Still, the more specific we can be about our present values the more likely we are to set goals that serve us well.

A. What do you consider to be the most important and noble virtues in life? (e.g., courage, fun, honor, love, adventure, service, building wealth, etc.)

1. _____

2. _____

3. _____

4. _____

5. _____

B. What interests (hobbies, activities, sports, etc.) are most important to you and what new interests do you think might contribute most to your future happiness?

1. _____

2. _____

3. _____

4. _____

5. _____

6. _____

7. _____

8. _____

C. At this point, what do you want most out of your life? Consider such things as wealth, service to others, power, interesting work, a happy family life, creative pursuits, lots of friends, spiritual peace, adventure, etc.

1. _____

2. _____

3. _____

4. _____

5. _____

D. What characteristics do you *like* best about yourself and what qualities and characteristics would you most like to develop?

1. _____

2. _____

3. _____

4. _____

5. _____

6. _____

7. _____

8. _____

STEP TWO: Identifying Academic Strengths and Areas to Develop

The purpose of this Success Step is to help you relate your awareness of your strengths and weaknesses to your college goals. Taking different college courses can be a major way of learning about new strengths as well as developing areas that need work. Often students underrate their true abilities, especially in such areas as math. We can compensate for our weaknesses by building on our strengths. But it's also sometimes important to develop strength in important areas of present weakness.

A. What are your major academic strengths? (e.g., knowledge of particular areas, specific interests, determination, writing skills, reading and study skills, creativity, experience in life, experience on the job, sensitivity, organization, etc.). Be open-minded as you compile this list; consider those things that can help you succeed academically.

1. _____

2. _____

3. _____

4. _____

5. _____

6. _____

7. _____

8. _____

9. _____

10. _____

11. _____

12. _____

B. What are your present academic weaknesses (e.g., writing, math, study skills, not open-minded, getting down on yourself, not taking time to check important details, disorganization, and so on.)?

1. _____

2. _____

3. _____

4. _____

5. _____

6. _____

STEP THREE: Setting Goals

Based on your answers to the above Success Steps, develop specific, realistic, MEASURABLE goals with time limits (exercises for deciding on a major and a career are included in Chapter 8). Don't try to work on too many goals at once. Concentrate your efforts and add new goals as you go along.

A. *Long-term goals.* Example: graduate (semester or longer)

	TIME FRAME	MEASURE OF ACHIEVEMENT
1. _____		
2. _____		
3. _____		
4. _____		
5. _____		

B. *Middle-range goals.* Example: Project grades, skills (week to semester long)

	TIME FRAME	MEASURE OF ACHIEVEMENT
1. _____		
2. _____		

	TIME FRAME	MEASURE OF ACHIEVEMENT
3. _____		
_____		
4. _____		
_____		
5. _____		
_____		

C. *Short-term goals.*   Example: bibliography for sociology paper (day to week)

	TIME FRAME	MEASURE OF ACHIEVEMENT
1. _____		
_____		
2. _____		
_____		
3. _____		
_____		
4. _____		
_____		
5. _____		
_____		

D. *Course goals* (learning goals, skill goals, grades)

	TIME FRAME	MEASURE OF ACHIEVEMENT
Course #1. _____		
_____		

	TIME FRAME	MEASURE OF ACHIEVEMENT
Course #2. _____		
Course #3. _____		
Course #4. _____		
Course #5. _____		

E. *Personal values and personal development goals*

	TIME FRAME	MEASURE OF PROGRESS
1. _____		
2. _____		
3. _____		
4. _____		
5. _____		

POST THESE GOALS WHERE YOU CAN SEE THEM OR KEEP THEM WHERE THEY'LL SERVE AS CONTINUAL REMINDERS. Write selected goals on your time schedule and action lists, which are discussed in the next chapter.

STEP FOUR: Using Campus Resources

Complete this list of campus resources at your school that can be of help to you. Include names, titles, department or office name, office and telephone number. Use the campus telephone directory and college publications as necessary. Some offices may go by different names at your college. Just telephone or stop by a related office to ask what office handles the area at your school. The Dean of Students office or Student Activities Office can give you a list of activities, clubs, and organizations, or they can tell you where to get one. Tear out these pages and keep them in an accessible place after completion.

A. My adviser_____

B. My instructors_____

_____

C. The dean (or director), associate deans (or directors) of my college or division

_____

_____

D. Department Office of my major and departmental chair person _____

_____

E. Health or Medical Center_____

F. Counseling Center_____

G. Career Development Office_____

H. Financial Aid Office_____

      Name of financial aid counselor_____

I. Campus and City Police emergency numbers_____

      (campus police) _____ (city/town police) _____

J. Writing Assistance Center_____

K. Math Assistance Center_____

L. Computer Lab_____

M. Tutors and other assistance centers_____

_____

_____

_____

N. List the names, locations, and telephone numbers of other offices and individ-

uals who can help you _____

_____

_____

_____

_____

_____

_____

_____

Chapter
3

Conquering Time

Most people waste enormous amounts of time, and students are no exception. This chapter will help you to overcome procrastination and develop a time management system that will serve you throughout college and your career. These methods have proven successful for tens of thousands of people just like you and me.

The mastery of time is especially important in college because much of your time isn't structured as it is in high school. There are no required study halls and no one to tell you to do your homework. On the other hand, college provides a great opportunity to learn tricks of time management that will reward you all your life and contribute greatly to your career success.

Don't count exclusively on sheer will power. Our unconscious needs and urges can sometimes overpower the best of intentions. Try to use the behavioral techniques of learning and reinforcement developed on the following pages and throughout the book. These, together with your conscious determination to succeed, will be enormously helpful in assisting you to get control of your time.

PLANNING AND TIME MANAGEMENT

No one has enough time. There are too many possible things to do: studying, working, socializing, taking care of kids, resting, watching television. Some tasks might

55

be worthy of a life's work. A term paper on the role of women in China could easily be developed into an entire book. The key is to organize, plan, and focus your attention on the task at hand. Limits have to be set; choices must be made.

Keep Action Lists

To make an action list, the first step is to decide what must be done and what can be left undone (or given very brief, cursory treatment). Simply list on a piece of paper all of your tasks and responsibilities. It's best to keep two lists—one long-term list that includes everything you have to do, and one short-term list. The short-term list can vary from one day to one week, though most people find it best to keep a daily list.

You may want to use two or more columns on your lists: one for course work and one for personal matters. Keep them handy. You might display your long-term list on a clipboard or in the front of a notebook you always carry. You can keep a daily action list on a 3 × 5 card, sheet of paper, or sometimes even write it on your daily or weekly schedule to avoid an excessive number of time-planning sheets.

For some matters you might want a fail-safe system so you don't forget. Stick-up notes work well for this purpose, with a short message such as "attend Bradley lecture 7:00 P.M." They can be put on a lamp, mirror, or any place you're not likely to miss.

Obviously you should include your course projects. It's a good idea to also list important responsibilities to others. Writing your parents or other relatives, visiting an acquaintance in the hospital, spending a few minutes helping a classmate who's really trying but just can't understand—these are all important matters. Figure 3.1 gives an example of a master action list. A sample form is available on p. 76.

Prioritize

Stars are a good way to delineate important tasks on your action lists: two stars for unusually important items and one star for items that cannot be ignored. Routine items get no stars. Numbers or letters work equally well (1, 2, 3 or A, B, C). Remembering your kid sister's birthday, completing your math project for the week, and writing up your chemistry lab assignment could rate two stars. One star could be assigned to seeing your adviser, deciding on courses, and compiling a bibliography for a sociology paper. Shopping for a new sweater and doing your laundry would usually rate no stars. You can even accomplish some tasks simultaneously, such as doing laundry while reading a novel.

How do you decide what items deserve high priorities? Those items related to your most important goals should get the stars, with the crucial tasks getting two stars. For example, important course assignments and personal responsibilities would ordinarily be top priority. Those items that could lead to problems if you fail to complete them by a certain date should be done when you can fit them into your schedule. If you've already selected your courses, turning in the registration materials may seem a formality. But missing the deadline could cause delay and present

ACTION LIST

ACADEMIC
★★ Math project
★ Sociology paper: bibliog.
Sign up for university chorus
★ English paper: outline
★ See adviser on courses
Attend Senator Bradley's talk
★ Decide courses (by Sept. 24)
Turn in Registration forms
★★ Chemistry Lab Project
Read New York Times
★ (Read Wuthering Heights)

PERSONAL
★★ Grandma's birthday,
(book, card and call)
Renew license
★★ Amy's birthday (card,
gift and call)
(Do laundry)
Buy sweater
★ Prepare financial aid forms
★★ See Bursar on tuition bill
Sunday news show
Balance checkbook

begin novel

Figure 3.1 Sample action list.

greater risk that you won't get the courses you want. If you're close to the deadline, this item should probably get two stars.

You must decide priorities within courses. Which assignments are most critical? Which are dangerously easy or appealing. In my classes I often assign a newspaper such as the *New York Times*, but I also typically assign two, three, or four textbooks as well. It would be a great mistake for students to spend two hours a day on the *Times* and fifteen minutes on the assigned text. The texts are ordinarily more central than the newspaper and deserve more time.

Don't put off doing important matters that turn you off. Maybe discussing a problem about your tuition bill with the bursar makes you feel nervous or angry. But if it's important, put it high on your list. It frees you from worry and anxiety and helps prevent needless complications.

The best policy is this: DO THE MOST IMPORTANT ITEMS FIRST, EVEN THOUGH THESE OFTEN WILL NOT BE THE EASIEST TASKS ON YOUR LIST. The idea is to enable yourself to concentrate on the important responsibilities in your life in an organized, systematic way.

This doesn't mean that you must tackle the hardest part of the priority task first. It's often best to begin with an easy or interesting portion of a tough project to help you get going. What's important is to focus your efforts on important, high priority activities. If secondary matters don't get done, there's usually no problem. Few people ever complete all the things they might want to do.

If you just can't get started on an important priority task, don't give up. Wasting time will just make it all the harder to get on with it later. It may be necessary sometimes to do a lower priority task, such as studying the assignment for an easier course, as a means of building confidence and momentum. You can then move on to the priority item.

Always Turn in Projects on Time

Begin your projects and papers on time, allowing sufficient time for each step, including final checking and corrections. Waiting until the last minute is one of the most common mistakes leading to lower grades. One trick is to set your own deadline well before the instructor's due date, and make yourself really believe in it. The steps below will help you get your projects in on time.

Maintain Weekly and Semester Schedules

Most students find it best to follow a study schedule, which helps provide structure and makes decisions in advance about what to do with your time. There's no one system perfect for everyone, but something along the lines of the weekly schedule in Figure 3.2 is an excellent system. You may be well advised to have to have two copies, perhaps one for your notebook and one for your desk. It should always be available. Blank forms are provided on pp. 77–78.

Note that substantial time is devoted to leisure and social activities. A useful trick is to shade in a bright color the spaces for all leisure and recreation time. This highlights the pleasurable features of your work plan and makes the rest seem less formidable. There'll be times, such as just prior to mid-term exams, that you will have to intrude on this time, but it's important to recognize that rest and leisure are essential to productive and happy living. Don't make your study schedule so heavy that you have no chance of sticking to it.

Although study periods are indicated as one hour long, the length of actual study should be determined by your ability to concentrate and work effectively. Fifty minutes is an ideal length of time for many people, allowing for breaks between study sessions. And a range of forty-five minutes to one hour probably covers the needs of most students. You should continue past the end of the study period if you're in the middle of an important part of an assignment or are working at peak efficiency. Occasionally you may need to step outside after half an hour to clear your mind.

Figure 3.3 gives a simplified example of a *semester* schedule. It combines a calendar and a bar graph. Notice that it indicates dates of projects due and allows for overlapping of different stages of the project. Consult your school calendar when constructing your semester schedule. Note holidays, final exam periods, and other important dates.

One of the great benefits of a bar chart is that it lets you know when each phase of a project should begin and end. You can shade in your progress as you go along. This gives you a clear measure of how you're doing from the standpoint of time. It's probably best to use this type of schedule only for major projects of some duration.

	Monday	Tuesday	Wednesday	Thursday	Friday	Saturday	Sunday
6:15-7:00 A.M.	Personal	Personal	Personal	Personal	Personal		
7-8 A.M.	STUDY HIST.	STUDY Eng.	REVIEW SOCIOLOGY	Study Eng.	REVIEW HIST.		
8-9		ENGLISH CLASS		ENGLISH CLASS			
9-10	Study Soc.	ENGLISH CLASS	See adviser	ENGLISH CLASS	Study Soc.		
10-11	Sociology Class	Notes + Study Eng.	Soc. Class	notes + study Eng.	Soc. Class		
11-12	Notes + study Soc	MATH Assign.	MATH Assign.	Study English	notes + study Soc.		
12-1 P.M.	Lunch	Lunch	Student government + LUNCH	Lunch	Student government + LUNCH		
1-2	Study math + Hist		Break + 15 min. review Hist.		BEGIN BIBLIOG FOR HIST PAPER	Budget + Balance Check Acct.	HIST. BIBLIOG
2-3	Math Class	Math. Assign.	Math Class	Math assign.	Math Class	COMPARE ALL CLASSES FOR IDEAS	Study English
3-4	Hist. Class	Math Study	Hist. Class	Math Study	Hist Class	Math Assn.	Review ENGLISH
4-5						Review Math + Prac. Problems	
5-6	DIN	DIN	DIN	DIN	DIN	DIN	DIN
6-7					WORK		WORK
7-8	WORK	CHORUS	WORK	CHESS CLUB	WORK		WORK
8-9	Revise notes + Study Hist.	study Soc	Revise notes + study HIST	Study Soc			study Soc
9-10	Study Eng.	study Hist	study Eng.	study Hist			Prepare weekly SKED.
10-11							

Personal Goals:

1. Quickly review previous assignments at beginning of each study hour.
2. One additional hour this week in outdoor recreation with children.
3. Make necessary decisions on history paper.
4. Take note of things I did better each day and that I enjoyed.

Notes:

Shaded area = Recreation and personal time. Take five to ten minute breaks each study session.

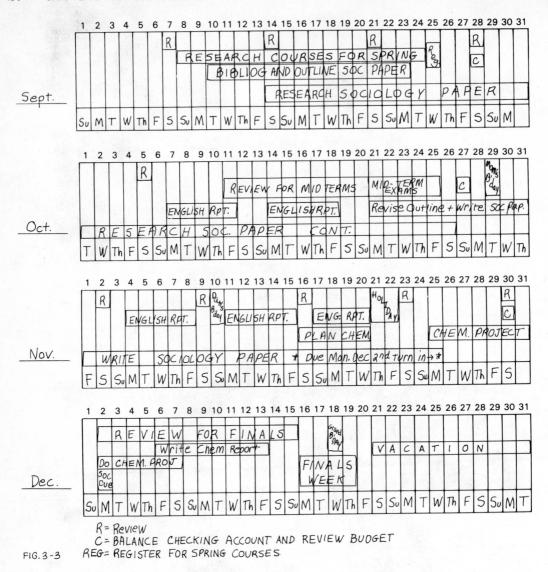

FIG. 3-3

R = Review
C = BALANCE CHECKING ACCOUNT AND REVIEW BUDGET
REG = REGISTER FOR SPRING COURSES

Figure 3.3 Sample semester schedule. Should include only major projects and reminders.

Be REALISTIC and FLEXIBLE in developing and following your schedules. Revise them as necessary and accept the fact that on many if not most days you will have to modify them. Some students perform better if they don't follow a weekly schedule. If you find that the weekly schedule make you feel trapped or slavish, try operating with a *daily* schedule in which the weekly plan is viewed merely as a set of suggestions.

Some students, especially high achievers, may do better without any formal schedule, perhaps deciding to spend certain parts of the day in the library or in a quiet room while their spouse watches the kids. But for most students, schedules provide a highly useful framework for managing time.

Allow Enough Time for Breaks

It's impossible to work efficiently or think effectively without sufficient rest. Taking regular breaks will help keep you alert. Five or ten minutes are often sufficient. If you picture breaks as a reward and if you try to do something pleasant during your breaks, you'll also help motivate yourself to continue working.

Breaks can be a source of ideas and insights about your work, because you'll tend to think about the material you've just been working on or anticipating the topic you're about to study. But try to avoid getting involved in a conversation or activity such as watching "five minutes" of "As the World Turns" that will tempt you from going back to studying when you should.

Organize Your Study Periods Around Logical Blocks of Work

Your goal for each study period should be to complete a logical block of work in one subject. You should take your break at a logical place, even if it means lengthening your study period by a few minutes. Say you're studying an anthropology chapter and haven't quite reached your goal of completing the chapter when the fifty minutes you've allotted to studying runs out. Here it makes sense to spend an additional ten or fifteen minutes to meet your goal. Stopping at a logical place facilitates learning and aids recall.

Protect Your Time

Among the most common obstacles to success are the demands of other people. Our friends, families, instructors, and others continually make demands on us for attention, participation, and our time. Many demands are legitimate. But you have to set limits if you want to be effective in achieving your goals.

Steve was a good student who began to have trouble with his grades. He explained that he had too many responsibilities in his student government work. As an effective person, Steve was continually asked to help out with projects undertaken by student organizations.

"I just hate to turn people down," Steve said.

When I asked him if the others did as much work, he said no. As we talked, Steve began to see that he was allowing himself to be used. "But it's really my fault for being too agreeable," he said. "I guess I have to set some limits."

He decided to tell the others that he would do his fair share but that he couldn't do any more. In a polite but firm way he'd explain that he wanted to go to graduate school and that getting excellent grades was his most important goal.

Steve's grades improved substantially. My guess is that like many of us, Steve had been afraid of offending people and may have underrated his own worth. He allowed his own primary goals to be comprised by the secondary needs of someone else. He seems to have made significant progress in standing up for his own needs, while retaining the human capacity to give time and affection to his family and friends. He has learned to set limits.

Consider Your Personal Biology

Try to accommodate your schedule to your own biological patterns of efficiency. Take advantage of the times you feel really sharp to do some of your studying. Sometimes we just have to "gut it out" and study or write when we're not at peak efficiency. But we optimize our time if we can achieve some balance. If necessary, don't be afraid to get up at five in the morning to have some quiet time to work on that psychology paper, catching up on sleep later.

Use Spare Bits of Time Effectively

Using little bits of time can pay tremendous dividends. Commuting time can be used for study or review. Even a ten-minute wait, say at the Health Center, can be used to plan a lab assignment. Sometimes you will be able to do course work while completing some personal chore, perhaps reviewing your notes while preparing dinner.

Three-by-five cards with key formulas, definitions, facts, and so on, are an excellent way to utilize spare minutes. You can easily carry these cards, pulling them out when you have an extra moment. They can be written while you're taking notes during study sessions as explained on pp. 159–164.

Don't Be a Drudge

Occasionally students make the mistake of becoming overly organized and working too hard. In the long run this is counterproductive. It interferes with thinking creatively and working energetically. It can even lead to serious psychological problems. People need to recharge their batteries and to have some rest, fun, and leisure.

Try to do something pleasurable every day. There are thousands of ways to add pleasure to life. Perhaps go for a walk at sunset, or simply take the longer but more scenic way home after class. Maybe just listen to your favorite music while you talk with a friend. The pleasures you choose will depend on your values and interests. The important thing is that these pleasures contribute to your feeling that life can be a beautiful thing and that you feel refreshed and good about yourself when you engage in these activities.

Take Time for Social Interaction

Spending time with friends and classmates is both worthwhile and necessary to successful living. Social activities, organized clubs, and sporting activities are all examples of ways for increasing your social contacts.

You may want to include reminders on your schedule and your action list to engage in social and other pleasurable activities. If you're walking to the library and an acquaintance stops to talk to you, spend five or ten minutes being sociable. You can always add the ten minutes to your schedule later. Even if you can't, it may still be a worthwhile choice.

Reinforce and Reward Yourself

Studying can be hard work. Sometimes our trouble isn't getting started; it's keeping at it. An important trick here is to give yourself small rewards *after you've done a block of work*. The idea is to motivate yourself to keep on working because you'll know it's not all drudgery. There'll be some fun as well. This simple procedure will go a long way toward the principle of rewarding yourself continually as discussed in Chapter 1.

The above discussion refers to your daily routine, keeping yourself going throughout the day. But YOU SHOULD ALSO GIVE YOURSELF SIGNIFICANT REWARDS AFTER YOU'VE COMPLETED BIG PROJECTS OR ACHIEVED SOME NOTEWORTHY GOAL. I know one student who likes to go on a weekend camping trip as soon as possible after completing a big assignment. It doesn't take a lot of money to create really good rewards for yourself.

Don't punish yourself when you fail. We all miss the mark sometimes. Punishing yourself by feeling guilty or telling yourself you're no good merely makes it harder to succeed next time. You're better off imagining what it would have felt like to have achieved your goal.

Reinforce the positive behavior, *however small the positive step may be*, and, if possible, ignore undesirable behavior. If you manage five more minutes than yesterday on your last hour of study, then give yourself some praise. You deserve it, and you are reinforcing your ability to work still more effectively in the future.

Pace Yourself

Most of the time frantic rushing is the enemy of effective work. Sometimes it's good to deliberately slow down. Too rushed a pace, and especially a rushed frame of mind, can wear you out. If you are trying to figure out subtle comparisons and contrasts between the ideas of the great psychologists Sigmund Freud and Carl Jung, sit down with something to drink and a piece of paper in front of you. Slowly develop subtle distinctions or ideas. A relaxed deliberate pace works best most of the time.

Tip: Often the beginning and end of a project require slower going for best results. Taking time at the beginning for effective planning and organization may actually save time. Taking time at the end to polish up loose ends and check for accuracy reduces your chance of a lower grade because of foolish errors.

There's a common myth many students hold: "I work best under pressure." Most people don't. Their thinking isn't as clear and their use of time isn't as effective. Letting your report go until the night before it's due means you may not be able to check a source or give it the careful proofreading that would have made it an "A" job. Besides, the relaxed, deliberate approach makes it easier to enjoy life.

Attend Every Lecture and Lab Session

There's one key strategy for organizing time effectively in college that hasn't yet been discussed. It's one of the easiest tricks to give structure and focus to the use of time and it pays enormous dividends. Simply GET IN THE HABIT OF ATTENDING EVERY LECTURE, LAB, AND CLASS SESSION.

Attending all classes is one of the keys to success in college, and it pays dividends in numerous ways. It makes some of your time-management decisions automatic. It greatly facilitates your learning and helps develop a variety of skills and abilities. Attending every lecture and lab session is an easy way to take a major step in giving structure to your college life and getting control of your time.

ENEMY NUMBER ONE: PROCRASTINATION

Getting started is often the hardest part. There's something within most of us that sometimes seems to rebel against work. We can have the best intentions, yet be unable to begin. It helps to know that this obstacle, commonly called procrastination, is a perfectly human trait and that even highly successful people must sometimes deal with it. Most important, procrastination can be beaten through a number of specific, simple techniques.

Sometimes the problem may be lack of concentration rather than not getting started. Concentration difficulties are often the result of lack of direction and purpose when studying. While effective goal setting is part of the answer, learning good study techniques is also crucial. Chapter 6 will give you sure-fire methods for developing focus and concentration.

Students often get discouraged and quit too soon. You may need ten to fifteen minutes to become fully focused. As we saw in Chapter 1, it's not necessary that you always feel motivated or enthusiastic. Just sitting there trying to work effectively is often enough, recognizing that you'll frequently become more effective as you get into the work and as you acquire more study skills.

Even with good intentions, students may get distracted by an interesting discussion, game, and a thousand other things. One way to get on top of this problem is to jot down distractions as they occur. Writing down sources of distraction can be done on a separate piece of paper or can be combined with the Measure Your Progress technique described later in this chapter on pp. 70–71.

Learning what your patterns of distractions are can help you more easily defeat them. It may be just a matter of getting out of harm's way, for example, refusing to even enter the television room if you're supposed to be studying, or going to the library to avoid temptation. Caroline came to see me during my conference hours after getting a "C−" on my mid-term exam.

"I really want to do well in college," she said. "I'm a nursing major and have always wanted to help others. And as the first one in my family to go to college, I feel a special obligation to succeed."

But she had a common problem. "I just can't seem to buckle down to work," she said. "I've got good intentions, but I seem to spend the days dodging my studies. Sometimes I sit at my desk and just stare at the book, daydreaming. Or I write letters, read magazines, shop, or just hang out."

Something seemed terribly wrong to Caroline. She wanted to work but couldn't. She was confused and unhappy.

"Don't worry about the mid-term exam; I take improvement into account," I said. "Being honest about procrastination is an important first step."

After going over her exam, we devised a plan to help her get control of her time. She set up strategies that are particularly relevant to students. Gradually Caroline got a grip on time. She had relapses, but realized these weren't permanent. She remained upbeat and positive. As she acquired good work and study habits, her grades and self-image improved considerably. The secret of her success is that she implemented the tactics discussed on the following pages and presented graphically in Figure 3.4.

Recognize That You're Procrastinating

You must recognize procrastination when it occurs. Usually this is easy, but sometimes we can fool ourselves. Letting trivial obstacles stop us is a common form of self-deception. Conditions may not be perfect (they hardly ever are). The desk is uncomfortable, the book you need is not available, the pencil is too short, or perhaps the wrong color. No excuse is too insignificant to the mind deceived by procrastination.

Another common form of self-deception is working on secondary or routine matters rather than the most important item on your agenda. Shopping or organizing your clothes closet when you should be studying chemistry is an example of this mistake. If you can't get started and don't know why, or if other things always seem to prevent you from doing what you should be doing, you're probably procrastinating.

Find a Good Location

A suitable location is critical. Most people require a quiet place to do homework; but be flexible. Soft music or irrelevant background noise actually helps some people. The idea is to GET AWAY FROM DISTRACTIONS TO A PLACE WHERE YOU CAN CONCENTRATE. Maybe this just means clearing your desk of distracting objects, asking that your roommate use headphones or turn off the radio, or going to the library.

Be imaginative in finding good locations. A number of years back as a junior professor I was working on a difficult project that could help determine my chances

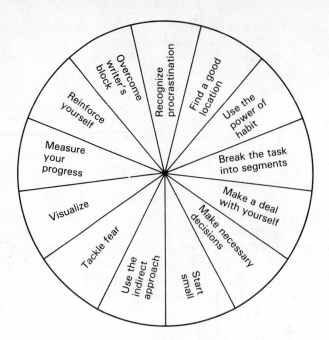

Figure 3.4 Ways to beat procrastination.

for tenure (permanent employment). My research was done, but nothing enabled me to begin writing. I spent several days struggling, taking unnecessary coffee breaks, and browsing in bookstores. My usual strategies to beat procrastination didn't work. Finally I decided to put myself in a place where there would be no possible distractions, no way to get away.

I went down to the bus station and asked for a round-trip ticket to any place that would take about three hours with no stops in between. The ticket agent looked at me in bewilderment but sold me the ticket. I rode the bus to nowhere in particular for three afternoons, my writing getting easier with each passing mile. I went on to finish the project efficiently, and it turned out to be one of the best pieces I've ever written. To this day I find commuting and travelling on a bus or train a great way to get work done.

I was able to defeat procrastination because I found a location that would virtually force me to work—no interruptions, no place to escape. Usually you will not have to resort to such drastic measures, but remember the importance of picking a suitable location if you can't get started. This strategy also works if you get bogged down and can't keep going. Sometimes just a change of scenery will provide the incentive you need to get back to work.

Use the Power of Habit

Many of our actions are automatic. We don't fret about what to do when getting ready for bed. Most of us have a ritual we follow about changing our clothes, setting the alarm, and so on. Force of habit saves us from wondering about what we should be doing or from being tempted away from completing the task.

You can do the same with study. If you've got two hours between classes, simply go to the library every time that interval occurs and work. Having a specific area of the library where you ALWAYS study and never waste time is a good idea. It may help to use the desk in your room for nothing but studying: no pleasure reading, letter writing, or anything else. These other chores can be done elsewhere. The idea is that habit will encourage you to study when you sit down at these places.

Break Down the Task into Manageable Segments

Maybe the idea of a ten-page term paper is frightening, but compiling a bibliography, reading one article, or talking to your instructor about your ideas for the project will seem less formidable.

Don't try to live an entire week or semester at a time. The age-old advice of living just for today (provided you have planned for the future) is sound. It's much easier to think about getting just today's work done and handling just today's problems.

Adam was a bright student who had a mental block regarding his term paper. He said, "I just can't understand why I can't get started." The paper was due in three weeks and should have been well underway. We discussed the problem and together developed a tactic of breaking down the work into stages. Adam wouldn't worry about the final product; he would just concentrate on each separate phase.

During the first week he'd finish his research and refine his outline. He'd complete a rough draft during the second week. In the third week he'd revise his paper and complete the footnotes, bibliography, final polishing, and typing. Adam stuck to his plan and went on to write a good term paper, although not nearly as good as if he had implemented this strategy a few weeks earlier. I saw him later next semester, and he said he was continuing to have success with segmenting difficult projects.

Make a Deal with Yourself

The idea of this technique is simple. JUST BEGIN, and tell yourself you can quit after twenty minutes if you simply can't continue. Sometimes it takes fifteen or twenty minutes just to develop real concentration on a subject. It's best to combine this technique with some of the other methods of beating procrastination. Begin with an easy and interesting part of the work you want to do. You'll build up momentum and confidence as you go along, and the shift to more difficult portions of the project will come more easily.

Make Necessary Decisions as You Go Along

Often procrastination is caused by indecision. Many projects require hundreds of decisions. What product will you choose for the marketing project in your business course? What unique quality will you focus on in your advertisements? How will you construct your advertising campaign? Often each step will have countless possibilities.

Just as personal decisions in our lives are fraught with uncertainty, so are decisions in college and on the job. We must simply accept uncertainty as a part of life, including college life. Maybe there will be insufficient data on a particular topic, but you can always change your focus. Don't be afraid to decide.

A simple "pro" and "con" list such as the one in Figure 3.5 can be a tremendous help. Specify your goals and objectives. List alternatives. Note pro's and con's as they relate to the objectives. Don't go by the number of pro's and con's but by the significance of the points for achieving your goal. Consider also relationships to other goals. SET A TIME BY WHICH YOU WILL MAKE THE DECISION. Make it by that point and immediately begin to work on the project.

In Figure 3.5 I've modified a chart used by Caroline. You'll notice that she allows herself one-half hour to decide whether to choose Nicaragua or China for her report on the role of women in revolutionary societies. She has done preliminary research and possesses all the information she needs to make the decision. She has determined that there are sufficient research materials to do a report on either country. Her instructor told her that either topic would be fine.

You can see that she chooses China. Although either choice would have been sound, writing about China will enable her to achieve more of her objectives. In particular, it will allow her to broaden her horizons and develop insight into a new major country. Even though the project on China will take a bit more time, it will contribute more to her education and probably be more interesting. Notice that she wrote down the actual time taken to make the decision and how she felt. She was reinforcing decisive behavior so that it would be even easier next time.

But be warned. Some decisions shouldn't be rushed. It may be that you should investigate further before committing your entire semester's grade to a particular engineering project.

Start Small

If you can't get started, accomplish an initial chore. Get your knapsack ready for the library, walk over to the library, go in and find a suitable place to sit, and begin to work.

If you still can't begin after sitting down in the library, do another beginning chore. Perhaps you need to arrange your note cards in logical order. The key is to make the small task related to the main project that should be the focus of your attention. But don't stay on the insignificant beginning task. Move on to the priority as soon as you are able.

If you have a report to write, sit down at your desk and put your writing tablet in front of you. Pick up a pencil. Write out the heading. Realize that you don't have to prove anything with the first draft. Even the best writers produce first drafts that are entirely unacceptable for publication. So begin. Not the entire paper. Just the first paragraph or first section. Then continue with your project.

Decision:	Choose either Nicaragua or China as subject for term paper
Objectives:	"A" for grade
	Understanding of major country
	Understanding role of women
	Practice setting time limits
	Improve writing skills
	Broaden horizons

Time allowed for decision: One–half hour

	Nicaragua	China
PRO	Research material okay Interesting country I read Spanish	Research material Interesting country Major country Little knowledge of China
CON	Small country Already know Nicaragua	A bit more time to complete report

Decision: Do paper on China
Time of decision: 23 minutes
How I felt after making decision: Surprised at how easy decision was
I wonder why I put it off?
Feel confident.

Figure 3.5 Sample pro/con decision chart.

Use the Indirect Approach

If you can't begin the central task, try approaching it sideways. Caroline said she sometimes worried too much, even about things beyond her control. But she found that she could get on with her work by doing a related project to the task at hand, one that was easy compared to the central difficult project on which she should be working.

If her mind was too cluttered with concern, she might begin by reading an article related to the material she was working on. Often within ten minutes she'd be attacking her immediate writing task. On occasion nothing succeeded. When this happened she just said, "Forget it. I'll do fine next time."

If you have trouble starting the tough new physics chapter, begin to plan the lab project, or take some easier aspect of the chapter such as writing down all the new formulas and definitions of symbols. For a writing assignment, do an interesting or easy part first, such as revising what you wrote yesterday. Use your imagination. There are typically dozens of ways to approach the task indirectly. Usually you will soon be working at the main project.

Tackle Fear

Fear is the cause of much procrastination. Fear that you'll get an "F," fear that you don't have the ability to do a good job, or perhaps fear that your instructor, who is an expert in the subject, couldn't possible be pleased by your work.

Try to see your task in perspective. You can ask yourself: "Realistically, what is the most terrible thing that can happen?" Usually it will not be all that serious. Don't be a perfectionist in the initial stages of the project. It isn't necessary that every undertaking be worthy of a Nobel prize or that every grade be an "A." Even less is it necessary to have your initial drafts of a report or project be excellent. So relax, you can do just fine.

The most important rule in facing up to unreasonable fear is to STAND UP TO IT. Naturally some fears are justified—things that can hurt you or get you into trouble. But for matters that require your attention, putting them off will make you more fearful and weaken your self-confidence. Confronting fear will build character and make it easier next time.

Carl was in big trouble when he stopped by to see me. He'd been arrested for drunk driving and causing an accident. A jail sentence at the upcoming hearing was a possibility. He was angry with himself for being so irresponsible, and felt terrible about the accident. Even more, he was scared to the point of being unable to concentrate on his work. I asked him what legal steps he had taken. He said, "None." I asked him what he planned to do. "I don't know," he replied. He was obviously frozen with fear.

We discussed possible responses to his trouble, and Carl decided to enroll in the student/staff legal plan which offered low-cost legal representation. He called to set up an appointment with an attorney. Knowing that he was dealing rationally and actively with his problem enabled him to resume studying, though understandably not with his previous efficiency.

Carl was lucky. He just got a stiff fine and a suspended license, along with significantly higher insurance premiums. Ideally, you won't have to deal with such an unpleasant or serious legal problem. But whatever fears you may face, *practice* dealing with fearful issues by taking appropriate action and you will eventually be successful most of the time.

Visualize

Try closing your eyes for a couple of minutes before you begin your project. Relax your muscles and take a few deep breaths. Imagine yourself breathing out feelings of anxiety and worry and breathing in feelings of confidence. Perhaps visualize some relaxing mountain scene to settle your mind. Picture yourself in detail accomplishing your task for the next hour. See the confident look on your face; imagine yourself opening the book, systematically surveying the chapter, stopping after each section to recall what you have read, going back to pick up any unclear points. View yourself being organized, systematic, and purposeful. Now open your eyes and begin.

On a regular basis think about your work as quite manageable. Picture yourself as believing deep in your heart and soul that you can study or work diligently for the next hour, week, and semester.

Measure Your Progress

Keep a record of time spent if you have trouble with procrastination, just a simple list that roughly estimates where you spend your time each day. Figure 3.6 gives

ACTIVITY	TIME	REASON
(Watched TV)	7- 9:00 A.M.	Dreaded math
Chemistry class	9- 10:00	Always attend classes
Review chem + began lab proj.	10 - 12:00	Followed weekly schedule
Lunch with Jim, went over chem.	12 - 1:00	Enjoy friend, planned chem. project
Library	1 - 2:00	Did math
Philosophy class	2 - 3:00	Always attend classes
Relaxed	3 - 4:00	Need break
Exercise group	4 - 5:00	Health & social
Socialize & dinner	5 - 6:30	Rest & relax
Library	7 - 9:30	Weekly sched.
(Actually studied	7 - 8:15	
read magazine till 9:30)		
TV	10 - 10:30	Relaxation time
Did schedule for tomorrow	10:30 - 10:45	Time management

20 MINUTES MORE STUDY THAN YESTERDAY, GOOD WORK!!!
Try going to library at 8:00 A.M. to avoid temptation.
Take break after one hour of study in evening.
Overall, continuing to improve. Continue to have fun, don't
overdo it. WAY TO GO !!!

Figure 3.6 Sample chart of time spent in one day.

you an example of how to do this. But don't devote a lot of attention to it. Write down why you think you spend your time on each activity. Don't condemn or criticize yourself. This merely makes developing good work habits more difficult. Just understanding what you do can make it easier to work effectively. Circle the items that indicate a waste of time. Write down suggestions for doing better next time. Keep the record for a few days and use occasionally, as long as it seems to help. A form is provided on p. 75.

The most important point is to NOTE ANY INCREASE OR IMPROVEMENT IN STUDYING. Be specific, noting number of additional minutes, degree of greater concentration, and so on. Remember to *emphasize the positive, no matter how small the accomplishment may be.* Write down the fact that you saved time by asking the librarian for help, that you had the courage to ask a professor for suggestions on sources. Any little step that you have taken to improve your use of time should be noted.

Reinforce Yourself

One part of reinforcing yourself requires setting up conditions that are like some pleasant or positive experiences you've had. It requires merely that you bring some aspect of these pleasant or successful associations into the present task you're trying to begin.

The idea is to create pleasant conditions WHILE YOU BEGIN TO WORK. Is there a quiet garden that can help inspire you to begin reading that novel? I know one student who loves sports so much that when he can't study, he sits on the bleachers while intramural teams play. The noise would distract most students, but it actually helps him get started. He's using pleasant associations to assist him in overcoming inertia. He shifts to the library once he develops momentum.

Can't get into that Spanish short story? Maybe you really enjoy coffee breaks. Try sitting in a quiet coffee shop and give yourself a one-hour limit while you have a favorite drink or snack. Allow yourself five or ten minutes to enjoy the surroundings; visualize yourself reading the story; then pick up the book and begin. The snack-bar technique should be employed with discretion, though, because of its effect on the wallet and waistline.

The second part of reinforcing yourself is to give yourself a little reward for successfully getting started. Next time you may not have to create the same pleasant conditions in order to begin, but it's a good idea to regularly reward yourself anyway to encourage yourself to work in the future. Pages 14–15 of Chapter 1 will help you establish appropriate rewards.

Realize That Good Techniques for Overcoming Writer's Block Exist

Many students have an especially hard time dealing with term papers and reports. Writer's block is one of the most common forms of procrastination. Pages 239–240 of Chapter 8, which deals with writing, describe several excellent ways to overcome this common difficulty.

Sometimes personal problems or underlying psychological difficulties such as depression can contribute to procrastination or lack of concentration. In cases where the above techniques don't seem to help, it's advisable to seek assistance at the school's counseling center. For most people the above techniques can bring dramatic improvement if they're seriously undertaken.

SUMMARY

Time management is simply an extremely effective form of planning. It's a way of linking goals to time that makes many of your decisions in advance. It's a technique that can free you from much indecision and worry and enable you to work effectively and efficiently. It's a major part of developing a decisive winning edge.

Most students sometimes have problems with procrastination, and for many students this is their number one obstacle to success in college. The techniques in this chapter can help you beat procrastination and get on with the task at hand. Almost always the actual work is far less stressful than the anxiety created by putting important things off. The trick is to remain positive and upbeat, building on your past successes in getting control of your time. For further reading I suggest Alan Lakein's *How to Get Control of Your Time and Your Life* listed in the Bibliography.

The strategies and tactics suggested in this chapter should be molded to your particular needs and judged on the basis on what works best for you. Coupled with the strategies developed throughout this book, time management gives you a powerful tool for maximizing your success in college and beyond.

SUCCESS STEPS

STEP ONE: Find Where Your Time Goes

The idea of this step is to get an accurate indication of where you're spending your time. Refer back to p. 71. Include only significant blocks of time, not a one-minute walk to find a paper clip. Remove this page and keep in a convenient place such as a notebook you use regularly. Circle the items that indicate a waste of time. Don't spend too much time on this process. You'll want to devote most of your time to your studies.

ACTIVITY	TIME				REASON
	Day 1	Day 2	Day 3	Day 4	

Positive Points:

Areas for improvement:

Words of encouragement:

STEP TWO: Make an Action List

Action lists should be kept in some convenient place. If you've not yet done one, simply fill in this sheet and tear it out when completed. Use it as a master or as a daily action list. Cross out each item as completed. Construct new action lists as needed. A notebook or 3 X 5 card is fine. DON'T FORGET TO PRIORITIZE THE ITEMS ON YOUR LIST: two stars for top priority items, one star for other priority items, and no stars for routine matters. Make revised lists daily, weekly, or as needed. Detailed instructions and a sample action list are provided on pp. 56–57.

ACADEMIC TASKS	PERSONAL TASKS

STEP THREE: Create a Weekly Schedule

See below for a sample time schedule and instructions. Modify the form as needed. Fill out one form now. Tear it out and keep it in a handy place. Use the form on the next page to make copies for your personal use as needed.

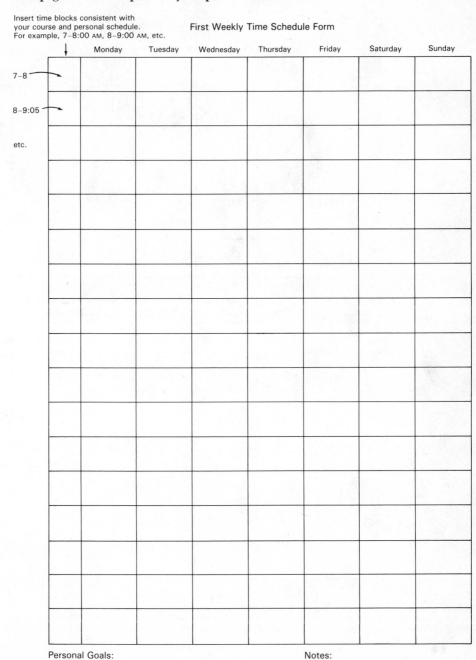

Insert time blocks consistent with your course and personal schedule. For example, 7–8:00 AM, 8–9:00 AM, etc.

First Weekly Time Schedule Form

	Monday	Tuesday	Wednesday	Thursday	Friday	Saturday	Sunday
7–8							
8–9:05							
etc.							

Personal Goals: Notes:

Insert time blocks consistent with
your course and personal schedule.
For example, 7–8:00 AM, 8–9:00 AM, etc.

Additional Weekly Time Schedule Form

	Monday	Tuesday	Wednesday	Thursday	Friday	Saturday	Sunday
7–8							
8–9:05							
etc.							

Personal Goals: Notes:

STEP FOUR: Construct a Semester-long Bar Graph Chart

Consult pp. 58, 60 and Figure 3.3 for further discussion and a sample semester schedule. This graph is easy to complete, but it's far more sophisticated than it looks. It allows you to plan complex projects such as term papers, showing you when each phase should begin and end. You should include only major projects from your courses, as well as major review periods for exams. Also include deadlines and exam dates. Shade in your progress on projects as you go along. This will give you a clear measure of how you are doing from a time standpoint. Tear out the following page when completed and post it in a conspicuous place.

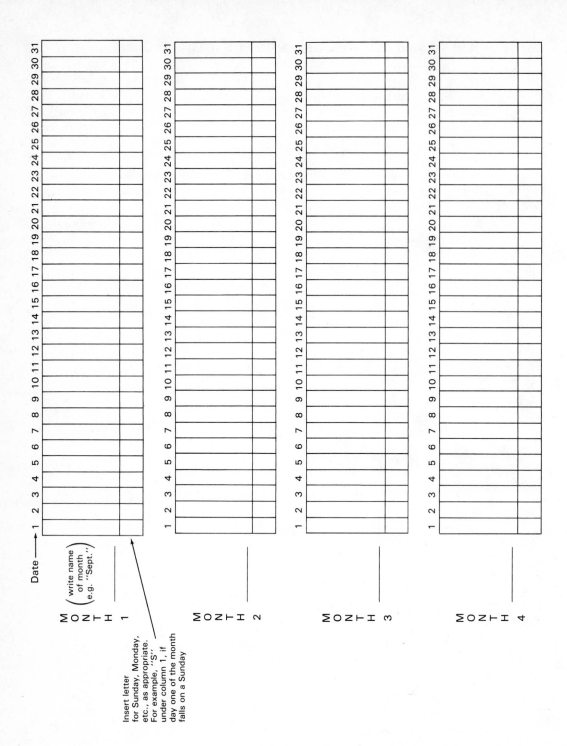

Date ⟶

MONTH 1

(write name of month
e.g. "Sept.")

Insert letter
for Sunday, Monday,
etc., as appropriate.
For example, "S"
under column 1, if
day one of the month
falls on a Sunday

MONTH 2

MONTH 3

MONTH 4

Chapter
4

Think Yourself to College Success

You can think yourself to college success. CERTAIN STRATEGIES OF THINKING CAN SHARPEN YOUR ANALYTICAL ABILITIES AND LEAD TO CREATIVE IDEAS THAT CAN RADICALLY IMPROVE YOUR GRADES. What's more, developing these thinking strategies will give you a significant competitive advantage in your career. They can improve your judgment and dramatically enhance your capacity to find solutions to problems.

The sad fact is that many students, like the driver in Figure 4.1, choose not to think. They just want to be told what they need to know to pass so they can parrot back the "knowledge" at exam time. Little do they perceive how much more interesting their studies would become if they tried to improve their thinking ability. Little do they know how much better they'd do if they developed their capacity to think. You'll see in this chapter that it's not nearly so difficult to think for yourself as you may imagine. Over time this ability can be increased significantly by habitually asking a few key questions.

Students who think really try to understand the subjects they're studying. They want to know why things are the way they are and why things work the way they do. They recognize that their instructors and their books might be wrong and that there are probably other points of view. So they try to evaluate ideas for them-

Figure 4.1 Good thinking is an essential part of doing well in college and in life. Thinking about your subjects makes it much easier to learn and remember, and your courses become more interesting. Developing the ability to think effectively for yourself is one of the most important things you'll ever learn and is a skill that will never become outdated.

selves. And they attempt to come up with new ideas. This makes their courses much more interesting because they become active participants.

Applying the basic thinking techniques in this chapter provides you with one of the most important ways of improving your grades

---

Thinking makes it easier to learn and easier to remember because things start to make more sense. Subjects become more meaningful because thinking makes us aware of the significance of what we're studying to our world and the people in it. It also makes us aware of the relevance to our own lives. Naturally, this increases our motivation to learn. The ability to think for ourselves may be the most important thing we ever learn.

In virtually every job a key to success is the ability to understand and solve problems. This capacity depends on the way we think. So developing our thinking capacity in college can pay high career dividends.

How can you improve your capacity to think? The ideas and techniques developed in this chapter will give you an important jump in developing a keen analytical and creative mind. But the development of thinking ability requires that you apply these ideas in your courses, for it is there that your analytical and creative skills will be refined to a sharp edge.

Sandy came to see me about improving her performance after receiving a "C" on my mid-semester exam. We talked about her course work and career plans as well as her mid-semester grade. She said, "My IQ is only a little above average, and I guess my 'B—' grade point average is about the best I can expect. I'd like to aim for at least a 'B—' in your course. Can you tell me how I can improve?"

I said, "You're quite right to accept yourself and your performance level if you're really trying, and 'B' students can achieve great career success. But are you sure you've done all you can to improve your grades?"

Then I explained to her that IQ had far less to do with academic performance, career success, or creative capacity than most people realize. Basically it measures a person's capacity to answer a bunch of questions quickly—questions that do measure some aspects of abstract reasoning ability but typically do not measure effectively many other aspects of intelligence. Sometimes these tests contain biases that distort their ability to give us reliable information about student capabilities.

Intelligence tests don't measure creative capacity, interpersonal sensitivity, administrative ability, drive, determination, interest, character, or attitude. And these latter traits of intelligence and character are usually more important in determining academic and career success. Students sometimes also sell themselves short because of scores on other tests such as the SAT, which have their uses but again are imperfect at predicting academic and career performance. They don't measure many basic components of intelligence and character that are fundamental to success.

So don't depend on IQ or other "ability" tests to assess your intellectual potential. Work with your instructors and with yourself to maximize your real potential.

"I try hard, but I just can't seem to get out of a 'B−' rut," Sandy said.

She'd spent a reasonable amount of time studying, and, unlike most students, seemed to have good study skills.

I asked her for her exam and read it again.

"Sandy this is basically okay," I said. "You presented many of the main points raised in the book and lectures, but your answer lacks originality and insight. It doesn't explain *why* these things happened. It doesn't put the material in perspective, answering the question 'How does this *compare* with other cases.' And it doesn't answer the question: *'What's the significance?'* That's why you didn't get a better grade."

We met several more times, on each occasion going over strategies for thinking more critically and creatively. After our second meeting Sandy said. "I'm sure I can learn to do it."

Indeed she did! She got a "B+" on her final exam and a "B+" for the course. Recognizing that she couldn't expect total success overnight, she continued to work on her thinking skills and eventually obtained consistent "A's" and high "B's" in all her courses.

How Did She Do It?

- She made herself *believe* she could do it. She rejected her stereotypes of herself ("I'm no good at math; I'll never be able to compete with the bright students"). She grew determined and positive about her ability to improve.
- She became independent-minded and continually tried to *critically evaluate* the material she was learning.
- During each class and study period she consciously looked for the *what, how,* and *why.*
- She always asked, *"What's the significance?"*

- She began to look for *comparisons and alternatives* as she proceeded through her courses.
- She tried to *classify* and *categorize* as she studied.
- She concentrated on *methods of analysis and thinking* used by the professors and authors in each of her courses.
- She took courses that would help her ability to think, courses such as logic, psychology, statistics, writing, and others.
- She began to apply critical and creative thinking to personal decisions and problems.

These steps dramatically altered the quality of Sandy's academic performance. Eventually, these higher level approaches to thinking became second nature. But Sandy didn't rest with these basic steps. She made the development of critical thinking ability a primary GOAL of her college education and a primary GOAL in each of her courses.

BECOMING A GOOD CRITICAL THINKER

Critical thinking is a process of analysis and evaluation. It relies on logical thought processes and makes evaluations on the basis of rational judgment. Don't be afraid of the word "analysis." At its simplest, this just means breaking the subject into easier-to-handle parts and looking at the problem from a specific viewpoint. "Evaluation" refers to the judgments you make about the material you're considering.

The purpose of critical thinking is to help us explain, solve problems, and discover truth. Critical thinking is essential to reading and studying effectively and solving problems in all our courses. It's also basic to intelligent decision making in all aspects of our lives.

The initial steps in learning to think critically are surprisingly easy. It's mostly a matter of getting into a few basic habits as you study or listen to lectures. And it gets easier with practice. The payoffs are an easier time studying and remembering, higher grades, and greater career and personal success.

Critical thinking tells us which information is important and should be remembered. It lets us know how ideas in a course fit together, and enables us to develop the best answers to exam questions. It helps us put knowledge into perspective and to evaluate and think independently. Later in this chapter we'll see that there's another important form of thinking called "creative thinking." But it's good critical thinking that forms the underpinning for effective creative thinking and constitutes the most important form of analysis for most college course work.

Good critical thinking can:

Help you understand your books and instructors.

Help you solve problems, both academic and personal.

Help you answer exam questions.

Help you make decisions.

Help you organize your course material.

Help you remember what you read.

Help you evaluate what you learn.

Give you a sense of pride in your ability to think independently.

The following strategies can greatly improve your ability to think critically and supply an almost immediate payoff.

Ask Basic Questions

The following key questions appear simple, yet they target core areas of critical analysis that can give your understanding and performance a significant boost. You should continually ask yourself these questions in your studies until they become internalized and automatic.

1. Ask Yourself "WHAT?"   In effective thinking DEFINITIONS ARE EX-TREMELY IMPORTANT. Typically, what's being defined is a concept, which helps you organize the subject and make sense of it.

It's difficult to understand something if you don't know precisely what it is. And it's even more difficult to communicate intelligently about a subject if you're vague about what it is. If you're going to do well in economics, you must know, precisely, what "supply," "demand," "gross domestic product," and other concepts mean.

Many students make the deadly error of thinking that definitions are unimportant. In reality, definitions deal with the *what* of the subject matter and are fundamental to understanding course material and handling exams effectively.

Observe the care your instructors and authors use to define their terms. Do they try to make clear their central concepts? Do their definitions contain hidden conclusions or value judgments? You can more quickly grasp the subject matter if you understand the implications of definitions.

Here's a quick method for learning and understanding key definitions and concepts. Imagine you have to explain them to a high school student. Use your own words, being as precise as possible. As you study, just pause for a moment until you can do this.

Next, consider your definition in light of the one given by the author or instructor. Be able to give both definitions without looking at your book or notes, modifying your own definition as necessary to conform to the one provided in your course. (If your own definition seems better, keep it in mind as you read to see if you can come up with new and interesting ways of looking at the material.)

Now you'll really understand what terms and concepts mean and how they fit into the subject. This short, little step you've just taken will enable you to understand and remember much better than you otherwise could.

If you carefully define basic terms on exams and term papers, you distinguish yourself from other students who don't bother, and give yourself an easy chance for a better grade (Chapters 6 and 7 show you how to do this).

2. Ask Yourself, "HOW?" In mathematics, the sciences, and technical courses, you should pay special attention to procedures, including the *reasons* for particular procedures. This increases understanding, recall, and the ability to solve problems. Focusing on "how" also aids understanding and remembering in other courses. Consider these examples.

As you read a novel for an English or modern language course, try to figure out how the author reveals the character of the major subjects. Does the author just tell you they're honest, disloyal, or whatever? Or is character revealed in some other way, say by the actions or words of people in the story. Knowing HOW an author communicates will make your understanding of the material sharper and greatly increase your ability to make independent judgments about it. You can also write more intelligently about the novel at exam time.

Sandy was careful to specify the "how" steps when she did a report on legislative process in the passage of a women's rights bill. She briefly discussed key steps. Interest groups lobbied; key senators and members of Congress introduced a bill and mobilized support; committee hearings were held. After passage by both houses the bill went to the President for his signature, and so on. Knowing how the bill progressed through Congress strengthened Sandy's grasp of the material.

Yet she evaluated this process for herself. She knew that just because these and other steps occurred didn't mean that any one of them was necessarily important to the bill's passage. Maybe the shots were really being called by a group of insiders, or outsiders for that matter. As she read books and articles for her report she observed the authors' line of reasoning.

AS YOU STUDY OR AS YOU LISTEN TO LECTURES, PAY PARTICULAR ATTENTION TO METHODS OF THINKING AND ANALYSIS. This was one of Sandy's most important new secrets. By paying attention to the way the experts reasoned, Sandy was able to pick up many good habits of thought. When she attended lectures she always bracketed material that indicated scientific method, proof, and lines of reasoning. She did the same thing as she read and took notes.

This helped her understand and remember, because it gave the subject more meaning. She did not, however, automatically accept what she read and heard as valid.

3. Ask Yourself, "WHY?"   This is sometimes the toughest question. It's often
possible to more easily explain *how* something happens than *why*. When we ask
why, we're seeking to understand *causes*. One of the reasons Sandy got an "A" on
her paper was her discussion of underlying and immediate causes for the introduction and passage of the bill. She dealt with these questions: Was it the increased
political power of women that determined the outcome? If so, why did this come
about? Was it that democratic ideas acquired such force that they became irresist-
ible? Was it that technological change minimized the male/female difference in the
workplace? Was male physical strength now less important in giving men a domi-
nant social role? If Sandy had just dealt with the "what" and "how" (describing the
bill and the stages it went through) her report would have been merely *descriptive*.
By dealing with the "why" she made it *analytical* as well. This greatly enriched her
paper and boosted her grade significantly.

   Answering these kinds of "why" questions with precision is especially difficult
in the social sciences, education, criminal justice, some of the humanities, or any
field that studies complex historical, sociological, or psychological processes. It's a
lot easier to prove that the National Organization for Women lobbied Congress on a
particular bill than it is to pin down the underlying causes for the evolution of
women's rights or even for the passage of a particular bill. But ultimately the why
questions are crucial. To understand something requires knowing the reasons it
happened.

   In the physical sciences it's often possible to reach a much more precise level
of explanation. Experiments can be conducted and controlled in a way that's impossible in many other fields. Here the importance of the why question is fundamental
in a practical sense. If you can understand "why" with precision, you can predict
what will happen in the future, given a particular set of circumstances. And if you
can explain and predict with precision, you may be able to control the forces you're
studying. Understanding the *causes* of a disease may enable you to cure it.

4. Ask Yourself "WHAT'S THE SIGNIFICANCE?"   When instructors grade exams and papers they typically look to see if the student understands the relevance
of the material. THIS IS ONE OF THE MAJOR DISTINCTIONS BETWEEN AN
EXCELLENT AND AN AVERAGE OR GOOD STUDENT. The excellent student
knows the significance of the material, how it relates to the course and other fields
of study, and its importance for the human condition.

   Sandy gave herself a decided advantage by dealing with the significance question. She asked, Does this law make any difference? Is it just a symbolic act designed to make women think they have a voice, but offering no real change, or is
there real substance to it? Is it one more indication that a worldwide struggle for
equality is succeeding? She put her paper into perspective sociologically, politically,
and historically. She attempted to answer this crucial question: *What can we learn*
from the case I've just analyzed: with respect to women's rights, the legislative

process, and national and social and political trends. She even briefly noted how her case fit into worldwide processes of social change.

Understanding and explaining the significance gives students a major edge when they take exams and write papers. It shows the instructor that students are doing more than mere rote memorization. They are giving the material *significance*. They show the instructor that they have developed the ability to think.

Here' how to look for the significance:

- Listen for the instructor's views on the significance of the topic during lectures.
- Watch for the textbook author's comments on significance as you read.
- Apply insights from other courses to the subject you're currently studying. Look for connections.
- Think about how the subject matter of the course might affect your personal life or the lives of people you care about.
- Consider how the the topic fits into current world affairs and how it impacts on the human condition. Try to empathize with those involved.
- Ask yourself how the topic can help you understand the human race and human behavior, the world, and the universe.

5. Ask Yourself, "HOW DOES THE TOPIC COMPARE?"   What are the similarities and differences between this topic or item you're studying and other cases? What can these similarities and differences tell me?

Sandy's comparison focused on this issue: How does the legislative quest for women's rights compare with the struggle for civil rights for black Americans. This comparison only took her three paragraphs but it added significantly to her paper.

It's often best to compare things that aren't too different, so the task of comparison is manageable. Systematically comparing General Motors with a neighborhood club of five-year-old-children is unlikely to make a good topic for a term paper, though we'll see later that such a comparison may be a good way to develop creative ideas.

For the student faced with a tough math or science problem, thinking about similar types of problems that have already been mastered is one way to find tipoffs to the solution. If you're studying about the organization of a giant corporation in a business class, ask yourself how the company compares or contrasts with with other large organizations such as a welfare agency or large charitable organization. How does it compare with small business organizations and other forms of private enterprise?

Comparison is a central part of effective critical thinking and it's one of the best ways to develop understanding and insight. It can help you see patterns, which can be basic to making sense out of something.

Comparing can:

- Alert you to possible explanations and causes for similar events.
- Aid you in seeing important differences or unique characteristics, which can give you insight and understanding.

- Assist you in making a stronger argument. By referring to other cases you may be able to give your ideas more credibility.
- Help you classify things so you can more easily understand and remember them.
- Enable you to show your instructor that you see the bigger picture.

6. Ask, "HOW CAN THIS MATERIAL BE ORGANIZED?"   Establish CATEGORIES AND CLASSIFICATION SYSTEMS. This allows you to *organize* your material and makes the tasks of analysis, study, and remembering much simpler. It's far easier to manage and remember a few major categories than a jumble of many different ideas and facts. But good classification schemes require a little thought.

Your categories should be chosen because they're useful. If you're studying world leaders it might make sense to divide them into categories based on whether or not they believe in western democracy, whether they're male or female, or many other variations. It probably wouldn't make sense to divide them on the basis of hair color or which flavors of ice cream they like best. Ask yourself, "What am I trying to explain or understand?" and try to choose your categories accordingly.

Your categories should cover the entire range of cases you're considering. Also, you should try to make each category distinct and not overlap with other categories. Sandy was stumped on this one. She couldn't come up with meaningful categories for her report. I asked what had struck her as most interesting as she did her research.

She said, "I'm amazed at how much of what governments do is pure fluff—just window dressing. How do they get away with it?" Sandy had found a useful way to classify government actions dealing with equal rights: actions designed to make a real difference and those designed to give the appearance of change.

She was concerned that some of her examples might not fit perfectly in one category or the other. I explained that this is often the case with real-world examples. Categories are concepts we create in our heads, so each one can be considered an ideal type. No need to worry if specific cases didn't fit perfectly into each box.

We talked about the possibility of a more sophisticated system, but both agreed that for her purposes the simple two-category scheme was fine. It helped give her paper organization and significance.

Evaluate as You Learn

We saw in Chapter 1 that a key academic value is the desire to discover the truth. In addition to being a value in its own right, there are many practical payoffs in seeking the truth, not the least of which is higher grades. Instructors are impressed with students who show they can think for themselves.

The nurturing of this value means that your studies will be much more interesting, and you'll be more strongly motivated to work. Because you're more involved, you learn and remember more. Here are some basic steps that will enable you to evaluate more effectively.

Try to Be Objective and Open-minded   Effective students are willing to consider the possibility that they, themselves, may be wrong. They recognize that highly intelligent and good people believe the opposite of many issues: the death penalty, gun control, nuclear disarmament, woman and the draft, the legal drinking age, legalization of marijuana, and so on. This suggests, at the least, that we should give the other side a respectful hearing.

Policies commonly considered "bad" may later come to be accepted. At one time many conservative politicians felt that mandatory government insurance for old age was wrong and dangerous. Now almost everyone accepts Social Security as good national policy. At one time some liberal politicians felt that rigid regulation of business was good policy. Now virtually everyone believes that too many stringent controls can weaken the economy. Today's liberals may be tomorrow's conservatives and vice versa.

In science the point is still more obvious. Even the most basic ideas—theories that are fundamental assumptions regarding the nature of the universe—may be disproven. Most scientists today accept the "big bang" theory of the creation of the universe, yet every competent scientist accepts the possibility that this theory might someday be undermined by new evidence. The very nature of intellectual inquiry in science and other fields assumes that truth is only temporary.

Perfect objectivity is probably impossible. Everyone to some extent has had their thinking molded by their environment. Even the effort to think objectively implies a value preference for objective thought. Still, we're more likely to arrive at the truth if we consider the matter as objectively as possible.

Tips for Developing Objectivity and Open-Mindedness
- Put yourself in the other person's position. Try to imagine their feelings as well as understand their ideas.
- Be able to argue both sides of the issue.
- Watch for loaded or meaningless words and phrases. Recognize when someone's trying to manipulate you.
- Recognize it's unlikely that any individual, group, or political party will have total truth or virtue on its side.
- Realize that there are very real rewards for objective and independent thinking. These rewards will be found in your grade report, your wallet or purse, your greater career and personal success, and the pride you take in your growing capacity to think for yourself.

Be Skeptical   Don't accept things at face value. And don't take anything for granted. Assume that everything you read and hear about is not necessarily correct or true. The instructor in the cartoon on p. 92 is too negative; he should be trying to show his students how to think critically. But this biting cartoon does illustrate an important point. Students who don't think critically are unlikely to impress their instructors and earn high grades. And they're unlikely to come up with the kinds of solutions and decisions that can propel them ahead in their careers.

It's possible to be too skeptical. The seemingly improbable event may sometimes be true. Consider conspiracy theories—these theories are quite attractive.

Figure 4.2 Always think critically as you listen and read. *Source:* DOONESBURY © 1985 G. B. Trudeau. Reprinted with permission of Universal Press Syndicate.

The idea is that someone must be responsible if things go wrong. So a bad event must be the result of a communist or capitalist plot or whatever. Or maybe it's the business or liberal elite that's blamed for engineering violence or drug abuse.

The wise student knows that conspiracies are difficult to prove and usually overrated. Once I included a few multiple-choice questions on a final exam. During the course the students had read about the extreme form of discrimination called apartheid that exists in South Africa. As a joke and as a little gift to students I asked: "What is the primary, underlying cause of violence in South Africa?" I gave several choices: (a) A KGB (Soviet secret police) plot. (b) Apartheid (the South African system of a racial segregation). (c) the decline in gold prices, and so on. The correct answer, of course, was apartheid, the system of racial discrimination and segregation.

The conspiracy answer (a KGB plot) was not a fundamental point. Sure, it's possible the KGB may have tried to influence events or groups, but from the standpoint of exploiting a basic problem. The exact degree and impact of their involvement is a matter for research, not uncritical belief. The clear underlying cause of the problem is a system of discrimination that is strikingly unjust. The reality is probably that most political and social events occur as the result of complex economic, political, and social forces—not somebody's planned actions.

On the other hand, the KGB (and American Central Intelligence Agency for that matter) have undoubtedly engineered some important political events. Clearly the role of the KGB in the post-Second World War politics of Afghanistan has been significant, while the CIA was involved in the politics of South Vietnam. Although many have a tendency to overrate conspiracy theories, they may sometimes be valid.

Be Conscious of Motives   Does the person making the argument have a vested interest in what is being presented? If an oil company executive is arguing for lower taxes for oil producers, you should obviously be alert to the fact that they want to pay less money to the government. The same principle holds for union officials advocating higher wages. Either or both may be correct in their assertion that their idea is best for the country. On the other hand, they may just be trying to convince us because it's in their own self-interest to do so.

Authors of books and instructors may also have a vested interest in the theories or ideas they argue. Maybe they're trying to make their academic reputation by promoting a particular hypothesis or theory. There's nothing wrong with this, and it will usually be perfectly sincere. But it may make their presentation less objective than it otherwise would be.

Assume that nothing you read, however praiseworthy or however well-respected, contains the whole truth. Few scientists, instructors, or authors will have the whole answer. The world is too complex for any one individual to possess total, cosmic truth.

Watch for Manipulative Language   Writers and speakers sometimes try to sway people to their point of view by the clever use of language. Suppose you read that a group of politicians is "un-American." Clearly the writer's goal is to weaken their support from the public. Yet the term "un-American" tells us nothing about the politicians' patriotism or the wisdom of their policies. We need, instead, to weigh independently the merits of their actions and policies.

Charges that certain politicians are "imperialists" or "war-mongers" may also be pure propaganda. We should decide for ourselves the wisdom of their policies and not be swayed by labels, whether negative or positive.

The bottom line is that students shouldn't allow themselves to be manipulated. It sometimes happens that instructors and writers will unconsciously use words that carry a hidden bias. It's the job of independent thinkers to be alert to this.

Make Sure the Conclusion to an Argument Is Justified   Ask yourself if the argument you're listening to makes sense. For an argument to be valid, the conclusion must logically follow from the premises that go before.

This is a classic example of a good deductive argument:

All men are mortal.

Socrates was a man.

Therefore, Socrates was mortal.

But suppose you hear:

John Smith is from Nebraska.

I was once cheated by a man from Nebraska.

Smith will try to cheat me.

Of course, Smith, like most Nebraskans, is probably a fine person. But the speaker draws an inappropriate conclusion. This may seem obvious, but often invalid conclusions are more subtle. The trouble is that the line of argument is often unclear, so you have to make sure you consciously understand the reasoning behind a conclusion.

Although I can't present all the formal rules of deductive logic here, I can suggest that *spelling out the argument in your mind or on paper will often reveal serious flaws that will enable you to independently judge a lecture, article, or chapter in a book.* Instructors are greatly impressed with students who show this ability to think independently. The more you practice, the easier this kind of evaluation becomes. Here are a few of the more obvious forms of invalid arguments, commonly called fallacies.

   a. *The slippery slope.* The school Department wants our kids to receive sex education. Pretty soon they'll be having orgies in the high school. (It doesn't logically follow.)

   b. *Post hoc, ergo propter hoc.* This problem occurs when someone assumes that because one thing follows another, the first event must have caused the second. Consider this: The crime rate has fallen ever since Dave Jones became chief of police. This shows that Jones is doing a great job. (Maybe something else caused the crime rate to drop, like a population change that included a drop in the number of young men, a group statistically more likely to commit crimes.)

c. *Using an analogy as proof.* The difficulty here is the assumption that because things are alike in some ways, they are therefore alike in every way. Here's an example of an invalid, horrifying argument of the type too often accepted uncritically: Society is like a plant. We prune weak and sick branches off plants. So we should kill weak and sick people in order to have a healthy, productive society. (Human beings are independent, living, feeling creatures; the branches of plants are not. Only in some limited ways are plants like human society. Stupid as the plant analogy may seem, many people have been swayed by such arguments, which have been used to justify mass killings of various groups around the world.)

Weigh the Evidence In inductive arguments, evidence is marshalled to support a claim. The logic of this kind of argument doesn't require an absolute claim of proof, merely a probability of truth. Here's an example of a person presenting a fallacious argument called a hasty generalization:

"I met a young couple from Iceland last year. They seemed to argue all the time. Icelanders sure have a hard time getting along. I'm glad none of them live around here."

The key problem is the sample size. It's obviously too small. Unfortunately this kind of thinking is a major source of prejudice. Here's an example of a more reasonable argument:

Three hundred students on campus were surveyed for their views on abortion. Care was taken to insure that the sample was representative of the diversity of students enrolled. Eighty percent said they favored the right of women to have an abortion, and twenty percent were against abortion. Therefore we estimate that approximately three-quarters of the student body favors the right of women to have an abortion.

Because the sample of students is large and representative of the entire student body, we can conclude that the argument is *probably* true. We should qualify our conclusions with such words as "we estimate" or "perhaps as many as . . . ." We must also consider other issues. Were students given a variety of options? How were the questions phrased? and so on.

If students had been asked slanted questions, the responses wouldn't let you draw good conclusions about campus opinion on the issue of abortion. Here are two obviously slanted questions designed to produce a particular result: "Are you opposed to the murder of unborn babies?" and "Should old men in government and the courts have the right to dictate how women manage their own bodies?" The first question would tend to produce "yes" responses, and the second would likely encourage people to answer "no."

In actual practice the biases in opinion-poll questions and many other fields are much less obvious and usually unintentional. Good critical thinking can help protect us from being manipulated and aid us to think for ourselves. It prompts us to look at the facts and assess them impartially, challenging even our own ideas.

Develop Your Moral and Ethical Sensitivities   People who think effectively look for ethical and moral implications. They are concerned with consequences for human beings. Sometimes people think that all ideas and beliefs are about equal. We see some beliefs and behavior as bad because of our cultural biases. So it makes no sense to try to evaluate things from the standpoints of right and wrong, good and bad, or just and unjust.

But this creates a problem: ideas and beliefs help determine behavior and action. If we don't attempt to evaluate them, we fail to perceive the real-world consequences of moral choice. Questions of the rightness and wrongness of actions, for example, can be assessed in terms of their consequences for the person taking the action as well as others affected by it.

We should certainly be aware that our view of right and wrong, good and bad, just and unjust, can depend on our cultural conditioning and biases. But this doesn't mean we have to accept everything, everywhere as equally meritorious. The Aztecs tore the hearts out of living human beings as a sacrifice to the gods. While we should try to be objective in studying that culture and recognize its many achievements, we're certainly not obligated to accept human sacrifice as a legitimate expression of religious ritual.

Effective critical thinking doesn't require that we ignore issues of ethics and morality. Nor does it demand that we abandon all moral and ethical beliefs. On the contrary, it requires that we view moral and ethical issues as a core part of good thinking. Not only will this help us develop better ideas, it will make learning a lot more fun. Considering the ethical and moral consequences of things often deals with issues that are hotly contested, significant for humanity, and therefore highly interesting.

Don't Be Afraid of Uncertainty   When Sandy first thought about evaluating lectures and textbooks she felt uneasy. She asked, "Shouldn't I leave it to people who know more than I do—people who are experts? How can I possibly evaluate independently?"

"That's a problem for all of us, Sandy," I said. "Even experts don't know everything."

The trouble with relying on your instructors and other experts is that the experts disagree with one another on most issues. So you still have the problem of deciding which experts to believe. Besides, experts are just people and can have unconscious biases. Experts also have interests that they may push unreasonably, and what's good for them may not be good for us. A surgeon may make money on an unnecessary operation, but the patient clearly loses.

After a few weeks, Sandy discovered that she could often make reasoned judgments even if she wasn't an expert. Although she would sometimes have to withhold judgment, she decided that she could usually form beginning opinions. She said, "Just because I evaluate something and form an opinion doesn't mean I'm locked into it. I'm free to change my mind anytime I see more evidence or hear a better argument. My opinions and judgments aren't rigid; I expect them to evolve. Besides, I can always try to get more information if I feel I don't know enough to decide."

What struck me most about Sandy was the newfound pride she felt as she shifted gradually into a thinking mode that puts her in charge of her own mind. She quite rightly felt that this represented a quantum leap in her intellectual ability and her confidence in herself as an adult person.

Uncertainly is something even top scientists accept. It's a virtue, not a vice. It keeps us open to new evidence and makes it more likely that we'll get closer to the truth. As we try intelligently to evaluate ideas and information, we acquire increasing independence over our lives. We perform better in our schools and in our careers. Good critical thinking won't prevent you from making mistakes now and then, but it will enable you to be right far more often in the many academic, career, and personal decisions that guide our lives.

THE POWER OF CREATIVE THINKING

The ability to think creatively is central to both academic and career success. Creativity and originality are core academic values. DEVELOPING CREATIVE INSIGHTS AND IDEAS IN YOUR COURSE WORK IS ONE OF THE BEST WAYS TO DISTINGUISH YOURSELF IN THE EYES OF YOUR INSTRUCTORS, and this can lead to higher grades. It can also make your studies more interesting and give you the satisfaction that inevitably accompanies creative achievement.

Many discussions of creative thinking fail to stress an important point: EFFECTIVE CRITICAL THINKING IS A POWERFUL MECHANISM FOR DEVELOPING CREATIVE IDEAS. As you think critically, you proceed systematically toward solutions to problems. A scientist trying to find a cure for a deadly disease might decide to experiment with a new chemical because it has similar properties to drugs that have worked. This can speed up the process of finding the right drug because there's a focus on the most likely prospects.

Yet CRITICAL THINKING CAN ALSO BLOCK OUT CREATIVE SOLUTIONS. In the example above, you might unwittingly exclude an unlikely drug that could save tens of thousands of lives.

Sometimes the key to discovery lies in abandoning old categories and concepts. Ceramics were thought to be poor conductors of electricity, yet major advances in research on electrical conductivity in recent years are partly attributable

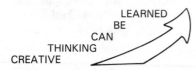

Figure 4.3 Learning to think creatively can pay high dividends.

to the use of this material, which had long been considered unsuitable. A significant advance occurred when scientists recognized that the old principles of conductivity might not be valid at super cold temperatures.

The most important element in developing your creative thinking ability is the *willingness to try*. Hang loose, have faith in yourself, and enjoy the unpredictability of your imagination. Creative thinking can be one of the most pleasurable and satisfying parts of academic life. Here are some practical, workable tips for increasing your creative thinking ability.

Reverse the Solution   If you're dealing with a physical problem, you can sometimes make a breakthrough by trying a reverse approach. Several years back a child was pinned under the frame of a car at a sand pit. Her life was being slowly crushed away. Rescuers worked frantically to save her, but every time they tried to jack up the car, the jack sank into the sand. No one thought of shifting their tactics, and the poor girl died. Only later did the rescuers realize that all they had to do was dig the sand from beneath the child, lowering her instead of trying to lift the car. Other more time-consuming options may also have been available, such as putting a wide board or other object under the jack.

David Perkins describes a more successful example of this point. NASA's scientists and engineers couldn't find a material that would withstand the fierce heat generated on re-entry into the earth's atmosphere. Finally someone solved the problem by changing the thinking process. Instead of looking for a substance that could withstand the heat, they decided to try something that would burn up but take the heat away from the re-entry vehicle. This breakthrough enabled astronauts to safely reenter the earth's atmosphere.

Consider Opposites   This is related to reversing the solution but refers more to the realm of ideas. The point is to consider the opposite of what you're being told to see if you can develop new insights and ideas. Systematically asking yourself this will sometimes yield surprising results. The idea for my first book was generated when I questioned the conventional wisdom concerning democratic political development.

Suppose an education major reads a statement like this: "The Parent Teachers Association (PTA) exists to serve the needs of parents and students." It might be interesting to consider the opposite. Maybe the organization exists primarily to serve the needs of teachers and school administrators rather than students and parents. Its primary function could be to build political support for ideas already decided by administrators or teachers.

Examine the Possible Benefits or Liabilities of Unanticipated Results   If you're doing an experiment for a biology or chemistry course, be open to the possibility that a flubbed result might still tell you something interesting. Analyze the possibilities. In 1928 Alexander Fleming noticed that bacteria had been killed by airborne mold that had contaminated a culture dish he'd been using in an experiment. This led to Fleming's discovery of penicillin, one of the century's most important medical breakthroughs.

In many complex problems there are so many factors with such complex relationships that it's often impossible to predict outcomes with certainty. Suppose you're taking a course dealing with welfare and you're trying to develop a program to decrease poverty. Might the program you develop have negative consequences you never considered? Perhaps some assistance programs would encourage recipients not to work because they'll lose money if they do. Other programs might provide the spark and training needed for many to break out of poverty. Being alert to the possibility of unanticipated consequences can greatly improve the quality of your academic performance.

Consider Whether There Might Be More Than One Result or Consequence of the Phenomenon You're Studying With respect to the welfare programs, a good creative thinker would recognize that there might *simultaneously* be benefits and liabilities resulting from the same anti-poverty program. This is often the case with programs in many fields. To continue with the example of the PTA, our education major might consider whether the PTA serves the interests of *both* the educational establishment and of parents and students.

Consider Variation; Don't Presume That Things Are Always the Same Some of the most important advances in studying electricity occurred when researchers recognized that certain materials behaved much differently at super cold temperatures. They offer little or no resistance to electrical current.

The economic and social implications are potentially massive. The generation and distribution of electricity could be much more efficient if power isn't wasted as it's transmitted over electrical lines. More generally, research in this field may produce major benefits in a host of areas such as medicine, third-world economic development, and environmental quality.

Or take the example of the education student studying the PTA. It might be important to ask whether the role of that organization varied among different kinds of school districts, under different management styles of school superintendents and so on. Asking these kinds of questions could provide valuable insight about how and why the PTA functions the way it does.

Use Offbeat Comparisons Try making absurd and offbeat analogies or groupings to spark your creative instincts. The person who invented velcro used as a model a burr that had the irritating habit of sticking fiercely to people who walked by.

If you're studying social or business groups, maybe you'll get some interesting ideas by comparing these to a biological organism, say the human body, or a colony of penguins, or whatever. Most offbeat ideas won't pan out, but the ones that do can pay great dividends. Even if you usually don't use these comparisons in your exams and papers, they can help you understand the significance of what you're studying and suggest ideas unconnected with the offbeat comparisons you employ.

Seeing Yourself in the Problem May Be a Useful Way of Generating Ideas This is useful in all fields, but has sometimes had spectacular payoffs in the sciences. Einstein imagined himself riding a beam of light as he pondered the questions of relativity. Seeing yourself as a character or director in a play, as a patient in a nursing course, or even as a rivet in an engineering project might give you good ideas and will certainly make learning more fun.

If Starting at the Beginning of the Problem Doesn't Yield an Answer, Try Beginning at the End or Middle   In an interesting problem presented by Edward de Bono, readers are asked to "divide a triangle into three parts in such a way that the parts can be put together again to form a rectangle or a square." As the author points out, this problem is tough because the shapes of the triangle aren't given.

   If you take it backwards, the solution is much easier. Start with a square since you know that it can have only one shape. Divide the square into triangles that can also be formed into a rectangle. Two of the possible solutions to the problem are shown in Figure 4.4.

Make Creativity a Game   Try BRAINSTORMING, that is, listing all possible ideas no matter how far out. Don't be afraid to be silly. Humor and creativity are closely linked. The idea is to generate as many ideas as possible. Maybe most won't be worth much, but it only takes a very few good ones to pay enormous dividends.

   There are a number of mind-bender problem books on the market that can be a source of entertainment as well as insight. Books analyzing the creative process, such as those by Adams, de Bono, Perkins, and Sternberg (included in the Bibliography) will probably be even more beneficial. Some of these include problems and can help you get into the habit of looking for alternatives and overcoming mental blocks to creativity.

Figure 4.4 Sometimes starting at the end of a problem makes it easier to find a solution. *Source:* Edward deBono, *Lateral Thinking: Creativity Step by Step.* New York: Harper & Row, 1970, pp. 177–79. Copyright © 1970 by Edward de Bono. Reprinted by permission of HarperCollins Publishers.

But it's important to focus on your courses in applying creative thinking strategies. This is where you can develop your thinking ability most effectively. I love to play chess, but I realize that most of the skills I've acquired from the game probably have only limited application to my professional work. I play mainly because it's a fun way to spend time with family and friends.

Let Simple Mechanical Steps Work for You Diagram the problem. Draw arrows to show cause and effect, interrelationships. Diagramming is thinking. And anything that improves your ability to think about your course work is a good investment.

In science, engineering, and similar courses, BUILD SIMPLE MODELS with paper, clay, pipe cleaners, paper clips, or any material that will allow you physically to play with the problem. One of the most important scientific events of the twentieth century was the discovery of the molecular structure of DNA, which contains genetic codes and is found in all living cells. Francis Crick and James Watson worked for months with hand-sized metal pieces representing the parts of the DNA molecule. Then one night Watson awoke after a dream of a spiral staircase, and he and Crick shortly thereafter completed their now famous double-helix model. These scientists revolutionized the study of genetics and received the Nobel Prize for their work.

Use Your Dreams, Fantasies, and Emotions as a Useful Source of Ideas The trouble is that we forget our dreams quickly, so it's smart to keep a notebook or note cards and pen handy. Reverie is a time of half-consciousness, between sleep and waking, that often yields useful ideas. If you're lying in bed half asleep, try bringing some project to mind and observe the strange combination of ideas that may emerge. Again write the ideas down because they fade quickly.

Many people use material from dreams. Several times when I was stuck on a particular problem in writing this book, I awoke at night to write down the answer. It's not surprising that we dream about things in which we're immersed and that we freely put together seemingly unconnected ideas and facts as we dream.

Bring Your Entire Life to the Learning Process Books, plays, travel adventures, movies, and other personal experiences can all be valuable aids to understanding. Take the 1980 movie *Nine to Five* starring Jane Fonda, Lily Tomlin, Dolly Parton, and Dabney Coleman. It's an entertaining film about some mistreated women employees who rise up against a tyrannical male boss and company that's been exploiting them and treating them like simple-minded people. In one hilarious part of the movie, Dolly and her friends kidnap their boss and implement some liberal company reforms, such as free child care.

This movie is a beautiful illustration of many principles of revolution, showing the corruption of the old system, the mobilization of exploited people, and so on. Comparing themes in the movie to your course work could bring a complicated academic subject down to earth. It could help you better understand your Russian history, sociology, or political science text. And you might get a unique insight into the possible causes of revolution. The point is to be alert to such comparisons and insights as you go about your daily life.

Your daily experiences can be a great source of ideas. Your interactions with people throughout the day can give you insights for your courses in psychology, business, sociology, anthropology, and many others.

ONE OF THE BEST SOURCES OF CREATIVE IDEAS IS YOUR COURSES. *Continually try to connect ideas among your different courses.* This will give you insights and will also help you think of interesting angles. Don't be timid. Try relating biology to economics. How is a mammal's generation of waste like (and different from) a country's generation of industrial waste? For example, animal waste produces benefits and liabilities (e.g., fertilizer as well as contamination). Can you develop any ideas about handling industrial waste from your study of animals?

Talk to Your Instructors About Your Ideas   They'll be glad to give you feedback and may be pleased that you suggested an idea or connection that had never occurred to them. One of the pleasures of teaching is having students come up after class with interesting ideas.

Pay Particular Attention to the Subjects in Which You Most Want to Develop the Ability to Think Creatively   Suppose you're an agriculture student with a particular interest in farm management. Stay alert to anything around you that could help you develop ideas for the operation of a farm. Maybe baggage-handling operations at airline terminals or the erection of a new building downtown can give you ideas. The possibilities are endless.

Visualize Yourself as a Creative, Insightful Person   Look for creativity in others and watch how they do it, including your professors and the authors of your books. See yourself as acquiring these same characteristics. As you improve your ability to think critically, you'll see more limitations in the ideas you read and hear about. Try to think of ways to overcome these limitations. BE POSITIVE ABOUT YOUR ABILITY TO DEVELOP CREATIVE INSIGHTS. As you proceed through your courses you will make drastic improvements in your creative abilities if you really want to and if you stick with it.

Follow the Principles of Good Time Management   Creative ideas almost always require a foundation of serious study. It's unlikely that you'll produce innovative insights and ideas out of thin air. You may have heard Thomas Edison's famous quote that "genius is one percent inspiration and ninety-nine percent perspiration." The ideas you get by applying these principles ordinarily won't require that much effort, but you've got to do your homework. You're unlikely to get a really good idea about astronomy if you haven't studied your textbook or attended the lectures.

FOR THE GREAT MAJORITY OF STUDENTS, MOST CREATIVE THINKING IS UNDOUBTEDLY THE RESULT OF STICKING TO THE TASK AT HAND. Many writers of term papers (or books) have kidded themselves into thinking that they can wait for the creative mood to strike or for the answer to appear out of thin air.

We also have everything to gain from building plenty of rest and leisure into our schedules. This rejuvenates us, and it lets us relate the subject to other courses and events. Rest, leisure, and fun are an important part of good thinking and good work. To the extent that creative thinking involves subconscious thought processes, rest and recreation can help us develop good ideas.

Don't Assume Uncritically Someone once said, "Assumption is the father of all foul ups." Certainly effective *critical* thinkers don't assume too much. They're careful to follow proper procedures and to be rational and orderly in their thinking. Who would want to fly in a plane whose pilot just assumed that the wing flaps were set for take off?

Assumptions can also block *creative* thought. The trouble is that many of our assumptions are unconscious and prevent us from approaching the problem from a different angle. Consider the following classic problem.

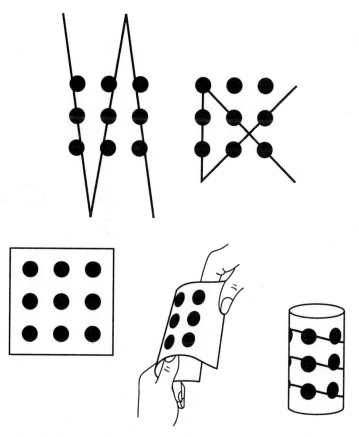

Figure 4.5 Don't let needless assumptions block your creativity.
Source: James L. Adams, *Conceptual Blockbusting,* © 1990 by Addison-Wesley Publishing Co., Inc., Reading, Mass. Diagrams, pp. 25–29. Reprinted with permission of the publisher.

You must keep your pencil touching the paper and draw no more than four straight lines that will cut across all nine dots. Three of many possible answers are be found in Figure 4.5.

Most people *assume* that the lines must not extend beyond the dots, that they cannot fold the paper, that they must keep it on a flat plane, and so on. They automatically set needless limits that prevent them from developing solutions.

Whenever you're stumped by a problem, whether academic or personal, consider whether some simple assumptions are limiting your ability to develop useful alternatives. As you try to develop interesting ideas for your papers and exams, set aside the assumed boundaries that can limit creative insight.

SUMMARY

One of the hallmarks of an educated people is the ability to think for themselves. Not everyone who acquires a formal education learns to think effectively. Students may acquire formal training and even a store of knowledge, but if they haven't developed their critical and creative thinking ability they will have missed a golden chance to develop skills they can use all their life. And their grades will usually reflect this failure to think. MANY OF THE FACTS YOU LEARN IN COLLEGE WILL BECOME DATED AFTER YOU GRADUATE, BUT YOUR ABILITY TO THINK WELL WILL NEVER GO OUT OF DATE.

Learning to think effectively is far less difficult than many people suppose. We've seen that continually asking just a few basic questions can make a profound difference in the quality of our thought and that a few simple strategies can help spark our creative capacities. Best of all, trying to think makes college and course work a lot more fun. It also helps us concentrate, understand, and remember.

The ideas and tactics presented in this chapter serve as a backdrop for some of the upcoming material. In one form or another, the practical application of thinking techniques has been a central theme of this book. By implementing the strategies and attitudes presented in this chapter you will have taken a significant step in maximizing your success in college as well as in life.

SUCCESS STEPS

STEP ONE: Handling Personal Problems and Relationships

Consider one of your personal problems, preferably involving interpersonal relations. Try to be open-minded and objective in analyzing the situation. Fill in the blanks.

1. Your point of view: _____

   _____

2. The other person's viewpoint _____

   _____

3. Mistakes the other person made in dealing with you _____

   _____

4. Mistakes you may have made in dealing with the other person _____

   _____

5. Possible areas of common goals or values _____

   _____

6. Using creative thinking strategies discussed in this chapter, devise eight possible solutions to the problem. Let your imagination run free in coming up with possible workable solutions (acceptance can sometimes be a solution):

   a.

   b.

   c.

   d.

   e.

f.

g.

h.

7. Which of the above ideas seem most feasible? _____

_____

_____

8. If helpful, consult others for advice. List best outside ideas if applicable. ___

_____

_____

9. What is your conclusion or decision? _____

_____

_____

STEP TWO: Thinking Effectively as You Study

This step anticipates some of the topics in the following chapter. It's designed to help you think more effectively in your courses. Take a current reading assignment in one of your most difficult courses that you haven't read yet. Use the following steps.

A. Scan the contents of the assignment, getting an idea of what's covered. Write down three main questions based on this survey.

1. _____

2. _____

3. _____

B. Now read the assignment one section at a time. Try to answer the three (or more) questions as you read.

1. Identify at least three important "what" items, including basic definitions. Write two entries each, one in the words of the text and one in your own words.

   a. _____

   _____

   _____

   _____

   _____

   b. _____

   _____

   _____

   _____

   _____

   c. _____

   _____

   _____

   _____

   _____

2. List three major "how" points (procedures, method of thinking or analysis, the evidence used to support arguments, and so on).

   a. _____

   _____

   _____

b. _____

_____

_____

c. _____

_____

_____

3. Now identify three major "why" points: explanations, underlying causes, reasons.

   a. _____

   _____

   b. _____

   _____

   c. _____

   _____

4. Next find four important "what's the significance" ideas, two of the author's and two of your own.

   a. _____

   _____

   b. _____

   _____

   c. _____

   _____

   d. _____

   _____

5. Now make two meaningful comparisons between the material you've just read and topics in your other courses.

   a. _____

   _____

   b. _____

   _____

6. Develop two simple ways to classify the material you've just read according to categories that will help you understand and remember.

   a. _____

   _____

   b. _____

   _____

7. After thinking about the material you've just read, how do you evaluate it with respect to quality and ethical or moral implications?

   a. _____

   _____

   b. _____

   _____

   c. _____

   _____

8. Using the principles in the present chapter on thinking, come up with five creative ideas that interest you in the difficult assignment you've just read.

   a. _____

   b. _____

   c. _____

    d. _____

    e. _____

STEP THREE: Spotting Faulty Thinking

Explain fallacies in these three arguments.

1. The Republicans were in office when the Great Depression occurred. If we elect the Republicans, we'll get another depression.
2. The Democrats want to cut out funding for the B-2 bomber. Next thing you know, they'll be dismantling the whole Army. Democrats don't give a damn about defense.
3. That guy rides a motorcycle. I've read about those motorcycle gangs. We don't want trouble around here, so we'd better not hire him.

Answers:

1. It doesn't logically follow. The fact that the Republicans were in office when the depression began doesn't mean they caused it. (Nor do current Republican candidates necessarily hold the same views as earlier Republican leaders.)
2. A slippery slope fallacy. Just because Democrats may want to control expenditures by cutting back on a particular defense program doesn't mean they don't recognize the importance of national defense or that they'll take extreme measures against the defense establishment.
3. A hasty generalization. Just because some motorcycle gangs may have terrorized people doesn't mean that everyone who rides a motorcycle is a thug. The job applicant should be evaluated on his merits. He may well be a first-class worker and is probably a decent fellow.

STEP FOUR: Generating Creative Ideas

Think up five offbeat uses for a frying pan.

    1. _____

    2. _____

    3. _____

4. _____

5. _____

STEP FIVE: Establishing a Base Line

Give yourself 1 to 5 points for each of the following questions. The more positive your response, the higher the number you should assign (1 = strongly disagree, 5 = strongly agree). Higher scores indicate a greater receptivity and capacity for critical and/or creative thinking. Remember, critical and creative thinking can be learned. THE PURPOSE OF THE EXERCISE IS TO HELP YOU SET NEW GOALS AND GIVE YOU A BASE FROM WHICH TO MEASURE YOUR PROGRESS AS YOU PROCEED THROUGH COLLEGE. There are no passing or failing grades.

1. Am I open to the idea that I can learn much from foreign cultures? _____

_____

2. Do I believe I can learn important ideas from writers who lived in earlier historical periods? _____

3. Am I willing to consider the possibility that some of my political beliefs might be wrong? _____

4. Am I willing to acknowledge that my country could sometimes be wrong in its foreign policies? _____

5. Do I recognize the central roles of critical and creative thinking in academic and career success? _____

6. Do I try to think actively, critically, and creatively in all my classes and study sessions? _____

7. Is one of my criteria for selecting courses their ability to develop my capacity to think? _____

8. When I see somebody "tried" in the press or on television for an alleged crime or offense do I withhold judgment, recognizing that I don't have all the facts and that the media personalities probably don't either? The more emotional people are about the matter the more determined I am to think for

    myself. _____

    _____

9. Do I try to judge things for myself in my courses and in life? _____

10. Do I go beyond my usual ways of thinking when I attempt to solve a problem

    or understand an issue? _____

STEP SIX: Setting Thinking Goals in Your Courses

Based on your answers to the above questions and the things you read in this chapter, set five measurable, specific goals to develop your thinking effectiveness in your current courses that you can begin working on immediately. Remove these pages and post or keep where they will serve as a continual reminder.

Goal 1. _____

_____

_____

Action I will take to achieve goal _____

_____

_____

How I will measure achievement of goal _____

_____

_____

Goal 2. _____

_____

_____

Action I will take to achieve goal _____

_____

_____

How I will measure achievement of goal _____

_____

_____

Goal 3. _____

_____

_____

Action I will take to achieve goal _____

_____

_____

How I will measure achievement of goal _____

_____

_____

Goal 4. _____

_____

_____

Action I will take to achieve goal _____

_____

_____

How I will measure achievement of goal _____

_____

_____

Goal 5. _____

_____

_____

Action I will take to achieve goal _____

_____

_____

How I will measure achievement of goal _____

_____

_____

Chapter
5

Understanding and Remembering What Your Instructors Say

*A*ttending class is often the key to enjoying a course and mastering its content. Instructors typically lecture on material they consider important, and they frequently ask a significant portion of the exam questions based on their lectures. Even for questions not based on class sessions, you can gain insights from class that will aid you at exam time. Lectures can put the textbooks into context and help save valuable study time.

Lecture and class discussions also help you develop concentration. Most people don't listen well, and the development of this skill can give you an edge in your profession or business after you graduate. Class sessions also provide an opportunity to develop public speaking ability and social poise. The capacity to feel comfortable in front of groups can increase your ability to be promoted into positions of leadership and enhance your effectiveness.

Kathy was a criminal justice major who recognized from the start how to handle attendance in her courses. She'd been slightly above average in high school but wanted to do much better in college. During her freshman year she achieved a very good 3.3 grade point average. Part of Kathy's success is the result of her decision to make every minute in class pay off. Here are the techniques she employed, though as you'll see she had a problem initially with participating in class discussion. You should follow these steps whenever possible.

OPTIMIZING CLASS TIME

1. Attend All Class Meetings   Kathy rarely missed a class. Only a major academic conflict or illness kept her away. On those rare occasions when she had to be absent, *she made it her responsibility to find out what had gone on in class: new assignments, announcements, and lecture content.* She got to know several other students who seemed serious about their work. Not only did this let her become part of study groups, but she could readily find out what she'd missed and make copies of notes when she couldn't attend.

When Kathy had to miss one of her smaller classes, she apologized to the instructor and explained her absence. Sometimes attendance will not be taken at the college level, but smart students make sure the instructor knows they're interested. If a student's course grade is on the borderline, instructors will often give the higher mark because of class attendance and other indications that the student took the course seriously.

Sometimes students have to miss a number of classes because of circumstances beyond their control. Last year two freshmen athletes inadvertently enrolled in one of my upper-level courses. I let them stay because of their apparent interest and commitment to the subject. They missed several classes while travelling with the team but always advised me beforehand when they had to be away.

They came to see me during conference hours, got copies of notes from their classmates, and participated in discussions. And *they attended every class* when the team was in town. Both got "B" grades, a fine showing in the course given their inexperience. Although they were at a disadvantage because of missed classes, they compensated by meeting with the instructor and other students. Of course, I knew they had a legitimate reason for not attending.

2. Sit Toward the Front   Paying attention throughout the lecture is crucial. Sitting a few rows from the front helps force you to concentrate on the material. Don't talk to classmates, and don't hesitate to move to a different seat if someone disturbs you. Consider lighting, noise, and other relevant factors in choosing your seat. You may also want to sit away from the doors to avoid disturbance.

By sitting near the front you gain several advantages. Kathy put it this way: "I'm amazed at how much easier it is to concentrate and understand now that I'm sitting up front. You can see your instructors' eyes and notice when they look at you. And you can't doze off when they can see you."

Sitting close to the instructor helped make class attendance enjoyable and facilitated concentration and understanding. Kathy got occasional feedback as the instructor looked her way, and she felt more a part of the class. Because she could see the instructors face more clearly she could get clues about meaning and importance from facial expressions.

Give occasional feedback to the instructor in class. Don't be afraid to nod occasionally if you like a particular point or look puzzled if you don't understand something. If I get such a look, I'll either go over the point again or ask the class if there are any questions.

I once heard the eminent psychologist B. F. Skinner relate an amusing example of this principle. In an undergraduate psychology class he had been lecturing on the mechanisms by which people can be conditioned to behave in certain ways. As a joke, the students deliberately conditioned Professor Skinner to address only one side of the room. They simply arranged that students on one side of the room would look bored, while those on the other side would display great interest through their facial expressions and body language. Professor Skinner unconsciously began to address only those students who looked interested.

3. Listen Objectively   Most people enjoy dynamic, enthusiastic lecturers. All the better if these speakers deliver witty remarks and tug at our emotions. Its fun to be entertained, and inspiring lecturers do help motivate students. But beware. Enthusiasm and great delivery have little to do with competence, truth, or wisdom. Adolph Hitler, Winston Churchill, John F. Kennedy, Fidel Castro, and Ronald Reagan were all leaders with great ability to captivate, motivate, and inspire. Yet their ideas certainly cannot have equal merit. ALWAYS THINK FOR YOURSELF, AND BE CONCERNED WITH CONTENT, NOT STYLE.

During the second week of the semester, Kathy told me about a problem she had with one of the instructors in a humanities course. He was an older man, a bit slow and halting in speech, who had the reputation among some students as a dull lecturer. Kathy found him boring and wanted to know if she should try to change courses. I knew the man to be an expert in his field and a person of great insight and integrity, and shared the thought with Kathy that she might gain great benefit from exposure to this distinguished professor.

She decided to stay in the course and later told me that it was one of the best she'd ever taken. She said, "It wasn't just that he showed us the importance of the subject; he also taught us a great deal about life. And despite his manner, I grew to really love his classes."

Sure, you'll occasionally come across incompetent or uninterested instructors, and these people should be avoided if possible. But if you get stuck with one, you can still learn a great deal by active listening and participation. And you'll find that some instructors judged less sparkling by superficial standards can nevertheless be teachers you'll remember all your life because of the meaning and depth they breathe into their subject.

4. Come Prepared   Have an organized notebook with plenty of spare paper and pens. READ THE CURRENT ASSIGNMENT BEFORE CLASS. This may help you understand the lecture and allow you to integrate course material. If you wait until later in the course, the relevant lecture won't be fresh in your mind. Preparing for class can save you valuable time comparing and integrating components of the course at exam time.

If you don't have enough time to read all of the assignment, at least look it over to get the main ideas. Doing the assignment before class is a simple principle that can greatly increase the benefit you receive from lectures. In those cases where the instructor doesn't lecture on the assigned reading, it's still an easy way to keep from falling behind.

5. Ask Questions and Offer Comments as Appropriate   Preparing for class will enable you to formulate intelligent questions or offer interesting insights. When the instructor asks for questions and comments, don't be afraid to raise your hand. It's natural to be fearful, but consider what you have to gain—you get experience and acquire poise before groups; you force yourself to think of the significance of the material during the lecture, and you help the instructor get to know you.

Avoid asking questions that show you haven't done the assignment, and save routine factual questions for after class. (If you didn't hear a point, a classmate may have gotten it.) Don't be afraid of looking stupid to your instructors or classmates. They're usually quite understanding of the insecurity you may be feeling. Use your discretion in deciding how frequently to comment. Some instructors spend a lot of class time on discussion, while other want little class participation.

Don't be intimidated by other students. It's easy to be fooled by students who speak well in public and appear to be highly knowledgeable. There's frequently a correlation between performance in class and performance on exams. But it's by no means perfect. Many times I've seen students speak up in class but do poorly on exams and vice versa, so don't sell yourself short by thinking that others must know a lot more than you.

BUT WHAT IF YOU'RE SHY? Every year I have a few students who are afraid to speak up in class or to visit during conference hours. Kathy was one of these students. She had faithfully attended every class and had gotten a "B" on her mid-term exam. One day after class I asked her why she never spoke up in class.

Kathy said, "It's nothing personal; I'm just shy."

"I know how you feel," I said. "So am I."

She looked surprised and a bit less nervous. "But you don't understand. I sometimes get uncomfortable around people. I like them, but I just can't help it."

"I occasionally have that tendency, too," I said.

"But you're a professor. You deal with people all the time. How can you be shy?"

I explained that lots of people have a tendency to be shy. Many professionals—teachers, actors, television announcers, and others—are basically shy. But they've overcome their shyness and often turned it to an advantage.

As we talked she began to see that fear of social interaction can be handled like any other fear. Not always beaten entirely, but brought under control. Even better, shyness and self-consciousness can be turned into a real advantage. It can make you more compassionate and motivate you to be a positive force in the lives of others. Shy people can learn to act with much greater confidence and enjoy social interaction more.

I suggested that Kathy spend a couple of minutes before class visualizing herself as relaxed, listening to the lecture and discussion rather than thinking about herself, and calmly and confidently contributing to the discussion when appropriate. Kathy raised her hand in the next class. She said, "I don't agree with the point you just made," and went on to make a very interesting brief argument. I was so pleased by her comments and her willingness to speak forthrightly that I could hardly keep from smiling while she made a serious point.

"Interesting observation," I said, and expanded a bit on the significance of her thoughts. After class she came up and told me that she'd been scared but thought she'd come up with a really good idea (she was right) and somehow summoned up the courage to speak. Kathy spoke occasionally in class and came to see me and her other instructors several times during the year. She gradually gained more confidence in herself and later told me that speaking in class helped her feel more at ease in social situations.

6. Think Critically and Creatively as You Listen   Look for the what, how, why, and the significance. Ask yourself, how does the material being presented COMPARE to the material presented so far? How does it compare with the textbooks? How does it compare with other courses? Think about how you can CLASSIFY the material and put it into CATEGORIES.

Try to anticipate as you listen. This will develop your analytical abilities and will help you understand and remember. You'll be able to see the big picture more easily. In short, think critically and creatively as you listen and take notes.

Thinking critically and creatively helps you concentrate and pay attention. It allows you to understand and remember. And it makes attending class much more interesting.

EVALUATE as you listen. Try to figure out the underlying values of the lecturer and the ideas being presented. What does the subject tell you about moral and ethical issues? Consider how the topic might contribute to your own moral and ethical outlook. Don't assume that what you hear is necessarily true or valid. Consider other possibilities.

TAKING GOOD NOTES

The steps above are just an introduction to getting the most out of attending class. Unless you write good notes you'll forget most of what you learned from your instructor. *Most students take far too few notes.* As a result they don't have an adequate source for review and preparing for exams. *Taking notes keeps you active, involved, and motivated.* It increases your ability to concentrate and dramatically strengthens your ability to recall what was said in lecture. *Taking good notes improves your thinking ability and enhances your understanding of the material.*

If you've already developed a good system of note taking that works for you, attempt to gain insights and tips from the following discussion that will help you further refine your techniques. Try the methods described below to see if they may be a significant improvement on your old system. Whether you've currently got a good system or not, realize that you may have to vary your note-taking style depending on the course, teaching method of the instructor, and your own best learning style.

The First Principle of Taking Good Notes Is to LISTEN ATTENTIVELY THROUGHOUT THE LECTURE, Including the Time You Spend Writing Notes   You shouldn't try to take down everything your instructor says. Copy the main ideas and key facts. Write down main points covering the *what, how, why, and significance* of the topic. Listen for comparisons and the instructor's method of classification. Don't take so many notes that you can't pay attention or think about what's being said.

Stay alert for *key words* that can help you grasp meaning, being sure to include these points in your notes, with appropriate abbreviations as necessary.

    a. Watch for words that indicate the instructor is defining something or describing basic characteristics. Phrases such as "by metamorphosis I mean . . . " and "deconstructionism refers to . . . " indicate a definition. Key descriptive points can also refer to space, distance, etc. Write "DEF" right in your notes or in the left margin to indicate a definition. For spacial/geographic characteristics its often best to draw a quick, very simple diagram.

    b. Words such as "procedure, process, method, means by which" and similar phrases indicate the instructor is dealing with the "how."

    c. Watch for words or phrases that indicate the instructor is dealing with the "why" of the subject. Phrases such as "the reason," "cause," "explanation," "this provokes, triggers," etc. can serve as cues.

    d. Stay alert for comparisons and contrasts. The instructor may say something such as "this is similar to magnetic force except that," or "unlike Locke, Descartes believed that. . . . "

    e. Be on the lookout for terms that can tell you how something is classified. "Like other animals that appeared to evolve during this period. . . . "

    f. Pay attention to qualifiers that indicate exceptions the opposite, or special conditions: terms such as "excluding, except, on the other hand, but, nevertheless, nonetheless, none of this should be understood as. . . . "

    g. Be alert for indications that the instructor is commenting on the significance of the topic. "The significance of this is . . . ; as a result of this experiment . . . , the human implications of . . . " and so on.

Keep alert for tipoffs. If the instructor says "this is a critical issue," or "one of the keys to understanding James Joyce is . . . " you know the points are significant. Instructors often show important comparisons and contrasts: "This is one of the central differences between the Aztec and Mayan cultures." They'll even sometimes indicate possible exam questions.

Try to figure out how the instructor feels as well as thinks about the topic. Pay special attention to points the instructor thinks are *profound*—ideas of unusual importance and insight. Put stars by these. Appropriately including these on your essay exams can improve your grade significantly. This is one secret of many "A" students.

You shouldn't accept the instructors' view uncritically, but chances are your awareness of their ideas on what is profound will help give you a deeper understanding of the meaning and significance of the topic.

Write Down Definitions Word for Word Copy everything your instructor writes on the board, including: charts and graphs, formulas, quotations, and outlines of the lecture. Write down everything your instructor emphasizes.

Use Separate Notebooks for Each Class Including all your class notes in one notebook invites disaster if you lose your notebook, and it's more tedious working from one thick notebook. A loose-leaf notebook enables you to move pages around and insert new ones. If you prefer to carry just one notebook you can transfer pages when you return to your home or dormitory room. Some students prefer spiral notebooks because they're less bulky, but this type limits your flexibility in moving and inserting pages.

Write on Only One Side of the Page The blank page opposite can remain blank, but it's a great place to draw charts and diagrams, put comments from the text, or write practice exam questions. Number and date the pages. Skip spaces and lines if you miss a point so you can fill in the space later.

Vary the Amount and Type of Notes You Take with the Format of the Class If the instructor is presenting an organized, systematic lecture, taking notes throughout the class period is usually essential.

If the class is conducted as a discussion, or if it's in the format of student debates, student reports, or simulations, you should usually take fewer notes. Write down new ideas or insights given by students that seem useful or significant, identifying the comment as being from a student. Leave space afterward to note your instructor's evaluation of the comment or for your own later evaluation. Focus on comments made by your instructor in your notes.

Take notes during movies, performances, and guest lectures as appropriate. At a minimum, note key concepts, facts, explanations and evaluations that can help you understand and evaluate for yourself.

Write Legibly, so You'll Be Able to Read and Understand Later Fast printing works for some students, while others prefer to write in legible longhand.

Economize, Using Abbreviations and Symbols Where Possible   Use abbreviations for frequently used words and terms. When possible, employ standard abbreviations used in the field; for example, in economics use GNP for gross national product.

Here are some examples.

Word	Abbreviation or Symbol
and	+
because	bec
causes	→
continue	cont
democrats	dems
different	difr
difficult	dif
equals	=
important	imp
subconscious	subc
therefore	∴

Use a System of Note Taking That Helps You Most Easily Learn the Material   The Outline System is a standard technique that works well. Later in this chapter you'll also learn how to use graphic organizers, which constitute an important supplement to the outline system.

The principle of the Outline System is to organize the material according to main ideas or topics, with successive levels of subtopics indicated by indentations, numbers, and letters.

The standard numbers and letters used in the outline system are shown below without any content.

I.
  A.
    1.
      a.
        (1)
        (2)
          (a)
          (b)
      b.
        (1)
        (2)
    2.
  B.
II.
  A. (and so on)

DON'T WORRY ABOUT FILLING IN ALL THE NUMBERS AND LETTERS AS YOU TAKE NOTES. Just use the indentations as appropriate, filling in numbers and letters only if it doesn't slow you down. If you don't get the organization immediately, simply indent as you think appropriate and sort it out later. For crucial material such as formulas and definitions, leave a blank line above and two or three blanks below, so you can add your own definitions or explanations later.

Center and write in capital letters all major topics. Write major subheadings flush against the left margin. Indent about one-half inch for major subdivisions, another half-inch for the next level of subdivision, and so on.

Here's a portion of a lecture on educational systems in the third-world countries of Africa, Asia, and Latin America, followed by an example of good outline notes. You can see that the instructor talks in a conversational manner. As in most classes, some of what is said isn't crucial to the topic and can be left out of the notes.

> Today we're going to talk about the role of education in the third-world. I sometimes include this subject as a short identification question on exams. This subject is important politically, sociologically, and economically. By education I mean formal schooling from kindergarten through college, graduate, and professional school.
>
> From a political perspective, education in the third world has many significant consequences, often negative. Government decisions about which language to use in the school can spark riots. Religious groups can also be contentious about religious aspects of the curriculum.
>
> Furthermore, unemployed graduates can become a volatile force contributing to political instability. Because political institutions are often weak in these countries, universities can be a focal point for democratic and undemocratic politics. Political pressures on campus can be so intense that instructors are pressured to spout the official propaganda of government or of powerful political groups on campus. If they try to uphold academic standards, they may be subject to verbal harassment or even violence.
>
> On the other hand, education in the third world offers many benefits, or at least it has the potential for offering many benefits. Educated people can more effectively judge the competency of government and more easily exert enlightened democratic control. They're less likely to tolerate dictatorial abuse for long.
>
> I'm not suggesting that in every case democracy is the best system, despite my own bias in that direction. It's easy to assume that democracy can be automatically transplanted to third-world countries, but this may not always be possible.
>
> An educated public, especially if they have skills needed by a developing economy, can contribute to economic productivity and therefore help government to function more effectively. In 1974, right after I got out of graduate school, I had a chance to travel throughout Asia and Africa. Let me tell you that sure was a low budget trip, but I learned a great deal. One of the things I noticed in my travels in India was . . .

and so on.

Notice how the lecturer gives a general structure but begins to ramble. This actually gives students more time to get down the main ideas. Some of the points raised during digressions are significant, such as the question of whether democracy is always the best system.

Whether the lecturer is highly organized or not, it's essential to *get down the main points*, not every word. Try to stay one step ahead of the lecturer if you can. Figuring out where the lecturer is going will help keep your thinking processes active.

Figure 5.1 is an example of how to record in outline form the lecture on page 125 (numbers, letters, and other material are added later as shown in Figure 5.2). Draw lines two inches from the bottom of your notebook paper prior to class for the bottom margin (a short, handwritten line do).

ROLE OF EDUCATION IN THE THIRD WORLD

- (eco = economy, ed = education, edd = educated, pol = political, t-W = third World)

look up contentious, volatile

Three aspects of ed in t-W: political, eco, social.
def of ed: formal schooling from kindergarten
through college, graduate and professional school.

- Polit. conseqns of ed (partly due to weak gov.)
  Ethnic conflict (lang, relig)
  Other polit violence (unemployed grads.)
  Politics on campus:
      Gov. pressure on instructors
      Student pres. on instrs.
      Low academic standards, violence.

Potential positive conseqns of ed (pol and eco):
    Edd people can better control gov (knowledge, self-confidence)
    + they're not as tolerant of dictators
- [instr. says democ may not always be best system?]

    Skills, eco. productivity

Figure 5.1 Sample notes, without revision.

Note that complete sentences aren't used and that the meanings of abbreviations not employed before are recorded. Plenty of space is left so that material can be added later. The information is clear but very compact. You'll probably need to write more extensive notes at first, but the example in Figure 5.1 is a model toward which you can strive.

Just how compact to make your notes is a judgment call. You should be as brief as you can and still recall the full meaning of relevant points later. Being concise helps you listen, concentrate, and think. But it's essential that you be able to understand your notes when you review. So *it's better to take notes that are slightly more extensive than necessary rather than notes that are too brief*. With practice you'll find an ideal style and length.

Review and Revise Your Notes That Same Day, as Soon after Class as Possible *Here's a crucial step where most students miss the mark.* Students who take no notes remember little of what's been said in lectures. Students who take notes and fail to review them until exam time must learn material all over again when the topics will have become vague and confused in their minds.

When you revise your notes, add numbers and letters to your outline if this helps you understand. Otherwise just let the intentions guide you. It's sometimes sufficient to number and letter only the major subtopics.

Use the top of the margin to write study HINTS. Write down key words and phrases in the top margin to spark your memory when you next review your notes. Put them in the order they appear in your notes. These hints should indicate the content of the notes and help stimulate your memory. You'll be able to test yourself on your recall before actually reviewing the page.

Use the left margin to write down symbols and words that will help you understand organization, meaning, significance, and relationships. The blank page opposite your notes can be used for charts and graphs or more extensive comparisons, ideas from textbooks, and so on.

Here are some key *margin symbols*, but develop others that meet your needs:

C = Cause

CP = Comparison

CR = Criticism

DEF = Definition

ETH = Ethical and moral points

EX = Possible exam question

I = Creative idea

KF = Key fact

M = Method

PF = Profound insights (stars can also be used)

SG = Significance

Some students prefer to underline key points instead of using the left margin. Another technique is to put stars beside these points. You can also use one or two stars to indicate degrees of importance and alert you to material that should get particular attention. Underlining, circling, and connecting key words, brackets, and parentheses can also be used.

Employing a combination of using the left margin with underlining, stars, and symbols within the text is a useful way to keep active as you review. The idea is to THINK, ORGANIZE, and to WORK EFFICIENTLY.

As with all strategies suggested in this book, you must make a cost/benefit assessment concerning how much time to spend on revision of your notes. Remember that the purpose of notes is to help you, so don't overdo it either.

Use the bottom margin to record your own OBSERVATIONS. These should include:

Your own critical and creative thoughts, including evaluations.

Comparisons.

Points to tie in from other courses.

Figure 5.2 gives an example of how to quickly modify notes as you conduct this first review, using the same notes presented above. Take special note of the student's observations that show good critical thinking and an effort to relate the lecture to material in the text.

Write Formulas, Definitions, and Other Items on 3 x 5 Cards to Review in Your Spare Minutes

Quickly Review Your Notes from the Preceding Class Before Each New Class   This step will help you concentrate and better perceive the instructor's meaning. It will also be an additional review that will keep you from forgetting.

Review All Your Lecture Notes at Least Once Each Week   *This is a major secret for doing well in your courses.* Reviewing your past notes every week helps cement the material into your memory. Even ten or fifteen minutes of review can have a dramatic effect on your ability to recall. This will save you much time in studying for exams. What you're doing when you review is keeping the material alive in your memory. **Reviewing your notes regularly is a key step in getting good grades.**

Before beginning, think about your goals for the course and for the next exam. Quickly look over your syllabus (course outline), book, past exams, and notes to determine which portions of your work need the greatest emphasis and to gain perspective.

Leaving the HINTS at the top of the page exposed, *cover the page of notes with a blank sheet of paper,* uncovering the notes as you answer or check the material as suggested by the hints. Proceed through each hint in order. As you uncover the page downward, you have the double advantage of having both the hints

[HINTS]	– 3 aspects of ed in T-W – def of ed	– political conseqns of ed – potential positive conseqns of ed

ROLE OF EDUCATION IN THE THIRD WORLD

● (eco = economy, ed = education, edd = educated,
pol = political, t-w = third world)

look up contentious, volatile

DEF — I. Three aspects of ed in t-w: political, eco, social.
def of ed: formal schooling from kindergarten
through college, graduate and professional school.

NEG — II. Polit. conseqns of ed (partly due to weak gov.)
●   A. Ethnic conflict (lang, relig)
   B. Other polit violence (unemployed grads.)
   C. Politics on campus:
      Gov. pressure on instructors
      Student pres. on instrs.
      Low academic standards, violence.

POS — III. Potential positive conseqns of ed (pol and eco):
   A. Edd people can better control gov (knowledge, self-
      confidence)
   B. + they're not as tolerant of dictators
●   [instr. says democ may not always be best system?]
   C. Skills, eco. productivity

OBSERVATIONS

Textbook says ed can cause conflict in modern world too.
   Ask instructor to elaborate on point that democ MAY not
   always be best system. Not sure I agree.

Figure 5.2 Sample notes, with revisions added during the first review after class.

and the uncovered notes serving as a prompt to encourage you to remember and connect material in your thought processes.

Try to combine your review of lecture notes with the review of your textbooks and text notes in the same course.

Get Feedback on the Quality of Your Notes Ask students you know who are top achievers to let you compare notes. Or explain to your instructors that you're working on improving your note-taking skills and ask them to take a quick look at your notes for the last lecture to see if they have any suggestions.

UNDERSTANDING AND USING GRAPHIC ORGANIZERS

Graphic organizers present complex information in condensed, easy-to-grasp visual form. Typically they help us understand relationships and view the big picture. Charts, graphs, stars, trees, chains, sketches, diagrams, maps, and tables are examples of commonly used graphic organizers.

Not only do graphic organizers facilitate understanding, they also make it easier to remember certain kinds of information. Students who learn especially well through visual presentation should pay particular attention to developing this technique. But all students can derive great benefit from knowing these handy learning tools.

It's important to be selective in using graphic organizers, because they can take longer than writing notes in outline form. Often you'll have to construct them as you revise your notes, though some organizers such as stars and simple comparison charts can sometimes be used while you listen to lectures.

Make Sure You Read Graphic Material Carefully in Your Textbooks

This will help you understand your texts, and *you'll gradually learn how to use these techniques more effectively.* Read and think about the *title* of the graphic organizer. What is the author trying to convey? Is the information presented from another *source* or is it the author's own creation? Knowing the source can help you evaluate the validity of the information. Make sure you understand *units of measure* or *headings* of the vertical and horizontal dimensions. Be able to explain to yourself the *purpose* of the graph, the *relationship* of the information, and how it ties into the text.

After studying a graph, chart, or table, look away for a moment and see if you can give a brief summary of the main points the author is trying to communicate. If you've forgotten or haven't quite understood it, read the description in the text again and study the visual organizer until you get it. If you don't understand a graphic organizer, ask a fellow student. If you still don't get it, ask your instructor.

Always read graphic material critically, just as you would the text itself. A line graph is a convenient way to show change over time. But Figure 5.3 shows an example of a misleading graph.

The improvement in the value of shares looks impressive visually. But when you consider that the increase is only about 2 percent a year, you can see that the gain is not impressive. You'd have earned much less than the average bank account. Had the vertical axis begun at 0 instead of 50, a more accurate picture would be communicated. The graph might also be misleading because of the years chosen. It's unlikely that textbook authors would try to mislead you intentionally, but you can evaluate all graphic presentations much more effectively if you think critically.

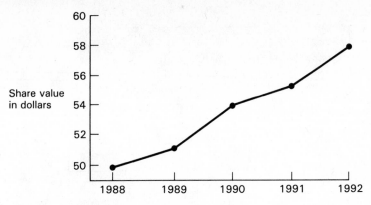

Figure 5.3 Example of a misleading line graph.

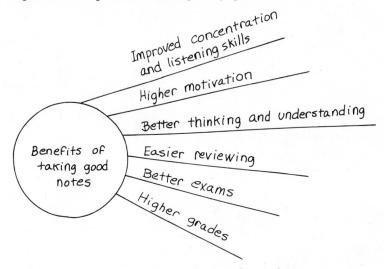

Figure 5.4 A star showing the payoffs of good notetaking.

Practice Using Visual Organizers as You Revise Your Notes and as You Study

Here are some examples of basic techniques for using visual organizers. Figure 5.4 shows a STAR that summarizes some of the main benefits of taking good notes. These stars can be used as a handy way to summarize main points derived from a single concept or event.

CHARTS are an ideal way to organize material for comparison and contrast. Figure 5.5 is a simple chart that visually displays part of a lecture that compared contemporary quality literature with best sellers. Note that the student includes critical comments at the bottom of the chart.

PIE GRAPHS are a handy way of displaying percentages and proportions. Figure 5.6 gives an example from a textbook in psychology. You can also use this technique to display concepts, as I did in Figure 3.4 on p. 66.

Popular Books   Quality Literature

	Popular Books	Quality Literature
Plot	Ordered	Often loose
Characters	Simplified and heroic	More real (weak?)
Theme	Shallow	Often profound
Complexity of Structure	Simple	Often complex
Setting	Glamorous	Real world, imaginative
Style	Often simplistic	Often creative, classy

Critical Observations: Quality and classic writings are sometimes harder to understand at first, but they're often more interesting and satisfying as I get into them and after I finish.

Not all "quality" literature stands the test of time, and not all popular writings are bad. Stephen King seems pretty good to me, and Charles Dickens was regarded as a pulp writer by some at first. I'll make up my own mind about books I read.

Figure 5.5 Comparison chart of popular and "quality" literature.

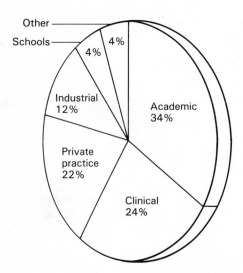

- Other
- Schools — 4%
- 4%
- Industrial 12%
- Academic 34%
- Private practice 22%
- Clinical 24%

Figure 5.6 Pie graph showing employment of psychologists by setting. *Source:* Wayne Weiten, *Psychology: Themes and Variations.* Pacific Grove, CA: Brooks/Cole, 1989, p. 17. Reprinted by permission.

TREES are a handy way of visually mapping hierarchies. As with most types of graphic organizers, trees work equally well for organizing either lecture or textbook material. By showing progression by rank, they help clarify relationships between higher and lower classes of information.

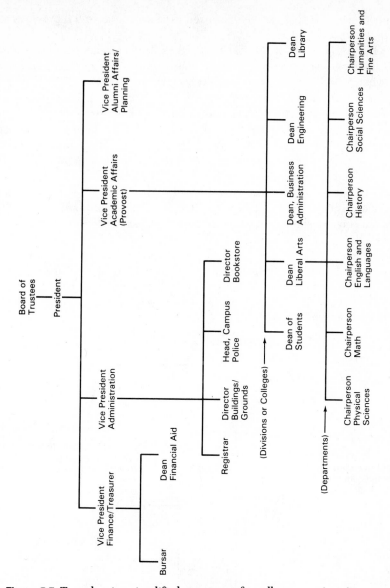

Figure 5.7 Tree showing simplified structure of a college or university.

You could organize the material in a chapter on the structure of government or other organizations with this technique. Figure 5.7 shows a tree that presents visually a simplified organizational structure of a college or university.

CHAINS and FLOW CHARTS are a simple technique for displaying processes and sequences, such as causal relationships and chronological events. Historical developments, biological processes, and industrial procedures are examples of the kinds of material that can be organized in chains. Figure 5.8 provides an example from a marketing textbook.

SKETCHES, DIAGRAMS, and MAPS all display location and spatial relationships in easier-to-perceive visual form. One useful learning technique is to trace the drawing, whether your own, the text's, or the instructors, omitting the descriptive words. This will help you test yourself. Instructors sometimes give these visual organizers on exams without labels and require students to fill in the information.

Drawing your own sketches and diagrams can help you understand the material and facilitate learning and remembering. Avoid the temptation of drawing something worthy of a prestigious art museum. It's okay to have a bit of fun, but the idea is to work efficiently as well.

TABLES can present vast quantities of information in a column format. The easy-to-read visual format of tables facilitates understanding and recall. They're a convenient way to show numerical relationships as well as relationships among concepts.

The table by Linda Lee Johnson reproduced in Figure 5.9 surveys some of the most useful graphic organizers and gives examples of how to use them. Read this table carefully to see which methods might help you in the courses you're now taking. Also give careful thought to the way in which Johnson puts together complex information into one table.

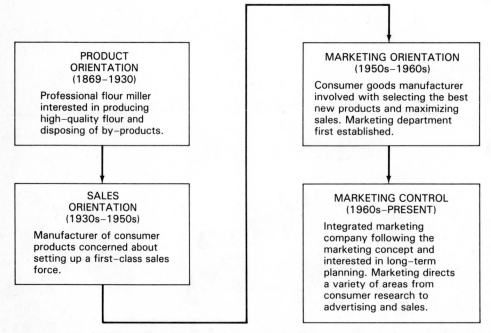

Figure 5.8 Flow chart depicting the evolution of marketing at Pillsbury. *Source:* Reprinted, with permission of Macmillan Publishing Company from *Marketing* Joel R. Evans and Barry Berman, Copyright © 1987 by Macmillan Publishing Company.

Graph type	Appropriate relationships for graph type	Examples			
		In the humanities	In the social sciences	In the life sciences	In the physical sciences
Star (for a concept)	Definitions Attributes Examples	Characteristics of cubism in art	Attributes of the demand curve in economics	Examples of echinoderms in biology	Attributes of sunspots in astronomy
Tree (for hierarchies)	Classification Pedigree Analysis Structure Attributes Examples	Family tree of Ming Dynasty in China	Organization of the White House staff	Parts of the alimentary canal	Classes of isotopes in chemistry
Chart (for similar concepts)	Compare and Contrast Attributes	Comparison of imagery in poems by Anne Sexton	Comparison of Viet Nam war to the 1988 war in the Persian Gulf	Comparison of endocrine glands	Comparison of planets of the solar system
Chain (for changes over time)	Process Sequence Cause/Effect Chronology	Plot sequence of a particular novel	Stages of Piaget's theory of cognitive development in children	Process of cell division	Geological development of coal
Sketch (for visualizing a description)	Physical structures Descriptions of places Space relations Concrete objects Visual images	Description of a stage set in a drama	Description of a complex apparatus for studying eye movements in reading	The structure of the epidermis and dermis, the two layers of skin	Description of layers of ice that form a glacier

Figure 5.9 Table showing methods of graphing, with examples. *Source*: Linda Lee Johnson, "Learning Across the Curriculum with Creative Graphing," *Journal of Reading* (March, 1989), p. 36. Reprinted with permission of Linda Lee Johnson and the International Reading Association.

The key thing in making graphic organizers is to keep them as simple as possible and still convey the information. If you practice, you'll soon learn to organize increasing amounts of material visually without wasting time. Remember that graphing is not an end in itself (though it can be fun and help keep you motivated). The purpose is to help you understand and remember. When graphs can help you do this more quickly than outlining, they're well worth the time spent on them. They can also help you evaluate and develop creative ideas.

MEMORY AIDS

THE MOST IMPORTANT MEANS OF REMEMBERING WHAT YOU LEARN IS THROUGH THE APPLICATION OF GOOD THINKING, LISTENING, NOTE TAKING AND STUDY TECHNIQUES, COUPLED WITH FREQUENT,

REGULAR REVIEW. The memory tricks presented in popular books do little to help your understanding or make your subjects meaningful. Nevertheless, memory devices can be useful for learning certain kinds of factual material. The main trick is linking difficult-to-remember information to things that are more easily recalled.

Create Words and Rhymes to Strengthen Your Memory

In the next chapter you'll learn a sure-fire method for successfully learning your textbook assignments that involve extensive reading. The steps are: Repeat, Scan, Question, Read, Think, and Reinforce. The first letters of these words are: RSQRTR. Tough to remember, right?

Wrong. Seemingly random letters can be made into words, often by omitting vowels. RSQRTR suggests this useful phrase: Remarkable Square Tree. If you look at the letters SQR, they clearly suggest the word "square." For the purposes of creating a useful visual image, the last two letters, TR, suggest the words "truck" and "tree," with "tree" being the better choice. For the first letter, R, the word "remarkable" helps create the easy-to-remember phrase "REMARKABLE SQUARE TREE." Now that we can recall the first letters RSQRTR, it's easy to remember the words "repeat, scan, question, read, think, and reinforce," once the meaning of those words is understood.

Words, sentences, jingles, or phrases can all be created around the information you want to remember. Make them bizarre or ridiculous. Some jingles are even a bit gross or saucy. THE IDEA IS THAT THE MORE ABSURD OR ATTENTION GETTING IT IS, THE MORE EASILY YOU'LL REMEMBER.

Here's a verse commonly used by human anatomy students to help them remember the three sacral nerves to the pelvic floor muscles (named S2, S3, and S4) as well as the cervical nerves to the diaphragm (named C3, C4, and C5):

S two, three, and four,
Keep your guts up off the floor.
C three, four, and five,
Keep your diaphragm alive.

It's not exactly an Elizabeth Browning love sonnet, but it does the job.

Another example from geometry helps students remember three basic formulas: SOH,CAH,TOA (pronounced soh-cah-TOE-ah) for

$$\text{sine} = \frac{\text{opposite}}{\text{hypotenuse}} \quad \text{cosine} = \frac{\text{adjacent}}{\text{hypotenuse}} \quad \text{tangent} = \frac{\text{opposite}}{\text{adjacent}}$$

Create Easy-to-Remember Visual Images

One of the best ways to remember something is to create a bizarre mental image that you're unlikely to forget. A Remarkable Square Tree is just such an image. (Figure 6.2 on p. 152 presents the Remarkable Square Tree visually.) With a mental picture of a square tree you've got a picture as well a words to facilitate recall.

Say you have to remember the following items for the staging of a play in a drama class: a toy panda, hammock, guitar, pitcher of mint juleps, and the facade of a house with four windows. You might visualize a giant panda sitting in a hammock in front of the house, playing a guitar with a pitcher and glasses balanced on its nose. This method is good for relating seemingly unconnected items.

The LOCI or place system is an ancient memory device. You simply visualize the objects or points you want to make as being in particular parts of a house, building, or some other place. This is a handy technique for remembering points you want to make in a speech. Figure 6.2 is partially based on the LOCI method.

For Remembering Numbers, Link the Numbers to More Easily Remembered Words

For short-term memorization of numbers you can use a phonetic system in which you assign a letter (just consonants) to each number from zero to nine. You then create words by adding vowels between the letters. Any time you need the number, just recall the easier-to-remember word. The word "kiss," for example, might stand for the number 355, with K representing three and S representing five. Long numbers can be broken into groups of three or four. You then LINK the words in some ridiculous way as suggested above.

If you want a ready-made system rather than developing your own, as well as many other useful techniques, I suggest *The Memory Book*, an easy-to-read paperback by Harry Lorayne and Jerry Lucas, available in most bookstores. This book will be especially useful if you're in a major requiring that you know lots of formulas, numbers, and abstract facts.

If you have to remember things in order, the PEG system makes the job simpler. Here you create a list of words for zero through ten (or zero to one hundred if you've got many complicated numbers or formulas to remember). In the Lorayne system the number six is represented by the word "shoe." If you have to remember that the sixth step in a scientific procedure is the sterilization of equipment, you might visualize a silly picture of a giant shoe going through the process of sterilization.

Other Principles of Remembering

The concept of overlearning is a useful technique, especially for factual and abstract material. The idea is to continue studying past the point where you think you know the material. The extra review helps anchor the material into memory.

You shouldn't spend more time devising a memory device than it would take you to remember simply by studying more diligently. Material for most courses can be best understood and remembered through basic study techniques such as the Remarkable Square Tree method discussed in the next chapter.

SUMMARY

Attending every class session is one of the easiest and most important ways to succeed academically. To help you concentrate, learn, and remember it's important to listen actively. This can be facilitated by sitting toward the front, coming prepared, and thinking critically. Participating in class as appropriate can help keep you interested, develop speaking skills, and often boost your grade.

Most students make the mistake of taking far too few notes, with the result that they remember little of what their instructors said. The Outline System works well for most students. It's important to listen even while you write, and to condense information effectively, getting down main ideas, formulas, definitions, and important details. Also record points relating to method, cause, comparison, and significance. Although you can't write down everything, be sure your notes are extensive enough so that you can understand them when you review.

It's crucial to revise your notes within one day of taking them so you won't forget. Writing review HINTS in the top margin and OBSERVATIONS at the bottom of the page will help turn your notes into a useful learning and review document. Using the left margin for symbols and words that help clarify, organize, and provide meaning further enhances the power of your notes to help you learn and get better grades.

Graphic organizers are one of the easiest and most interesting ways to get actively involved in your courses. Making charts and graphs can help you condense complex information and remember. These devices often make it much easier and faster to get the big picture and retain it. By reading carefully the graphic material in your texts and by practicing making your own, you'll soon become proficient. Graphic organizers can help you evaluate and develop creative ideas.

Weekly reviews of your class notes (as well as your texts) is one of the major secrets of doing well on exams. These reviews will help you to remember, to develop good ideas, and to have most of your studying accomplished before you ever arrive at examination time.

Remembering abstract material from your classes and your books can sometimes be facilitated by such memory devices as the creation of words and jingles that are easier to recall. Visual images and memory techniques for recalling numbers can also help, especially in courses that have many formulas, abstract numbers, and terms. But most information is best learned through effective study techniques such as those presented in the next chapter.

SUCCESS STEPS

STEP ONE: Measuring Your Progress

This Success Step will enable you to establish a benchmark and measure your progress on actions that can dramatically improve your academic performance. It will also assist you in setting goals.

Rate yourself on the following questions. Give yourself 1 to 5 points for each question; the more positive your response, the higher the number you should assign (1 = strongly disagree, 5 = strongly agree). If the question doesn't apply to you, write "N.A." for not applicable. Remember that the purpose of the exercise is to help you set new goals and chart your progress as you proceed through college. There are no passing or failing grades.

Reevaluate yourself again after two and four weeks, and at the beginning of each semester thereafter. Jot down the date beside the points you assign, for example: 2 (10/3/92) 3 (10/17/92) 5 (1/93).

Measures by Which You Can Gauge Your Progress

Maximizing Class Time

1. Do I attend every class? _____

   _____

2. Do I sit toward the front? _____

   _____

3. Do I listen actively and objectively? _____

   _____

4. Have I read my assignment before class, even if it must be just a quick scan?

   _____

5. Do I think critically and creatively during the lecture? _____

   _____

6. Do I try to participate in class as appropriate without underrating myself or

overrating my classmates?_____

_____

7. Do I evaluate the lecture material for myself? _____

_____

Taking Good Notes

1. Do I listen attentively, even while I write? _____

_____

2. Do I keep basic thinking questions in mind (what, how, why, comparisons, what's the significance, classifications, etc.)? _____

_____

3. Do I listen for tipoffs and key words? _____

_____

4. Am I developing a good system for taking notes, with plenty of space for additions, review HINTS, and my OBSERVATIONS? _____

_____

5. Do I use abbreviations and other devices for economizing, but make sure my notes are complete enough so that I will understand them when I review?

_____

6. Do I revise my notes no later than one day after taking them? _____

_____

7. Do I review my notes from the last class in the subject just before attending the next class? _____

_____

8. Do I review my class notes at least once a week? _____

_____

9. Do I seek feedback on the quality of my notes? _____

_____

10. Do I use graphic organizers as appropriate, and am I working on my skills in

this area? _____

_____

STEP TWO: Establishing Goals

Based on your answers to the above questions and the things you read in this chapter, set five measurable, specific goals to develop your in-class effectiveness that you can begin working on immediately. Remove these pages and post or keep where they will serve as a continual reminder.

Goal 1. _____

_____

_____

Action I will take to achieve this goal _____

_____

_____

How I will measure achievement of this goal _____

_____

_____

Goal 2. _____

_____

_____

Action I will take to achieve this goal _____

_____

_____

How I will measure achievement of this goal _____

_____

_____

Goal 3. _____

_____

_____

Action I will take to achieve this goal _____

_____

_____

How I will measure achievement of this goal _____

_____

_____

Goal 4. _____

_____

_____

Action I will take to achieve this goal _____

_____

_____

How I will measure achievement of this goal _____

_____

_____

Goal 5. _____

_____

_____

Action I will take to achieve this goal _____

_____

_____

How I will measure achievement of this goal _____

_____

_____

STEP THREE: Qualitative Indications of Progress

Answer these questions one week after establishing the above goals. Use the same 1–5 grading scale as above. Revise your goals as needed.

1. Do I feel I'm getting more out of class sessions?_____

2. Am I beginning to enjoy my classes more?_____

3. Am I starting to feel more confident about my ability to succeed academically?

   _____

4. Do I feel a bit more in control of my life?_____

5. Have I been patient with myself as I change my class attendance and note-

   taking habits?_____

6. Do I encourage myself positively?_____

7. Am I continuing to engage in constructive leisure and recreation?_____

   _____

STEP FOUR: Developing Skill in Using Graphic Organizers

Based on either your class notes or reading assignments in your current courses, make simple graphic organizers as indicated below that will help you organize, comprehend, and remember the material. Construct these on a separate sheet of paper and keep them in the appropriate set of notes.

A. Line graph, pie graph, or table (see pp. 131, 132, 135).
B. Chart (a simple chart comparing two items is one possibility (see p. 132). You might also use the following method:

DISTINCTIVE CHARACTERISTICS OF A	SIMILARITIES OF A & B	DISTINCTIVE CHARACTERISTICS OF B

C.   Star showing major subdivisions of a major concept or category you must remember (see p. 131).

D.   Create a tree to organize one of your recent lectures or reading assignments (see p. 133).

E.   Choose suitable material from your lectures or textbooks and draw a chain, diagram, or map that will help you organize, comprehend, and remember (see p. 134).

STEP FIVE: Building Your Memory Skills

As you study for any of your current courses this week, create two memory devices for remembering material that seems amenable to this approach. (Techniques for creating these devices are discussed on pp. 135–137.) Write them down below.

1.   _____

_____

2.   _____

_____

After your weekly review, evaluate the effectiveness of the technique. How might you use this and other memory aids more effectively next time?

_____

_____

_____

_____

Continue to practice using these methods where you think they will be helpful, especially for abstract and numerical material that is not easily handled through the Remarkable Square Tree method, discussed in the next chapter.

Chapter
6

How to Get Better Grades by Studying Smarter

*I*magine a farmer spending back-breaking, sweaty days in the sun, plowing earth but never planting seeds or harvesting crops. Digging and digging with nothing to show for it except sunburn, insect bites, sore muscles, and headaches, all through the spring, summer, and autumn, just plowing foolishly away.

Most students resemble our imaginary farmer when they study. They sit down with a book and start reading and keep on reading until they decide to quit. Frequently they quit rather soon after beginning because they believe—correctly— that they're not learning anything.

Seldom can college textbooks be comprehended and remembered simply by reading. Human psychology and brain physiology combine to prevent learning and recall. You'll jumble up what you've just read with what you read half an hour earlier. You'll forget unless you reinforce your memory as you go along. And you'll fail to understand much of what you read unless you use the guideposts and study techniques available to you.

This chapter presents the Remarkable Square Tree method of studying—a technique that can dramatically increase your learning and improve your grades. Before showing you how to use this method, this chapter will discuss and review some preliminary basics.

Accommodate and Expand Your Learning Styles

People have different styles by which they learn best. Some can hardly remember without writing everything down; others respond particularly well to the spoken word. Some naturally prefer a logical, organized approach, while others like best a free-wheeling, creative style. We all have different backgrounds, personalities, and brain physiologies that make some techniques good ways to learn and others less so.

In college the reality is that often you don't have much choice in the way material is presented. Most texts follow one particular style, as do many instructors in class. So, much of the time you'll have to adapt. You can turn this to your advantage by developing several different learning styles. These techniques will reinforce one another and give you more ways to understand and remember. At the same time, you can emphasize things that work particularly well for you.

Out of habit, many students stick with their old ways of studying that may give adequate but not good results. This book, and the present chapter in particular, show you how to improve your academic performance dramatically. Try to develop new ways of learning. If a particular technique doesn't seem to fit in with your own psychological makeup, give it a reasonable try to see if you can benefit from it. Modify as necessary to suit your own needs. Effective students become aware of what works best for them, but they also have the flexibility and insight to develop new approaches that can help them succeed.

Choose Surroundings That Work for You

As we saw in Chapter 3, for most students it's best to have a place or places where you ALWAYS study. Never sit daydreaming or wasting time at these places. If necessary, get up and move to another chair for a few minutes. You don't want to weaken the power of PLACE to make you work. The idea is to USE LOCATION AS A TRICK FOR CREATING AUTOMATIC SELF-DISCIPLINE.

Find somewhere compatible with effective study. Have your pen, calculator, or any other material you need ready in advance so you don't waste study time getting ready. Your desk, a particular chair at home, the commuter train, or a special area of the library are locations you can choose. A quiet library is good because it removes you from temptation. It's best not to have a nice view or interesting distractions. Plain surroundings, books, and academic objects all help keep you targeted on your work.

There may be occasional exceptions to the desirability of a quiet setting. As explained in Chapter 3, if you suffer a mental block, you can sometimes get started by going to someplace you really like. But when you get there you must really work. Do this only if absolutely necessary and if the surroundings actually enable you to get work done. Shift back to an academic setting as soon as possible.

Sometimes a change in location, say from the desk in your room to the library, will refresh your spirits and help you keep going. The idea is to be a friendly manager to yourself—someone with determination, a sense of humor, and a light, affectionate touch. You'll soon figure out a number of good study tactics, without laying a guilt trip on yourself when you don't succeed.

Figure 6.1 Finding a good location is crucial to successful studying.

Make sure you have plenty of light, not glaring, too dim, or flickering. This will enable you to concentrate and keep fatigue at bay. KEEP YOUR DESK AND SURROUNDINGS ORDERLY. Staring at a mess can be depressing and distracting. A simple trick is to spend two or three minutes straightening your desk after each study session; then it will always be reasonably neat.

NOISE, INCLUDING MUSIC, USUALLY CAUSES DISTRACTION AND FATIGUE. Again, there are exceptions. Quite candidly, I'm listening to some lively harpsichord music as I write this. After an afternoon of busy errands, I'm tired and don't really feel like writing, but I'm using my environment to maximize my motivation and concentration. Tomorrow morning the music stays off.

Set Specific Goals for Each Study Session

Decide *how long* you intend to study. Ideally, you'll have already determined this through your study schedule. Be flexible. If you're on a roll, you may want to keep going until you finish those math problems. You should also plan to stop at some logical point. If you have to go on ten minutes longer than you've planned or stop five minutes earlier in order to complete a key section or chapter, you're controlling your learning in an intelligent way. The advantage of a schedule is that you make decisions in advance and help free yourself from indecision and temptation.

Next, set a target for *how much* you intend to read or how many problems you intend to complete. You may have to modify this goal so that you finish an assignment or avoid stopping at an illogical place. Still, these goals give you clear targets and will help you concentrate.

Before beginning, VISUALIZE yourself concentrating effectively, employing good study practices, and achieving your goal. Focus only on the next hour. Forget your course grade and your degree. Now only one thing counts: your IMMEDIATE GOAL. Don't waste time or impair your concentration worrying or fantasizing about long-term matters.

Set Priorities When You Study

You've got to make judgments about what's really important. If you're supposed to read a newspaper for one of your classes, it usually won't be necessary to apply the complete Remarkable Square Tree techniques discussed below. Some articles will be important and others won't. Probably few will merit the attention that your textbooks require.

You also must make judgments about the material within your textbooks. Portions may be primarily illustrative. Other ideas will be central. Sometimes it's not necessary to know the details in books of readings that accompany the main text. Critical thinking is essential as you study—you must try to assess the relative importance of different assignments and even portions of your assignments.

Here are some ways to tell what's really important; you should already be familiar with most of them.

- Your instructor tells the class that a particular book, idea, topic, or assignment is important.
- The book emphasizes a particular point through repetition, italics, or some other technique.
- The book is focusing on the basic what, how, why, and significance of a topic.
- The material compares the topic to something else, because comparison helps give you insight and understanding. The material is being classified.
- The material is discussing the *moral, ethical,* or *human* dimensions of the subject.

Develop Your Vocabulary

This will improve your reading comprehension and your ability to understand lectures. Write down words you don't know on 3 x 5 cards, which can be arranged alphabetically for review in spare bits of time. Include brief definitions and a shortened version of the sentence where the word first occurred. Try to use it several times in written or spoken sentences. Next time you come across it you won't have to look it up.

Appendix A contains a list of common prefixes and suffixes that will help you develop your vocabulary more quickly (pp. 311–316). This appendix will show you how to figure out the meaning of many words for yourself.

Get Physically Involved and Use Your Creative Imagination

Active participation helps ensure concentration and minimizes boredom or drowsiness. Taking good notes is one of the best ways to stay actively involved and alert. Making charts, graphs, tables, and diagrams requires activity and helps you think and understand as well.

Say or whisper aloud key points you want to remember. Gesture with your arms, hands, or fingers. Even if you're in the library you can mouth the words to yourself as you repeat key points, though it's better not to do this as you read.

There's a time and a place for everything, but if you're in your room why not act out one of the characters in a play if it helps you learn, remember, and enjoy?

Generally speaking, it's good not to get too comfortable when you study. You may be tempted to lie in bed as you read a novel for your British Literature class, but you may be hurting yourself in two ways. First, you'll probably become less alert and may get sleepy. Second, you'll have a harder time writing notes and engaging in the kind of action that contributes to motivation and learning.

Be creative. If you're reading a novel for a literature course, imagine yourself as actually present as the events unfold, perhaps as one of the characters. As you study a physics chapter you might imagine yourself as an astronaut who needs to understand the assigned problems in order to rescue colleagues stranded in orbit around the earth. You could conduct the music as you listen to a recording for a music course.

It may be helpful to view each study session as a game in which you try to learn and remember as much as possible. The idea is to create action, drama, and meaning that works for you, so you'll generate additional interest in the subject at hand. Not only will the material become more interesting; you'll also understand and remember more.

The above principles can help you set the stage for successful learning, but the most important thing is the technique you use as you study. The Remarkable Square Tree method discussed below provides a mechanism that can dramatically improve your understanding, recall, and performance on exams. It's a major key to effective study.

THE REMARKABLE SQUARE TREE METHOD: LEARNING MORE AND GETTING HIGHER GRADES AS YOU STUDY YOUR TEXTBOOKS

The Remarkable Square Tree method is a tool designed to improve dramatically your academic performance. It expands on and modifies the classic SQ3R method developed by Francis Robinson (see Bibliography). Unlike some other techniques, it places great emphasis on thinking and psychological strategies as ways to boost learning and recall as well as analytical skills.

At first, it may take more time to study using this method. But you'll save time in the long run. And, used effectively, it will help you learn much more and get better grades. Eventually you'll find that using the Remarkable Square Tree method becomes automatic.

The steps for maximizing your success in study are: Repeat, Scan, Question, Read, Think, and Reinforce. Recall from the last chapter that you can remember this sequence by *Remarkable* (for Repeat) *SQuaRe* (for Scan, Question, and Read), and *TRee* (for Think and Reinforce). We've seen that one of the best ways to remember is to create an unusual mental image that you're unlikely to forget. A square tree is just such an image. Figure 6.2 presents the REMARKABLE SQUARE TREE visually.

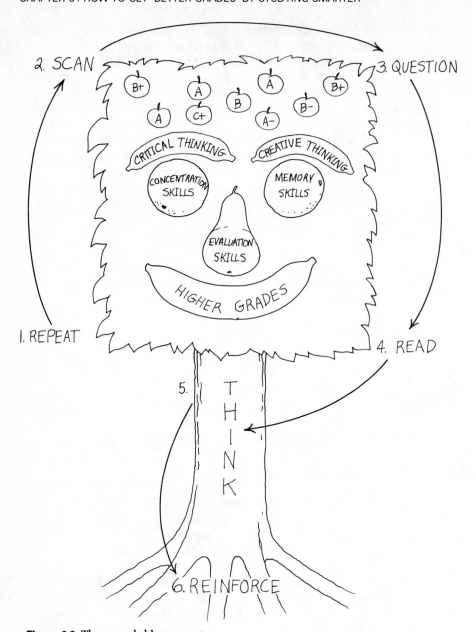

Figure 6.2 The remarkable square tree.

The First Step of the Remarkable Square Tree Method Is to REPEAT

The principle is to review and rethink earlier chapters and notes on those chapters. Ordinarily you should briefly review the lesson immediately preceding the one you plan to do during the study session.

This technique is as old as academics itself. Instructors often begin lectures with a brief review of the preceding lecture, offering some additional interpretations. This aids memory, puts the current day's topic in context, and gears up students psychologically for the task ahead. Often it makes getting started easier because you've already done the assignment and are less intimidated by it. A major difference in the Repeat step and traditional reviewing is that you're asked briefly to RETHINK the earlier lesson.

THE REPEAT STEP IS CRUCIAL FOR CEMENTING EARLIER COMPLETED ASSIGNMENTS INTO YOUR MEMORY. Automatically and in advance it accomplishes much of your studying for exams.

The Repeat step should take no more than about five or six minutes at the beginning of regular study sessions. Don't merely glance over the earlier chapter or your notes on the text. Scan quickly, looking at headings. Then turn away from your book and try to recall the material. Also look at the HINT in the top margin of the textbook or the notes (discussed on pp. 159–164), and try to repeat the items to yourself. For things you've forgotten, look at the book or your text notes, then turn away and repeat them again to yourself to sink items into your memory.

Also briefly RETHINK the material. Have you changed your mind about any points since you last read it? Does anything you've heard in lecture or read in other books cause you to reinterpret anything?

The Second Step of the Remarkable Square Tree Method Is to SCAN the Material to Be Read

When you quickly scan the material you help orient your mind to what's ahead, increasing your comprehension. It's like cross-country runners walking or jogging an unfamiliar course before the race. They don't have to hesitate and be hampered by uncertainty during the actual race because they know where they're going. All their energies can be concentrated on winning.

a. Always scan your textbooks *when you start a course*. First look at the *title page*. THINK about the title and subtitle to the book, trying to get a clear idea of the precise subject matter and its meaning. Note the edition number of the book. Turn the page and check the copyright date as well as the publishing history. Get in the habit of doing this for every book you read.

Next read the *preface, acknowledgments*, and the *"about the author"* sections of the book. Usually you can read these very quickly because there's no need to remember details. These sections will explain why the book was written and give you insight into the author's purpose, thinking, and even personal background. Not only will this help you better understand the book, you'll also have a greater personal connection with it and greater incentive to learn.

Next read the *table of contents*; this will provide a road map for your journey ahead. Glance over the *glossary* and index to get an idea of major terms that will be used.

If the *introduction* and *conclusion* to the book are reasonably short rather than full-length chapters, read them next. Even if they're long, at least look them over. The introduction prepares you for the rest of the book, and the conclusion often summarizes and helps explain the significance of the book. You'll know where you're headed and may even understand some of the major points of the book before you begin your assignments. If your courses are already underway, take time to scan your textbooks sometime during the next week.

b. Always SCAN CHAPTERS before reading them. First quickly read the *introduction* and *conclusion*, looking for the broad picture rather than the details. If there is no formal introduction or conclusion, glance over the introductory and concluding paragraphs to get the gist of what the chapter will cover and what its conclusions are. Determine the number of pages in the chapter and make a time estimate for its completion.

Sometime chapters will have a *summary, review,* or sections marked *key terms, major ideas,* and the like. Be sure you quickly go over these.

Glance at *charts, graphs,* and other visual displays. What are they trying to get across? Don't spend much time here; if you don't get it right away, move on. You don't need to learn the content at this point.

Observe how the chapter is organized, noting *major headings* and *major topics.* Then look away from the book for a few seconds to go over in your mind the material you've just glanced over. Quickly see if you can relate it to lectures or other readings. Usually three to five minutes on the SCAN step will be sufficient.

The Third Step of the Remarkable Square Tree Method Is to QUESTION

As you read, turn each heading into a question so that while you're reading you'll look for the answer. The idea is that supplying questions as you read orients your mind and helps you to think and comprehend.

Aaron was a student who stopped by my office to discuss some of his academic difficulties. He felt overwhelmed by everything he was expected to learn during his first-semester courses.

"My psychology course is especially rough," he said. "We've got dozens of new terms to learn as well as knowing the people who developed the ideas. It all gets kind of confusing."

I explained the Remarkable Square Tree method to Aaron, showing him how to apply it to his textbooks.

When I saw him during the next week he seemed more upbeat. "This Square Tree idea is great," he said. "I feel like I'm even getting a grip on psychology."

"Can you give me an example of how you've applied it?" I asked.

He took a book entitled *Psychology* out of his backpack and flipped through it until he came to a heading called "Reinforcement-Induced Behavioral Stereotypy" (Benjamin, et al., pp. 187–88). He said, "When I got to this section I actually felt confident. I'd already gotten the gist of it when I scanned the chapter and went over the summary at the end of the chapter. When I started reading the section I had in my mind the question 'what is reinforcement-induced behavioral stereotypy?' I also set in my mind other questions like who was the psychologist behind this idea and when and where did the work take place and what's the significance?"

"How did you remember and understand a tough phrase like Reinforcement-Induced Behavioral Stereotypy?" I asked.

"No problem. I remember the words with a couple of the memory tricks you showed us. I picture a giant plate of barbecued ribs, with a stereo sitting on them and a typewriter piled on top. And I remember the word "RIBS."

"Will you run that by me again?" I asked.

"It's easy. The first letters of each word make the word 'RIBS.' For the visual image I just take r-i-b for the first letters of reinforcement-induced behavior, stick a stereo on the barbecued ribs with a typewriter on top for the word, 'stereotypy.' Kind of weird, but it helps me remember. The main thing is that I really tried to learn the meaning of the words as I began to read that section."

The Fourth Step of the Remarkable Square Tree Method Is to READ the Material

Follow the guidelines suggested below as you read.

a. *Read with the goal of answering key questions*, including the questions you've created based on chapter headings. Also, read to answer the key questions posed in Chapter 4: WHAT, HOW (including methods of analysis), WHY (causes and explanations), WHAT'S THE SIGNIFICANCE. Look for key facts such as WHO, WHEN, WHERE, as well as COMPARISONS and CLASSIFICATIONS.

b. *Keep alert for possible exam questions as you read*. This will be discussed more fully in the next chapter, which shows you how to get better grades on exams.

c. *Vary your reading speed according to the difficulty and importance of the material*. Read as quickly as you can and still get the meaning you need to successfully complete the assignment. Sometimes for background reading it's enough to carefully skim for the main ideas. Most of the time, you'll have to know the material in your textbooks very well, especially the most important sections.

Make a judgment about the importance of the assignment as a whole and each section of it. Vary your speed as necessary within chapters. When you come to key definitions, pause to say them to yourself to make sure you understand. Pause at graphs, tables, and other visual displays as necessary to make sure you've got the meaning.

d. *Use cues within the text to help you understand*. Most texts will help you understand the organization of the material by presenting headings and subheadings in different sizes and colors. Sometimes authors will number and letter sections of the reading to help you see the organization and keep the material straight in your mind. Often capitalization or underlining will be used to help students get crucial points. Use whatever means are presented to help you learn and remember.

e. *Use the structure of written English to help you understand.* Punctuation, sentences, and paragraphs all give you important clues. The next sentence, for instance, contains a colon, which is used to introduce a list. Watch for key words as you read: negatives such as none, not, never, and qualifiers such as but, however, and nevertheless. These change significantly the meaning of the words that follow them.

One of the most important devices writers use to organize their thoughts is the PARAGRAPH. Almost always each paragraph contains a main idea, just like the one you're reading now. Look for the topic sentence, which gives the main idea. In this paragraph it's the first sentence. But sometimes the writer will put it last or even in the middle of the paragraph. Sometimes you'll just have to infer the main idea from the context of the sentences in the paragraph.

A key to improving your reading comprehension and speed is to build a good vocabulary. KEEP A GOOD DICTIONARY HANDY SO YOU CAN LOOK UP WORDS YOU DON'T KNOW. Write these down as explained on p. 150.

f. *Read only one section before pausing to think about and reinforce what you've just read* (these can be as short as one paragraph, a brief subsection, or a couple of pages). Let your ability to remember determine how much to read, or follow your instructor's directions if you're using this book in a reading or study skills course. Generally speaking, its unwise to read more than two or three pages of a textbook at a time before stopping to think and reinforce.

"Aaron, did you have problems when you proceeded to read the section about Reinforcement-Induced Behavioral Stereotypy?" I asked.

"Actually it wasn't bad at all," he said. "The questions I had in my mind seemed to make it come together."

"What did you learn about it?" I asked.

"Well, this guy Barry Schwartz found that when some pigeons learned to push buttons and light up a certain part of a matrix board, they'd stick with the original solution that gave them food as a reward. Even when a new solution was needed, they rigidly stuck to the old pattern, cheating themselves out of a lot of food."

After Reading an Appropriate Section, the Next Step Is to THINK About What You've Just Read

Of course, you're thinking when you follow the steps outlined above. The point here is to STOP after you read a section and *really* think. If you've read only a short section of your assignment you'll usually have to spend only a couple of minutes. If you can't remember something from the section, check back as explained in the Reinforce step, then think.

After you've completed the chapter or study session, again stop to think about what you've read. This time try to think in greater depth and develop more creative insights about what you've been studying.

Here are some of the most important things to think about:

How does this fit in with other things I've read in the book, the course and with lectures?

How does this compare with other courses, with what I know from my job experience, and from life?

Does it make sense? What limits or weaknesses are there in the material? How do I feel about it?

What are the moral and ethical implications?

In commenting on the thinking step Aaron said, "I found myself doing several steps at once. While I was reading, I was thinking all the time, like why is this stuff important and what does it mean to me? But when I finished reading a section I paused to think some more, and asked myself things like what are the comparisons?

"Did you come up with answers?"

"Sure," he said. "In fact, the authors told me some of the main comparisons."

"How about reinforcement-induced behavioral stereotypy and the experiment where pigeons wouldn't try new solutions?"

"Well," he said, "the textbook authors explained that Schwartz also tried a similar experiment with college students, where students were required to try new solutions on the matrix board in order to get rewards. What really got me was that these students also tended to hang on to the original solution, without trying new answers. They stuck with an old method when trying something new was needed to get rewards."

"What's the significance?" I asked.

He said, "That's where I began to think, maybe I'd locked myself into old patterns of studying and learning because they let me just get by. Maybe if I tried some new ways of studying I'd get a lot better grades."

"That's great," I said. "You related your studying to your own life. What about evaluating Schwartz's research? Evaluation is one of the most important parts of thinking effectively."

Aaron answered, "The work seems reasonable. But I'm not really qualified to judge the research itself. I do know that any research might later be disproved, so I'll assume it may be true until proved otherwise or until I see evidence to the contrary."

"Moral and ethical consequences are also an important part of critical thinking," I said. "Did you happen to think of any regarding the experiment with pigeons?"

"One thing that kind of bothered me was the way animals are used in experiments. I guess it's got to be done sometimes, but I sure hope they're treated well. Is that what you're getting at?"

"Maybe I'd have come up with something different," I said, "but your answer shows ethical sensitivity and independent thinking. And that's impressive. Students often surprise themselves when they discover the many ethical and moral consequences of what they're studying."

"It seems to help keep my interest," Aaron said.

The Next Step Is to REINFORCE

Here's a place where most students miss the mark completely. They fail to stop and see if they understand and remember what they've just read. Instead they just plow on and on like the farmer who never reaped a harvest. Because they remember little, they're less motivated to keep trying.

This step reinforces in two ways. It helps lock the material you've read and thought about into your memory. It also encourages you to continue to study in the future by prompting you to reward yourself. It builds confidence in part by demonstrating to you the power of effective review.

The key point of the Reinforce step is to stop at the end of each paragraph, section, or every couple of pages, look away from the book, and say to yourself the key points in the material you've just read. Again, how much you should read before doing this depends on how much you can comprehend and remember as you read. This step tests your understanding and recall, so that you can go back to reconsider points on which you're confused.

GLANCE BACK TO PICK UP ANY POINTS YOU'VE FORGOTTEN. Then look away and try again. Do this until you can remember the key points. You should be able to give important definitions, explain methods, causes, and show the significance of what you've just read. You should also know important factual material such as the who, when, where, and the evidence offered to support a conclusion. This is the point at which you should underline or take notes, as explained in the next section.

By taking time for the reinforce step, you accomplish several things: you understand better, remember more, and give yourself motivation to keep going because you can see the clear results of your efforts. You're testing yourself and proving that you know your stuff.

Also, *after* you finish the chapter or study session, go over everything in your mind. Recite the material to yourself again. *If you've forgotten anything, quickly go back and look at the section in doubt or consult your notes.* You'll pick up anything you forgot or didn't understand. This will help anchor the lesson in your memory.

Look over any questions and study aids at the end of the chapter and test yourself. Go back to the reading as necessary. Read and think about material at the end of the chapter to see how it can help you better understand and remember what you've read.

When I later asked Aaron about the Reinforce step he said, "This final step is really a second review because I've already done it at the end of each section. In fact it's more than that because I'm also reviewing and reinforcing when I'm thinking about the material. The thinking and reinforcing steps sometimes blur together, because I often have to look back when I'm thinking. And when I'm at the Reinforce step I sometimes think of new ideas."

"That's good. You're showing flexibility. What seems to reinforce you to continue using the Remarkable Square Tree method?" I asked.

"Easy," he said. "I can see results right away; I understand and remember better. I've pulled my psychology grade up to a 'B,' and I hope to do even better."

"Are there any negatives?" I asked.

"Well, it took some patience when I first started to apply the method," he said. "I had to be careful not to get so bogged down with each step that I didn't get much done."

"Anything else?" I asked.

"Well, I thought of something else when I was studying for my psychology exam. I don't want to let the success of this method go to my head. Maybe I can modify it into something even better for myself."

"Good," I said. "Everyone's got to adapt their studying to their own learning style. You're showing an ability to adapt and to try new things, and you're beginning to take charge of your own learning."

It's important to be flexible when you employ the Remarkable Square Tree Method. It's more suitable for textbooks made up of reading assignments rather than problems. Books and articles for research projects should be handled differently (see Chapter 8, pp. 224–227).

Readings for literature courses should be read through once for pleasure before applying the technique, and you'll probably want to work on a chapter-by-chapter basis rather than stopping at shorter intervals. Naturally, you'll be looking for character development, theme, plot, style, and other important facets of literature. Modifying as necessary, you'll find that the Remarkable Square Tree method makes you more organized and effective in understanding and analyzing readings in literature courses.

Sample readings from college textbooks are provided in Appendix B (pp. 317–327). These provide an opportunity to apply the Remarkable Square Tree method to readings from different fields.

In addition to the personal reinforcement you get from seeing good results, the reinforce step should also prompt you to give yourself rewards, such as pleasant, refreshing breaks after your study sessions and a little praise for your efforts. It's also important to engage in some pleasurable activities each day, even if they must occasionally be brief.

UNDERLINING AND TAKING NOTES ON WHAT YOU READ

Underlining and taking notes are an important part of effectively learning from your textbooks. Both underlining and note taking should be done during the RE-INFORCE STEP. Basic underlining and note taking should be accomplished after completing each section. Concluding thoughts and summaries should be written after finishing the chapter or study session.

The advantages of writing separate notes are considerable. Writing is a process of thinking. It's an excellent test of your understanding and a way to develop new ideas and insights. It lets you compare your own written presentation with the book. It's also excellent practice for exams. Taking good notes has the added benefit of improving your skill as a writer.

Sometimes there may not be enough time to take an extensive set of notes on all of your assignments, and compromises may have to be made. The following discussion of different methods will show you how to maximize the benefits of each technique. At a minimum try to combine underlining with writing notes in the textbook itself. Provided you can complete all your assignments, the more time you invest in writing separate notes, the further ahead you'll be in learning.

Underline and Write Your Notes in the Textbook

If you pick up the average used textbook in college bookstores, you'll see that most students use colored highlighting pens to mark their texts. As much as 50 percent or more of the typical chapter is highlighted, suggesting that the major accomplishment of all this marking is to inflate the profits of the manufacturers of these markers. Buy new textbooks if possible, because unmarked books give you a real advantage in studying in that you can add your own marks to your texts. If possible, try to economize in areas other than buying textbooks but, if you must buy used books, avoid ones that are heavily marked.

With the proper use of this note-taking technique you do more than merely underline, you also use graphic organizers, symbols, and short written notes. There are decided advantages to writing out notes and symbols. You're more actively involved in studying and thus are more likely to concentrate and think effectively. You aid the process of remembering, and you have more useful material when you later review.

Ordinary ballpoint or fine-tipped marker pens are more versatile than wide markers, because you can write many more symbols as well as notes with them. Following these simple guidelines will make the effort more worthwhile:

1. Don't underline or highlight until AFTER you've completed reading the section you're working on currently. Mark the section as part of the RE-INFORCE step. At that point you'll know what's important.
2. Resist the temptation to underline or highlight everything. Ideally, no more than 10 percent of the words should be highlighted or underlined, including: definitions, methods, causes, consequences, and key facts. BUT YOU MUST BE ABLE TO MAKE SENSE OF THE UNDERLINED MATERIAL WHEN YOU REVIEW, so don't underline too little, either.
3. Abbreviate and use symbols as described in Chapter 5 (pp. 124, 127).
4. Use the top margin to note HINTS to prompt you as you review, just as you did for lecture notes (p. 127).
5. Use the side margins to write down major clues to the organization of the material that is not clear from the reading itself. For example, if the author says that four causes of deviant behavior will be discussed, simply write 1 C, 2 C and so on in the side margin beside each point for the first cause, second cause, and so on. Also indicate crucial characteristics of the material you want to remember, for example, "DEF" for definition, "EX" for possible exam question. Use brackets, enclosures, arrows, and lines to show relationships within the text itself.

6. Use the bottom margins for OBSERVATIONS, writing down comparisons with lectures, other courses. Your evaluations of the content can go here. Also, ideas you develop as you think critically and creatively should go in the bottom margin.

7. Write a brief mini-essay at the end of the chapter. Sometimes this can be done right in the book, or use a separate sheet of paper. This essay should not only present the main idea of the chapter and key supporting points; it should show the relationship of the material to lectures and the course. This mini-essay should also show key insights, criticisms, and creative ideas.

8. Write graphic organizers as desirable (see pp. 130–135 for a discussion of graphic organizers). You will probably need separate pages for this step.

9. Review at the REPEAT step before beginning new assignments as well as during your WEEKLY REVIEWS. Cover the page with a blank sheet of paper, uncovering the text as you answer, or check the material as prompted by the HINTS at the top of the page, just as you do with lecture notes (pp. 128–129). During weekly reviews, GO OVER BOTH THE TEXTBOOK AND LECTURE NOTES DURING THE SAME REVIEW SESSION TO HELP INTEGRATE THE MATERIAL.

Figure 6.3 gives an illustration of how to underline and write notes in your textbook.

If Possible, Write a Separate Set of Notes in a Notebook Designated for That Purpose

These notes are more extensive than those written directly in your book. You should probably not try to use both methods unless you have a great deal of time to spare. The idea of writing separate notes is that you'll more thoroughly learn and remember by taking more extensive notes. You'll also have a handy source for the Repeat step, weekly reviews, and reviews at exam time.

Use the techniques presented in the last chapter regarding abbreviations and form (outline, graphic, etc.). Be concise but not so brief that you can't understand the notes when you review. Better a touch too long than too short.

1. Don't write your notes until you've completed reading and thinking about each section. The actual writing should be combined with the Reinforce step of the Remarkable Square Tree method. Briefly recite to yourself the material presented, going back to check on points you've forgotten. Then write your notes, checking back as necessary. Go over your notes to see if you've forgotten anything.

2. Use a separate notebook, with a standard one and one-quarter inch lefthand margin. Write on only one side of each page, indicating at the top of the page what book and page the notes are drawn from. Keep the left margin blank to write in organizational points as well as key symbols. Mark off the bottom section of each page as you did for lecture notes. The blank page opposite the notes can be used for charts, graphs, or other material.

Concept Formation

In beginning our discussion of concept formation, we would like to show you something that you have never encountered before in your life. In fact, until we wrote this book, we are pretty sure that no one in the world is likely to have ever seen what we are about to show you. Look at the following number.

even/
odd
concept

$$27,943,008,873,619,488,500,037,113,096,842,656,125,334$$

While looking at this number may not have provided much of a thrill for you, we hold to our contention that it is the first time you have seen it. You probably cannot even say the number, other than merely repeating the digits. By that we mean that most people do not know what comes after billions, and trillions, and since this number far exceeds those sums, they do not know what to call the various higher number groups. Still, even though you may not be able to say the number and even though you have never seen it before, you can probably answer a question about it. Is the number odd or even? Look at it again. If you said even, then you were right. The interesting question here is how you knew it was an even number if you had never seen it before. The answer is that you have learned the concepts of "evenness" and "oddness" as they apply to numbers. Early in your mathematical education you learned a few simple rules about what makes a number odd or even. This kind of learning is an example of concept formation.

def

def
def

examp

A concept is a symbol (most often a word) that represents a class of objects or events that share some common properties. These common properties are called the attributes of the concept and they are related to one another by a rule or set of rules. Thus, concepts are abstractions: they represent classes of objects rather than any particular object. "William Golding," author of *Lord of the Flies* and the recipient of the Nobel prize for literature, is not a concept, but "novelist" is. The concept of novelist includes a number of people who write fiction of some reasonable length. "Poet" represents another concept, as does "biographer." These concepts may all be subsumed *examp* under another concept, namely "writer."

Many concepts are nested in this way, arranged in a hierarchy in which more specific concepts become part of broader concepts. The phylogenetic scale in biology is an example of a hierarchical arrangement of concepts because it classifies plants and animals under various phyla, classes, orders, suborders, families, and so forth. "Penguin" is a concept that includes a number of adorable creatures including Opus of *Bloom County* fame. But penguins are also members of a broader concept known as "bird," *examp* and birds are part of a still broader concept known as "animal," and animals are included in an even broader concept known as "living organism." If you examine a concept hierarchy, you will note that concepts at the bottom include objects or events that are more alike in terms of their common attributes. In other words, as you move up the hierarchy, members of the conceptual categories are related in increasingly general ways.

Observation: concepts help us think and organize the world around us.

HINTS: SIGNIFICANCE
Relationship to novel situations

Are concepts important? We can answer this question by describing what life would be like without concepts. First, we would not be able to eat since we would not have a concept for what things are edible, nor could we drink. We could not play sports nor tell time. There would be no mathematics. Science would not exist without a conceptual structure. According to Moates and Schumacher (1980), without concepts "we would as likely make love to telephone poles as to people." examps.

Children begin to learn about the orderliness and regularity in the world through the formation of concepts. The cognitive structures so important for learning, memory, thinking, and other processes continue to develop as children establish categories to classify the objects and events of the world. Perhaps a child learns that cows are furry things with four legs. The child may overgeneralize and use the word "cow" when a horse is first seen because the horse meets the child's conceptual definition of "cowness." Corrections are quickly made (often by older siblings—"You dummy! That's a horse.") and the child's use of concepts becomes more sophisticated. There is also much novelty in the world, even beyond the world of children, and concept formation is essential for providing a framework from which to deal effectively with novel situations. sig.

OBSERVATIONS: Thinking conceptually is at the heart of good thinking. It's not really so difficult. I can define things precisely and think about how they form categories. Instructors and books do a lot of this for me.

Figure 6.3 Sample of making notes by underlining and writing in the textbook itself. *Source:* Reprinted with permission of Macmillan Publishing Company from *Psychology* by Ludy T. Benjamin, Jr., Roy Hopkins, and Jack R. Nation. (Copyright © 1987 by Macmillan Publishing Company.)

3. Write brief phrases and key words as HINTS at the top of the page to indicate the content of the notes. These will serve as a prompt when you review, so you can test yourself on your recall before actually reviewing the page.
4. Use the bottom margin to record your own OBSERVATIONS.
5. Briefly summarize each major section or chapter. Here use complete sentences. Write out your conclusion in as clear English as possible, because this will assist you in clarifying your understanding and help your recall. It's also a good way to develop writing skill.
6. Graphic organizers such as charts can be drawn on the blank page opposite your notes. Other more lengthy material can also go here.

Figure 5.2 on p. 129 can serve as a model of how to write notes, since the system for lecture notes and textbook notes is basically the same.

Write Notes Selectively on 3 x 5 cards

This technique is best combined with one of the note-taking or underlining methods just discussed. The idea is to allow you to review important ideas and facts during your spare moments. Three by five cards can be used for important definitions, formulas, summary of causes, and so on.

Keep the information on each card as simple as possible: one item to a card, using abbreviations and symbols as necessary. Adapt the cards to your needs. For example, one side of the card can be a HINT, with the answer on the reverse side. In a language course, the English version would appear on one side with the foreign language version on the other. This will enable you to test yourself. (Although language cards are available in many bookstores, writing your own will help you remember and allow you to adapt them to your own needs.)

As with other written notes, you have to balance the benefit of making these cards against the time it takes. It may prove very effective for an economics, chemistry, or language text with many formulas or definitions. You should still do the Repeat step as well as conducting regular reviews, but you have the added benefit of using the cards in spare minutes to learn important items cold.

THE IMPORTANCE OF WEEKLY REVIEWS

At least ONCE A WEEK, spend thirty minutes to an hour per course reviewing your previous lessons. Because you've already gone over them a couple of times at the Repeat and Reinforce steps, this step can be accomplished more quickly. THIS IS A CRUCIAL STEP IN PREVENTING THE MEMORY LOSS OF ALL YOUR WORK TO DATE.

It's a good idea to designate special times for these reviews and to regard them as important as going to class. This way you won't let the pressures of keeping up with assignments and projects prevent you from doing this essential step. Try to separate review sessions for each course by at least two hours.

Not only will weekly reviews help keep you from forgetting, you'll actually be learning new things. Before you begin reviewing, think about your goals for the course and for the next exam. Glance over your syllabus (course outline), book, past exams, and notes to determine which portions of your work need the greatest emphasis and to gain perspective.

Follow the procedure that you use for reviewing class notes. Leave the HINTS at the top of the notes or text exposed, and *cover each page with a blank sheet of paper*. Uncover the notes or text as you answer or check the material as prompted by the hints. Proceed through each hint in order. As you uncover the page downward, you'll have the hints and the uncovered notes to stimulate your memory and help you integrate the lesson's ideas.

Begin by reviewing your assignments from the previous week, to help implant these in your long-term memory. Then review other assignments you've chosen for emphasis. Finally, review everything you've learned to date, even if this must be done quickly.

Review your lecture notes during the same session. One of the most important benefits of these reviews is that they help you to put things together.

SUMMARY

Effectively using the learning and study techniques presented in this chapter can dramatically improve your academic success. You'll understand and remember far more than would otherwise be possible. Studying will become more interesting because you'll be more actively involved. Preparing for exams will be far less of a burden because most of your reviewing will have been done during your regular study and review sessions.

The Remarkable Square Tree method is a major key to learning more and getting better grades. As with any method, you've got to use common sense and judgment. Don't be so meticulous that you can't complete the work you've got to do. The trick is simply to employ effective study techniques every time you study. By applying the Remarkable Square Tree method consistently, you'll find that it soon becomes automatic, making your use of study time even more efficient.

Effective underlining and taking notes can help you concentrate and develop better ideas. It makes reviewing far more profitable and efficient, and it can improve your writing ability. Most students make the mistake of underlining too much and failing to take useful notes. How many notes to take and which system to use depends on your own individual learning style, the course and textbook you're studying, and the time available. One of the major benefits of taking good notes is better grades at exam time. The following chapter will show you specific techniques for maximizing your success on exams.

SUCCESS STEPS

STEP ONE: Measuring Your Progress

This Success Step will enable you to establish a benchmark and to measure your progress on actions that can dramatically improve your academic performance. It will also assist you in setting goals.

Rate yourself on the following questions. Give yourself 1 to 5 points for each question; the more positive your response, the higher the number you should assign (1 = strongly disagree, 5 = strongly agree). If the question doesn't apply to you, write "N. A." for not applicable. Remember that the purpose of the exercise is to help you set new goals and chart your progress as you proceed through college. There are no passing or failing grades.

Reevaluate yourself again after two and four weeks, and at the beginning of each semester thereafter. Jot down the date beside the points you assign, for example: 2 (10/3/92) 3 (10/17/92) 5 (1/93).

Measuring Your Study Habits

Reading and Studying

1. Do I always follow the REPEAT step (review and think about past assignments) before beginning new assignments?_____

   _____

2. Do I SCAN the chapters or lessons before I begin?_____

   _____

3. Do I set key QUESTIONS in my mind before beginning to read each section?

   _____

4. Do I READ attentively and actively, trying to answer key questions?_____

   _____

5. Do I vary the speed of my reading and the need to know details, depending on the importance and difficulty of the material?_____

   _____

6. Do I always pause after reading an amount of text that I've decided is a manageable segment and THINK about the material I've just read? Do I also think

   about the material after completing the assignment or study session?_____

   _____

7. Do I ALWAYS include the REINFORCE step in my studying? Do I pause after each segment not only to think but to see if I can remember and to cement the material in my memory, checking back if I've forgotten something?
       Do I do this after completing each section and after completing the entire

   lesson?_____

   _____

8. Do I UNDERLINE and take NOTES *after* reading, as part of the REINFORCE step? Do I also write concluding thoughts and summaries after completing and thinking about the assignment?_____

   _____

9. Do I reinforce myself as well as my memory by trying to give myself appropriate rewards for my efforts? Sometimes these rewards may be just a bit of self-praise and encouragement as well as a brief pleasant break._____

   _____

STEP TWO: Establishing Goals

Based on your answers to the questions in Success Step One, establish five measurable, specific goals for improving your studying effectiveness. Begin working on these goals immediately. Remove these pages and post or keep where they will serve as a continual reminder.

Goal 1. _____

_____

_____

Action I will take to achieve this goal _____

_____

_____

How I will measure achievement of this goal _____

_____

_____

Goal 2. _____

_____

_____

Action I will take to achieve this goal _____

_____

_____

How I will measure achievement of this goal _____

_____

_____

Goal 3. _____

_____

_____

Action I will take to achieve this goal _____

_____

_____

How I will measure achievement of this goal _____

_____

_____

Goal 4. _____

_____

_____

Action I will take to achieve this goal _____

_____

_____

How I will measure achievement of this goal _____

_____

_____

Goal 5. _____

_____

_____

Action I will take to achieve this goal _____

_____

_____

How I will measure achievement of this goal _____

_____

_____

STEP THREE: Qualitatively Measuring Your Progress

Answer these questions after one week and again at three weeks after establishing the above goals. Use the same 1–5 grading scale as above. Revise your goals as needed.

1. Do I feel more purposeful when I study?_____

2. Am I starting to feel more confident about my ability to succeed academically

    according to my goals?_____

3. Am I feeling a bit more in control of my life?_____

4. Have I been patient with myself as I change my study habits?

    _____

5. Do I encourage myself positively?_____

6. Am I continuing to engage in constructive leisure and recreation?_____

    _____

STEP FOUR: Applying the Remarkable Square Tree Method to Excerpts in Appendix B

Turn to Appendix B, pp. 317–327, and apply the Remarkable Square Tree method to the reading samples provided. Be patient and good-natured as you apply the technique. It becomes easy with practice, and some steps become virtually automatic. This technique will actually save you valuable study time and help you remember far more than would otherwise be possible.

STEP FIVE: Applying the Remarkable Square Tree Method to Your Courses

Choose one of your current reading assignments. Complete this assignment using the Remarkable Square Tree technique. DON'T AIM FOR PERFECTION. *Instead let the method guide you as you proceed efficiently through each stage, doing the best you can in the time you've got.* Be determined, but good-humored as you apply the technique.

STEP SIX: Underlining Effectively and Taking Good Notes

1. Choose a long reading assignment of moderate difficulty in one of your current courses. Apply the underlining techniques as described in this chapter in the first half of that assignment, ending at a logical place.

    Before underlining, wait until after you've completed a reasonable segment of text and have thought about it and begun the reinforce stage by checking your recall. After underlining and marking half the lesson write a brief summary in which you evaluate the assignment.

    Try to underline no more than about 10 percent of the words, but make sure you underline enough so that you can understand just by reading the underlined material. Underline key facts, definitions, methods, significance, comparisons, etc. Further mark your text by writing review HINTS at the top of each page as well as notes in the side margin using appropriate abbreviations and symbols. Use the bottom margins for your own critical and creative thoughts. Use arrows, stars and other symbols within the text as applicable. But consider the cost in time as well as the benefit for review.

2. Take the other half of the assignment that you underlined and marked in the text. This time write out a separate set of notes in a notebook. Use abbreviations and symbols as indicated.

    Use the outline form and graphic organizers as appropriate. Use the top margin for HINTS, the side margin for appropriate symbols on content, and the bottom margin for your own thoughts and evaluations. Be concise in your note taking, but be sure to take sufficient notes so that you can understand them when you read them a week later. Write a brief concluding essay in which you evaluate and focus on the significance of the lesson.

3. Wait until tomorrow and try reviewing the text you've underlined and marked. Hold a blank sheet over the text and note pages except for the HINTS in the top margin. See if you can remember the points referred to by the hints. Pull the cover sheet down the page as you answer the points or recheck the answer.

    Next, continue the above review by shifting to the notes you've written in a notebook, using a cover sheet in the same manner.

4. Now compare the two techniques. Consider the amount of time you have, your ability to stay interested and the benefits to be gained from each method.

    a. In which courses and assignments is the underlining and marking technique likely to be superior?

    _____

    _____

    _____

b. In which courses and assignments is taking separate notes in a notebook likely to be superior?

_____

_____

_____

STEP SEVEN: KEEP PRACTICING

Continue to use the Remarkable Square Tree Method in each assignment for which it's applicable. Apply good underlining and note-taking techniques as appropriate. During and after each lesson reflect on which steps seem most useful, and think about ways to make each step more helpful.

Chapter
7

Maximizing Your Success on Exams

*N*othing worries most students as much as examinations. And it's a fact that exams are important. They determine the major part of your grade in most courses. And grades can have a significant impact on your career options and employment opportunities. But several simple techniques can help you do much better on exams, and test anxiety can be greatly reduced. *Although there is nothing that can substitute for preparation,* using good techniques for taking examinations can significantly increase your scores.

Few students like exams, though good students see them as challenges rather than threats. Linda was initially terrified by the examination process. She attended every class, sat toward the front, and was beginning to use the thinking and study techniques discussed in the last three chapters. But she only got a "C" on my mid-term examination and stopped by during my conference hours to discuss her performance.

"Linda, I liked your answers to the main question and the two short essays, but you didn't answer all three short questions called for in the directions. Have you figured out what happened?" I asked

"I just panicked and didn't look at the instructions carefully," she said. "I always freeze up on exams; I'm just no good under pressure I guess."

"Many people feel that way about themselves," I said. "But they can learn to cope with the pressure and even to turn it to their advantage. I've known dozens of students who have dramatically improved their grades by learning strategies for taking exams."

It was clear that Linda knew the material. She'd just made a couple of basic, easily corrected mistakes in exam-taking techniques. She was also hampered by a negative attitude.

"Linda, I'll take improvement into account so this exam doesn't have to prevent your getting a high grade for the course. But you need to approach exams differently. Are you willing to try?" I asked.

Linda was no quitter. "Sure," she said. "But you don't have any idea how scared I get."

"You can learn to handle test anxiety," I said. "It's a common problem that thousands of students have overcome. Sometimes students may need to get assistance at the Counseling Center, but most students can learn to deal with their fear of exams just fine. So why don't we give it a try?"

Over the next few weeks we worked on exam-taking strategies as well as thinking and study skills. Linda got a "B+" on the final exam, in part because she implemented the strategies discussed in this chapter. She got a "B+" in the course because of her improvement as well as a very good term paper. Her marks began to improve on all of her exams with a corresponding rise in her grade point average. These are the key steps she took:

- She tried to acquire a more positive attitude, replacing negative thoughts with hopeful ones.
- She sharpened her thinking and study skills.
- She implemented a system of time management *during* exams.
- She carefully read and underlined key points in the directions.
- She quickly outlined her answers to complex essay questions to ensure she included all relevant material, and she made sure she answered the entire question.
- She learned strategies for taking both multiple-choice and essay exams.
- She began to see exams as a source of motivation for learning and studying as well as a means of seeing how much she was learning.
- She never missed a chance to use feedback on her exams to help her perform better next time.
- She learned to deal with her exam stress and anxiety, part of which seemed to evaporate automatically as she began to take personal control of the exam process.

LET A POSITIVE ATTITUDE HELP YOUR PERFORMANCE

A more positive attitude won't alter the fact that exams can be very important and that you'll have to study. But negative fears can be turned to an effective source of motivation. Instead of letting your fears immobilize you, try regarding exams like this: "Since I'm afraid of getting a poor grade and disappointing myself and my family, I'd better start studying smarter and learning how to handle exams. It's natural to feel some pressure. I'll just turn it to my advantage and let it be a source of motivation to work more effectively."

Nowhere is negative thinking so common as it is about exams. Here are some typical erroneous ways of thinking:

"I always freeze up on exams."
"The other students are smarter than me."
"I'm probably going to flunk or do poorly."
"It's not fair that we have to take exams. It's a rotten system."
"I just can't handle math."
"I'm just no good at taking exams."

If you dwell on negative stereotypes about yourself, you can create a self-fulfilling prophesy that prevents you from doing as well as you might. It's actually more realistic to take a positive view. Start by substituting realistic positive thoughts for negative ones:

"Maybe I really can learn to do well on exams."
"Maybe I can act as if I'm good at taking exams."
"How do I know those other students are smarter? Maybe I'm selling myself short and maybe they're just as scared as me."
"Tens of thousands of students who have been afraid of exams have learned to handle them well. I'll bet I can, too."

Of course, *positive thoughts must be backed by action.* But they can make it easier to begin and to follow through.

HOW TO STUDY FOR EXAMS

THE MOST IMPORTANT TECHNIQUE FOR GETTING GOOD GRADES ON EXAMS IS CONTINUAL PREPARATION. If you've implemented the steps discussed in the preceding chapter, your work is more than three-quarters done. The "Repeat" and "Reinforce" steps coupled with the somewhat longer weekly reviews help ensure that you know the material when exam time comes.

Briefly reviewing and rethinking earlier assignments *before* each study session and reviewing and reinforcing *after* each study session is half the battle. Weekly reviewing all earlier lessons is the other half. As we've seen, even brief reviews can have a profound payoff in how much you learn and remember.

Conduct an Intensive, But Paced Review over Several Days Prior to the Exam This review should accomplish three goals:

1. To integrate all the course material thus far into a meaningful whole.
2. To THINK systematically about the material, organizing it into useful categories for analysis, comparison, and evaluation.
3. To cement essential material into your memory.

The idea of integrating the material is to determine how everything in the course thus far fits together. If you've thought about the subject as you've gone along, much of this work will already be done. Your main task is to put the broad pieces of the puzzle together and subject the material to a final critical and creative analysis, making sure it's firmly locked in your memory.

During these final reviews be sure to do the "Repeat" and "Reinforce" (pp. 152–153, 158–159) steps at each session. Also use the possible exam questions you've identified as well as HINTS you've written in your notes and textbooks to check your recall. It's excellent practice to write out answers to possible exam questions as a means of identifying areas for further study and refining your thinking.

Don't forget to refresh and reinforce yourself with sufficient breaks. Try to do something pleasant and interesting that won't tempt you from going back to work. Building some brief pleasure into your preparation for exams helps motivate you to keep at it and keeps you mentally alert.

Do a Quick Review Just Before the Exam   The purpose of this review is to ready your mind for the examination. Don't get bogged down in detailed study that might make you lose sight of the big picture. If you've done your studying, a light once-over is all that should be necessary. Try to avoid studying other subjects within an hour of the exam so that your recall doesn't become confused.

THE PITFALLS OF CRAMMING

Cramming is a final resort. If you wait until the last minute to study for an exam you handicap yourself in several ways. You don't have time to think and evaluate. You don't have time to relate the material to other subjects. You don't have time to digest the material for full understanding. You tend to more quickly forget the material. And you'll probably be so anxious when studying that your concentration will suffer.

Still, if you have no choice, cramming is better than not studying at all. Since you won't have much time to think and evaluate as you read, your main focus should be on understanding, remembering, and reviewing as you go along. Aim for the basics:

Knowing key concepts and definitions.
Remembering basic facts.
Understanding principle causes and relationships.
Knowing the major significance.

Even though you haven't enough time to study for the exam, allow for rest breaks as you study. Otherwise the material you're currently reading will become jumbled up with things you've studied a few minutes before.

Before taking each break, review what you've just done. See if you can remember the basics; if not, go back to refresh your memory. After each break, review what you studied earlier so that you reinforce it on your memory. Only then proceed to new material.

Unfortunately, cramming works best for remembering factual information, and even here it's far inferior to the paced studying recommended in the last chapter. You'll forget fairly quickly unless you review after the exam according to the principles discussed in the preceding chapter—an essential task if you'll need to know the material on a future exam.

Get at least a few hours sleep, and wake up two or three hours before the exam so that you have time to review again. Go for a quick walk. Eat a good though not heavy breakfast. Drink no more than two cups of coffee.

Don't run yourself down for waiting until the last minute. Instead, try to use the experience to do better next time, and follow the other techniques discussed in this chapter for taking the exam successfully.

EXAM SUCCESS TACTICS

Manage Your Time Effectively

The main principle is to not lose points because of poor time management.

- Allow plenty of time to get to the exam. Use a fail-safe wake-up system for early morning exams. Don't rely on your electric alarm clock or clock radio. Have someone check to see if you're awake or use an extra alarm clock, especially if you've had to stay up late studying.
- Always take a watch with you in case the clock in the examination room isn't working.
- Determine the amount of time you can spend on each question. USE THE POINTS ALLOTTED TO EACH QUESTION TO APPROXIMATE THE TIME YOU SHOULD SPEND ON EACH ONE. Allow enough time to review your answers. *If it's an essay exam, write the time allowed for each question right on the question sheet, noting as well the time you must switch to the next question.* Check your watch periodically to see if you're on schedule. DON'T WASTE TIME IF YOU'RE HAVING TROUBLE WITH A QUESTION. Move on to others you can handle more easily and come back to it later.
- If you see you're running out of time, don't panic. Simply alter your tactics. Abbreviate and use outline form if necessary. If you're taking an objective-type exam, make sure you're answering the easiest questions first.
- Use leftover time to recheck your answers. *Don't be concerned with students who leave early.* If you've checked your answers once carefully, use any extra time to double check. The exception is when you have an examination in the next period. In this case you're probably better off leaving AFTER you've gone through your answers once. This will let you clear your mind and quickly review your notes so you can get mentally prepared for the next test.

Come Prepared with All the Equipment You'll Need

Double check to see that you have all the pencils and pens, calculators, and other supplies you might need, making sure you have backup supplies. Use a dark blue or black pen for essay exams, unless your instructor requests otherwise. Pencil and odd-colored pens are hard to read, and you want to be as legible as you can.

Choose a Good Location

Sit in quiet spot. Avoid sitting right in front, so you won't be disturbed by noise as people pass in their papers. But don't sit so far back that you might not hear important instructions. If there's noise or disturbance around you, politely explain to the instructor that you need quiet or request to sit someplace else if necessary.

Be Physically Prepared

Try to get a good night's sleep before the exam. If you have to study late, get at least several hours of sleep. Don't take tranquilizers; they'll dull your mind. If stress is a problem, use some of the anti-anxiety techniques discussed later in the chapter.

Eat light meals. A reasonable amount of caffeine, say a cup of coffee or two cups at most may help you stay awake, but avoid so much caffeine that you become jittery. Amphetamines and other stimulant drugs will interfere with your thinking ability. They have highly dangerous side effects, and you may crash in the middle of the exam. A little light exercise such as shooting a few baskets, doing some light aerobic dancing, or walking for ten minutes can stimulate and refresh your mind.

Read and Follow Exam Instructions to the Letter

Read carefully, and underline or highlight key points right on the question sheet if possible. If you don't understand something, ask. Instructors usually are quite willing to answer questions regarding instructions and procedure. FAILURE TO FOLLOW INSTRUCTIONS IS ONE OF THE MOST COMMON AND EASIEST-TO-PREVENT ERRORS.

Pay Attention to the Instructors Whenever They Speak to the Class

Clarifications or new instructions may be given. Perhaps the instructor is saying something like: "I've reconsidered the format of the exam. You only have to answer one of the long essay questions, not two. This will give you time for an in-depth answer." Or maybe an error is being corrected: "On line three of question two, the word should be 'demand,' not 'supply.' "

A Note on Cheating

The pressures of exams and the false belief that "everyone does it" sometimes lead students to cheat. There are many ways it's attempted: bringing in crib (cheat) notes or a pre-written blue book, having someone else take the exam, and buying copies of exams in advance from students who claim to have stolen a copy (often a sure invitation to being caught) are a few. Cheaters frequently spend more time and emotional energy trying to cheat than it would take to study for the exam.

The risks in cheating are high. Your instructors probably know all the tricks. They have no choice but to enforce the rules against cheating; otherwise they're letting down the great majority of honest students. So they'll be put in the very unpleasant position of having to confront the cheater. Sometimes the matter is handled informally—the student may be assigned an "F" on the exam but is not reported to disciplinary committees. Sometimes the student must appear before a student or faculty court, which can often exact serious sanctions up to and including expulsion. At the very least cheating creates extreme embarrassment for students when they're caught.

Cheaters kid themselves. They almost always underrate the intelligence of the person they're trying to cheat. While they try to justify their own behavior, they won't acknowledge anyone's right to cheat them. The potential "benefits" of cheating are always outweighed by the inevitable, even if unconscious, loss of self-confidence and self-esteem—not to mention the lost opportunity to learn by studying. Add to this the triviality of the gains compared to the potentially serious consequences and the choice is clear.

TAKING ESSAY EXAMS

Recognize the difference between an extended or long essay question, a short essay, and a short answer. *An essay is an argument that is backed by evidence. Its quality is judged by logic and quality of thought, clarity, coherence, and substantive content.* In a long essay you'll have the opportunity to more fully develop ideas, especially as they relate to illustrations, comparisons, significance, and evaluations. On shorter essays you must focus on the point of the question, though it's still advisable to distinguish your answer briefly by the techniques discussed below.

Short answer and identification questions require a direct, thorough response as allowed by time available for each short question. Even on these questions you can sometimes help ensure full credit by a brief reference to the significance of the subject. Here's an example from a business course exam on organization theory.

Briefly identify Max Weber:

Max Weber was a German sociologist who wrote varied works of great importance in the late nineteenth and early twentieth centuries. His development of the concept "bureaucracy" profoundly advanced the study of formal organizations. Despite today's emphasis on human and interpersonal aspects of management, Weber's ideas remind us of the continuing importance of organizational structure and of values such as professionalism.

One of the keys to success on essay examinations is *organization*. The first step is to use the instructions as a planning document.

Quickly but Carefully Read and Outline or Highlight the *INSTRUCTIONS*

Here's one way to mark the instructions to make sure you understand and don't forget:

Part I Answer two of the following 3 questions:

Part II Answer fifteen of the following twenty identification questions:

If you answer all three or all twenty questions the grader may just read the required number; you're unlikely to get credit for the best answers. Instead you shortchange yourself on the time you have to answer the questions carefully or deal adequately with the remaining portion of the exam.

Outline the *QUESTIONS*

Read through all the questions. If there's a choice factor, decide which questions you feel you can answer best and mark those. Determine the amount of time available for each question before you begin, and write the time beside the question.

ONE OF THE MOST COMMON ERRORS STUDENTS MAKE IN ANSWERING ESSAY EXAM QUESTIONS IS FAILURE TO ANSWER THE ENTIRE QUESTION. The best way to prevent this is to read the question carefully and outline the question itself. Say you're taking a history exam and the subject is the colonization of Africa by European powers. You might get a question something like:

Contrast French and British colonial policies in Africa. Pay particular attention to strategies and structures of control. Analyze the relationship of these differences to the problems faced by newly independent African nations.

Underline key words and insert numbers and other symbols to make sure you understand and have identified everything called for in the question. Make a simple outline beside the question if necessary. DO THIS QUICKLY BUT CAREFULLY. Here's one good way:

Contrast French and British colonial policies in Africa. Pay particular attention to strategies and structures of control. Analyze the relationship of these differences to the problems faced by newly independent African nations.

Now you've identified all parts of the question and are unlikely to lose points because you failed to answer every part of the question. You've drawn attention to the need to emphasize both strategies AND structures of political control. And you've outlined the need to relate the differences to problems faced by these new nations.

Here is a list of key terms used in instructions, followed by their meaning:

ANALYZE   *Explain*, showing causes, relationships, and significance.

COMMENT   This instruction is often given as an open-ended directive to test the student's creative and analytical abilities as well as capacity to evaluate. Identify the appropriate material, then show the significance, offering a reasoned evaluation. Evaluate critically showing your insight. Be creative in a way that sticks to the subject and shows its importance.

COMPARE	Describe the similarities *and* differences. Note the significance of these comparisons.
CONTRAST	Describe the differences, noting the significance of the contrast.
CRITICIZE	In a reasoned and objective manner, show the strengths and weaknesses. Provide arguments, evidence, refer to authorities as appropriate. Take a thoughtful position (you can be for, against, further information needed, etc.). Show the significance.
CRITICALLY EVALUATE	Same as above.
DEBATE	Present the arguments on both sides. If appropriate and time allows, conclude your answer with the strengths and weaknesses of each position, giving your reasoned judgment.
DEFINE	Give the meaning (definition). Be accurate in presenting the formal definition provided in the course. Sometimes a critical or creative evaluation of the definition can strengthen the answer.
DESCRIBE	Identify the key people, materials, events, dates, processes. Sometimes it's essential to include explanations. For long or short essay exam questions it may be helpful to show briefly the significance.
DEVELOP	Create whatever is called for, explaining, elaborating, and justifying.
EVALUATE	Same as CRITICIZE, with emphasis on the pros, cons, and significance. (In mathematics, evaluate means to show numerically).
EXPLAIN	Focus on the WHY, showing causes, reasons, purposes or motives. Include appropriate comments on the significance of the matter.
ELABORATE	Show further connections, reasons, consequences.
ILLUSTRATE	Provide examples, taking care to include important cases that cover the appropriate range of possibilities. Show relationships and significance if time allows.
LIST	Put in sequential order key components or items, being as thorough as possible.
OUTLINE	Organize the topic called for in a logical framework, showing clearly all major components and subcomponents.

REVIEW   Provide an overview of important components. Evaluate critically and show the significance if appropriate.

SUMMARIZE   Present the essential, key points, facts, arguments, etc. Condense the material showing what's most important.

TRACE   Show the sequence, carefully identifying key components and their relationships.

After Outlining the Questions, the Next Step Is to Write an Outline for your *ANSWERS*

Again, it's important to work fast. Unless you're taking a two- or three-hour final exam, you're probably not going to have enough time to construct a detailed outline. Jot down quickly any key points that come to mind for each question you're going to answer so you don't forget them later, but don't do a thorough job at this point. The insides of the cover pages of the exam booklet are good places to outline your answers. If permitted, you can also use the question sheet.

Outline each answer as you come to it. Use your judgment. Short identification questions may not require an outline. Think back over your lectures and assigned readings for the course. Consider your own insights and ideas (you may also develop ideas as you write the exam). Quickly add other points and ideas to the preliminary list you made when you first looked over the questions. Use an abbreviated form to save time. If you've got thirty minutes to answer a question, three to five minutes of thought and outlining will enable you to write a much better answer. Carefully reflect on the meaning of the question to make sure you consider all possible angles.

Think Your Way to High Achievement on Essay Examinations

A theme of this book is that you can learn to think in ways that will dramatically increase your level of performance in college. You can be sure that most instructors will recognize and reward evidence of good thinking on exams.

Most instructors are not impressed with exams that simply parrot back information from the textbooks and lectures. While such answers—if relatively complete—may get you a "C" or sometimes even a "B," they're less likely to earn you distinguished grades. Even answers that omit some information can often be considerably strengthened by evidence of independent thought and insight.

These points are especially crucial in developing your answers; you'll already have given them thoughtful attention as you studied:

- INCLUDE THE "WHAT" (especially definitions). You can't define everything, but you'll impress many instructors if you carefully define key terms. Using important terms correctly is one way to give your exam an automatic boost in grades, provided you don't overdo it.

  Here's one example: "Informal organization, defined as the actual relationships of power and influence among individuals within the organization, often differs significantly from the official organization chart . . . " or you could say simply, "Informal organization is defined as . . . " followed by your definition.

- INCLUDE THE "HOW" AS APPROPRIATE (procedures, methods of analysis). You might say something like this: "Henderson was careful to establish a control group for comparison, to ensure that any changes noted were the result of her new program of treatment. Specifically, she established a double-blind procedure by . . . "

- INCLUDE THE "WHY" AS APPROPRIATE. If the question calls for you to "explain," or to show the "causes," or "reasons" you should focus on WHY. If you're asked to "analyze," you should describe as well as explain. Many other answers can be strengthened by including the WHY.

  You might say something like this in responding to a question that asked you to explain the fall of the Roman Empire: "The decline of the Roman Empire was the result of a long, evolutionary process. There were a number of key causes for this decline, many of which reinforced one another.
  First, [followed by a paragraph developing the point]
  Second, [followed by a paragraph developing the point]
  Third, [and so on.]"

- INCLUDE THE SIGNIFICANCE. Again, one of the major differences between an "A" and a "B" or "C" answer is often that the "A" student shows the *significance* of the issue. INCLUDE PROFOUND IDEAS AS APPROPRIATE THAT YOU'VE IDENTIFIED IN LECTURE AND IN THE READINGS. Offer as appropriate your own insights and profound ideas that you've subjected to your critical thinking.

  Here's an example of a conclusion to an essay describing practical applications of genetic research: "These new techniques of genetic manipulation present both opportunities and difficult problems. Already treatment of various illnesses has become possible, and great future benefits in areas such as agriculture seem probable. A host of problems await resolution, such as legal questions of patent rights and the controversial question of abortion. It is unlikely that the advance of scientific capabilities in this field will be reversed. The challenge will be to balance fairly and wisely the many competing values involved."

- INCLUDE COMPARISONS as appropriate to show the instructor that you have perspective. Like this, "Unlike the French Revolution, the American

Revolution did not fundamentally alter the internal economic and social systems. Specifically, the American revolution produced these more limited changes. . . . " IDENTIFY CATEGORIES AND CLASSIFY.

- Sometimes questions will call for your evaluation and critical judgment. THE ABILITY TO EVALUATE SHOWS YOUR INSTRUCTOR THAT YOU CAN THINK. Even if you've not been asked to evaluate, briefly indicating the moral or ethical consequences of the topic may enable you to distinguish yourself as a superior thinker. Use your judgment when you include more than is requested. Don't let it weaken your response to the question; gradually you'll gain confidence in making these decisions.

    Avoid saying, "I feel," "I think," or similar phrases that suggest you're merely giving your opinion. The idea is to evaluate critically.

Writing the Exam

WRITE LEGIBLY, WITH DARK BLUE OR BLACK PEN, unless the instructor requests otherwise. Studies have shown that poor penmanship can significantly lower grades, so work on your penmanship if your handwriting isn't legible.

Printing rather than writing out your answer in longhand may be a solution if you can develop a technique that doesn't slow you down excessively. Instructors will appreciate legibly printed answers, but they sometimes find that printed answers are excessively brief and superficial.

Single-spacing is probably best on the typical exam booklet unless the instructor requests otherwise. Although double-spacing allows you to insert material, it spreads out your thoughts so that your instructor may lose your underlying organization. You should leave a narrow margin to make reading easier and allow space to insert additions.

Make the Job of Grading as Easy as Possible for the Instructor   It's a tough and tedious job grading essays, and graders will appreciate, if only subconsciously, that you made their job easier. There's nothing like a clear, effectively developed examination to make an instructor say "excellent."

Begin by answering the easiest question first. MARK CLEARLY THE NUMBER OF THE QUESTION YOU'RE WORKING ON so the instructor can follow what you're doing. If you use more than one exam booklet be sure to number them clearly. If the beginning of the second booklet is a continuation of an earlier question, clearly label where the continuation takes place ("Question 3 cont.").

Begin with an INTRODUCTORY PARAGRAPH in which you present your theme or main argument. Don't repeat the question. It wastes time and some instructors find it annoying. Check off each item on your outline when you've finished writing that portion of your answer.

Paragraphs should stress major themes. As with most writing, it's usually best to begin your paragraph with your topic sentence: the main point that introduces the material to follow. This main point should support your theme and should be in direct response to the question. The remainder of the paragraph should be a development of this main thought through illustrations, qualifications, and analysis that elaborates on the main point. A common error is for students to get off the subject.

EVERYTHING YOU WRITE SHOULD BE IN DIRECT RESPONSE TO THE QUESTION. *Stay on target.* Make sure your paragraphs follow a logical sequence.

End your essay with a short CONCLUDING PARAGRAPH (unless it's a short identification-type essay). Don't merely recap. Try also to distinguish yourself as a student who can think. Show the significance as appropriate, clearly indicating why it matters. Comparisons and evaluations can also often strengthen the conclusion.

Overgeneralizations Are One of the Most Common Mistakes Students Make in Writing Their Answers   Avoid statements that imply "every" or "all," unless you're really sure of your facts. Here's a typical question on a political science exam:

> Please analyze changing patterns of political legitimacy (public support and acceptance) in Cuba.

One student began his answer this way: "Cuban citizens hate their government and they hate communism." He failed to qualify his statement and went on to write a brief answer that amounted to a shrill attack on the Cuban political system. Naturally he didn't receive a good grade for his response. One of his problems was overgeneralization. Is it really possible that every single Cuban citizen, numbering about 10,500,000 people, hates the government and communism? Sure, the Cuban political system may very well change because of popular discontent, but this idea could be developed analytically.

Instructors look for sophisticated, careful thinking. You should note, explicitly, significant exceptions and qualifications. Here are two paragraphs from a much better answer to a question on legitimacy in the Soviet Union.

> The Communist Party was firmly entrenched in the Soviet Union prior to 1989, partly because of its dictatorial nature and partly because it had the support of many Soviet citizens. Although violations of human rights may have helped give the government short-term control, they weakened its moral authority and thus its legitimacy in the long run.
>
> Problems of legitimacy may have grown worse in spite of (perhaps also because of) the reforms attempted by Gorbachev. Inefficiencies in the Soviet economy have undermined legitimacy in several ways. The failure of collective farms to produce adequately, the ineffective system of harvesting, transport and storage. . . .

The above answer avoids simplistic either/or thinking. Its tone is reasonably thoughtful, not hostile. It shows an awareness of the complexity of the issue. The idea that reform might have negative as well as positive consequences shows good thinking. The answer also includes specifics, such as the problems in the agricultural system. Try to avoid presenting only vague generalities in your answers. CONCRETE EXAMPLES WILL HELP SHOW THAT YOU KNOW YOUR STUFF.

Watch Your Tone   A common problem on essay exams is the use of inappropriate tone. Your textbooks and instructors can usually serve as a good model for appropriate style. In answering a question about the drug problem, an instructor in a public health course wouldn't say: "Druggies and drug dealers are a bunch of thugs." The instructor would show an ability to see subtle distinctions and the capability of thinking rather than mere emotional reaction.

Usually inappropriate tone isn't quite so extreme. But keep in mind that you're not writing to appeal emotionally to a crowd but rather to show your instructor that you're capable of reasoned analysis and judgment. An answer that began this way would be much more impressive because it shows more careful thinking and an awareness of the complexities of the problem:

> The drug problem in the United States has many roots and therefore requires a variety of government responses. Among the causes of the problem are poverty, changes in the family and educational systems, discrimination, law enforcement deficiencies, and current public health policies. The international nature of the problem further complicates the quest for solutions. . . .

The Importance of Good Writing

So important are the matters of style and accuracy in college-level writing that I'll go into more detail in the following chapter, which covers the subject of writing. For now, be aware that AS YOU IMPROVE YOUR WRITING YOU CAN PROFOUNDLY IMPROVE YOUR PERFORMANCE ON ESSAY EXAMS. You're graded on what you say and *how* you say it.

Next to knowing the subject matter, nothing is as important for good grades on essay exams as learning to write well. Clear, well-organized, well-written answers give you a tremendous advantage.

Never Leave an Essay Exam Question Blank, and Never Walk Out of an Examination in Frustration

It's tough for your instructor to give you credit when there's nothing written down. Occasionally a student will try to be funny, thinking everything's lost anyway. Writing an essay on the virtues of Mickey Mouse is unlikely to win you any points.

Try to WRITE SOMETHING INTELLIGENT, as closely related to the subject called for as possible. Most instructors actually look for ways to give their students points, but you've got to help. The first step is to realize that you probably have some knowledge about the topic. If you've gone to some of the classes and done even part of the reading, you should be able to think of a couple of key ideas. You can then try to develop these as best as you can. You won't get full credit for such an answer. Even if you have to write about a closely related matter, tying it into the question as much as possible, you'll still probably get some credit.

Allow Time to Proofread Your Answers

Always proofread your answers. The purpose is not to correct spelling and grammatical errors, although you should correct any obvious mistakes; it's rather to see if your ideas are logically related to one another and discover any errors or omissions. Simply make changes as in this portion of a World Literature exam answer:

> The link between literature and freedom is imperfect but nevertheless real. Good literature ~~always~~ teaches us to value human life and sensitizes us to the human condition. It typically generates a sense of hope that makes people more likely to stand up for their rights.
> Work as diverse as that of Achebe, Dunleavy, . . . etc.

If you start to run out of time, IT'S USUALLY BETTER TO OUTLINE AND ABBREVIATE TO GET ALL YOUR MAIN POINTS IN THAN TO KEEP ELABORATING ON ONE OR TWO. You'll probably lose fewer points writing in outline form (listing in brief words or phrases) and abbreviating than you will in leaving out large chunks of your answer. Your instructor might not even deduct anything, being thankful for the easier job of grading you've presented. But don't do this unless it's really necessary. One purpose of an essay examination is to see how you think and how you communicate your ideas.

TAKING OBJECTIVE-TYPE TESTS

Objective tests require that you choose the proper answer from two or more options or supply missing information. Multiple-choice, true/false, matching, and "fill-in-the-blank" questions illustrate this kind of exam.

Questions written by instructors often contain errors or tipoffs that can help you choose the right answer. Even questions from test booklets supplied by textbook publishers are often flawed. Students who know how to look for these mistakes can sometimes improve their scores. It's perfectly legitimate to take advantage of this information. Your use of these techniques will help compensate for the disadvantage of having to take tests that may contain poorly designed questions. Besides, some of the other students will have this knowledge, and you shouldn't be at a competitive disadvantage.

Make Sure You Understand the Instructions

Underline key words in the *instructions* if you're allowed to write on the question sheet. Also, underline key words in the *questions* as explained below.

Find out if there's a penalty for guessing, ideally before the day of the exam. Make sure you use the right kind of pencil for computerized answer sheets, and take great care not to make stray marks. Erase all changed answers completely.

Look over the entire exam before you begin so that you can budget your time effectively. ANSWER THE EASIEST QUESTIONS FIRST, going on to the progressively more difficult questions as time allows. (On standardized exams the

easiest questions sometimes come first.) LOOK AT ALL POSSIBLE ANSWERS
TO ENSURE THAT YOU CHOOSE THE BEST ONE.

True/False Questions

While many of these questions may appear simplistic, they can be tricky. If part of
the question is true and part of the question is false, the "false" choice is the correct answer. The statement in the question must be totally true all of the time for
the correct answer to be "true."

Watch for and underline key words such as "all," "always," "completely," and
"totally." There are usually exceptions to most things, so be observant. Statistically,
questions with words like this are more likely to be false, though sometimes they'll
be true. The important thing is to take the question precisely as written and answer
it on the basis of your knowledge.

Take this example from the "true/false" portion of a history exam:

> Historically the Conservative Party of the United Kingdom has represented
> Britain's privileged classes and has never supported welfare-type legislation.

It's true that the Conservative Party has tended to represent the interests
of the "privileged" classes, but that party has also drawn substantial support from
working-class citizens and in some instances has supported welfare measures. So
the correct answer is clearly "false."

Words such as "frequently," "many," and "often," "some," and "sometimes"
allow for the possibility of exceptions. They are not absolute and so from a statistical
standpoint are more likely to be true, though you should decide on the basis of
your knowledge.

Simplify double-negative sentences by making them positive in form. Take
this example:

> President Lincoln was not unsympathetic to the plight of slaves.

Simply cross out the "not" and the "un," and answer accordingly:

> President Lincoln was n̶o̶t̶ ̶u̶n̶sympathetic to the plight of slaves.

Clearly, President Lincoln was sympathetic to the plight of slaves, so the answer is "true."

Generally speaking, a higher percentage of correct answers will be "true"
rather than "false," so there may be some advantage in guessing "true" if you're
unsure. But an instructor who has read widely on the subject of exams will not
make the mistake of routinely giving more questions with "true" answers.

Matching Questions

These questions can vary from simplistic to highly complicated. As with other types
of objective questions, significant clues can sometimes be obtained from the wording or structure of the questions.

There are typically two columns, in which you choose the best answer from
column "B" to match each item in column "A" (or vice versa). Unless you can use

entries more than once, put a mark beside them as you use them. This way you won't have to consider them for every question. But don't make items illegible because you'll need to double check your answers.

Here's an example of a matching portion of an exam:

Instructions: Using each item only once, choose the entry in column B that best matches the items in column A.

Column A		**Column B**
Impeached president	_____	a. Italy
Date of U.S. entry into the first		b. Woodrow Wilson
World War	_____	c. Abraham Lincoln
Ally of the United States in World		d. 1920
War One	_____	e. Turkey
President who favored the league		f. Andrew Johnson
of nations	_____	g. 1917
A possible cause of World War		h. Theodore Roosevelt
One	_____	i. 1914
President whose assassination led		j. The system of Alliances in Europe
to civil service reform	_____	k. 1896
Date of *Plessy* vs *Ferguson*		l. James Garfield
decision	_____	

Instructors often mix up different items in matching questions, as in the example above. The first thing to do is figure out the categories being asked. In this case it's presidents, allies, dates of historical events, and a cause of war. Next, go down the lefthand column, answering questions you know for sure.

The idea is to work down the column with the more involved entries, so you can quickly go over the easier-to-read items looking for the match. Even if you're not yet familiar with this period of history, you might guess that three great presidents—Lincoln, Theodore Roosevelt, and Wilson—were not impeached. You'd then have a good chance of guessing the correct answer, "f," Andrew Johnson.

Answer the easy questions first, then quickly and systematically narrow the range of possible choices of those that are left. On matching tests there's usually no penalty for guessing, so your chances of improving your score are substantially higher if you let the system work for you. The correct answers from top to bottom are f, g, a, b, j, l, and k.

If you're stuck, see if the structure of the lists provides useful hints. In the example above only one possible answer matches "A possible cause of World War

One." The answer has to be "j," because no other possible causes are given on the righthand side. Of course, it usually won't be that easy, but you can frequently narrow down possible choices.

Completion-type Questions

These questions place a premium on remembering factual information. If you know your instructor will ask completion questions, it's important to learn well significant facts and definitions from readings and notes as you study.

Completion questions ordinarily don't exact a penalty if you choose the wrong answer, so you should guess at the answer if you don't know it. Even the layout of the question can give you a tipoff—you've got nothing to lose and a chance to improve your grade. Say you get the following question on an economics examination and your memory deserts you:

"_____ _____ _____ was a founder of the idea that government should play a key roll in the regulating the health of the economy."

Here you have two tipoffs: the word "was" suggests that the person is dead, and the three dashes implies that the person had three names. This might help you remember that the answer is John Maynard Keynes. Few instructors would be so obvious, but this question illustrates the value of being alert for clues.

If you're not sure of the answer, read the question carefully for grammatical and other clues that may spark your memory.

Multiple-Choice Questions

These questions can be the most useful of the objective tests from the standpoint of measuring analytical ability and understanding. Yet even these tests have serious limitations and often are weak in design. You can help protect yourself and improve your grades by keeping several points in mind as you take these tests.

1. Use the techniques discussed under true/false questions for underlining key words and crossing out double negatives.
2. Ordinarily you must choose the *best* answer. This requires that you consider every possible response. Sometimes you'll be asked to identify *all* correct answers, which also requires considering every possibility.
3. GUESS if there's no penalty for guessing or if you can eliminate one or more questions. Determine in advance the exact penalty for guessing.
4. Where numerical choices are given, the correct answer may tend to fall in the middle in a poorly designed test. Say you're given the choice of five numbers: 9, 10, 7, 40, and 32. If you have no clue about what the correct

answer is your chances of a correct guess may be increased by excluding the numbers 7 and 40.

5. Look for clues within the question, using your critical thinking ability. Grammatical and contextual clues can help narrow your choices. If you're stuck, THINK about the question and the way it's worded compared with the wording of the possible responses.

6. Read each question carefully as you proceed through the exam. Students are sometimes tripped up because they'll misread or misunderstand key words. Take this example:

Which of the following is not an Anglo-Irish literary figure?
(a) William Butler Yeats (b) George Bernard Shaw
(c) Henry Wadsworth Longfellow (d) James Joyce

The correct answer is (c), the American Henry Wadsworth Longfellow. Students who read the question too hastily might miss the word "not," which is critical to understanding the question. This is why underlining such key words is a good idea. Thinking they're asked to name an Anglo-Irish figure, they may put down the first answer (a). If they looked at all possible responses as they should, they'd see that (a) made no sense since two other Anglo-Irish literary people are also included.

Simplify complex multiple-choice questions that give you choices combining possible answers (all of the above, none of the above, "a" and "b," etc.). The trick is to answer each possible choice on a true/false basis and then choose the correct answer from among the possibilities presented. Take this example:

Which of the following countries are members of the European Community:
    A.   United Kingdom
    B.   France
    C.   Switzerland
    D.   Germany
    E.   Republic of Ireland

1.   B, C, and D
2.   A, B, D, and E
3.   A, B, and C
4.   None of the above
5.   All of the above

To answer this seemingly complex question, simply proceed down the list from A through E, marking each country that applies. Only Switzerland among these countries is not in the organization called the European Community, so you rule out entry "C." Draw a line through entry "C" or place an "X" beside it if you're allowed to write on the question sheet.

Next, choose the correct answer from the list of choices 1 through 5. Look carefully through the choices and you'll see the only possible correct answer is number 2.

Some instructors may deliberately construct the exam in order to mislead those who haven't studied. They may reverse some of the tendencies noted above, such as the greater probability that true/false questions will be true. Probably most of the time these principles will hold.

THESE TIPS ARE NOT A SUBSTITUTE FOR STUDY. You should always go with your knowledge rather than choose an answer on the basis of something superficial such as grammar. But your awareness of some common weaknesses of these exams can help you protect yourself and perform better than you otherwise might. Developing test-taking awareness lets you do as well as you possibly can with the good work you put into preparing for exams.

HANDLING ANXIETY AND STRESS

Exams and other pressures in college can produce anxiety and stress. Basically, anxiety is fear that can produce various unpleasant physical symptoms that can limit your ability to concentrate, study, and have fun. In extreme form this fear can produce "anxiety attacks," resulting in a variety of symptoms: racing heart or chest tightness, rapid breathing or shortness of breath, dry mouth and tightness in the throat, sweating, disorientation and dizziness, stomach queasiness, and a sense of panic. THESE SYMPTOMS ARE SOMETIMES PRODUCED BY SERIOUS DIS-EASE such as stroke, asthma, heart attack, and many others. The first step is to get a medical diagnosis to rule out a physical problem. Obviously, severe chest pain demands immediate medical attention.

If you have an almost continual feeling of generalized or specific anxiety or panic, you may have a psychological condition that sometimes first emerges during the late teenage years. This condition can be treated effectively in a variety of ways, usually with dramatic results. For generalized feelings of anxiety the Counseling Center is the place to start.

Often anxiety and anxiety attacks are merely the result of stress associated with specific situations. There are a number of ways to deal with the problem. If disease has been ruled out, you should realize that symptoms associated with minor anxiety attacks (dry mouth, rapid breathing, and lightheadedness) won't hurt you. If you don't let these physical reactions cause you to panic, you can get a grip on yourself.

The first step is to quit thinking panic thoughts. Try to relax and breath more slowly and deeply. And THINK. Substitute constructive thoughts for destructive ones. *Visualize yourself reacting calmly and imagine your emotions calming down.* Act *as if* you were in control of the situation.

Linda began to practice these and other techniques whenever she was hit by anxiety. She bought several good books on anxiety (see those by Sheehan and Wilson listed in the Bibliography) and read them thoughtfully. Had these steps not worked, she planned to see a counselor in the Counseling Center.

She said, "The most important thing I do to control my anxiety during exams is to prepare myself beforehand. I study for exams as I go along, try to anticipate questions, and just try to be philosophical. All I really have to do is just sit there and answer some questions. No evil monster's going to attack me. If I should happen to do badly, I'll live and still have a good life."

"Have you done anything else to achieve such a change in attitude?" I asked.

"Well, I meditate briefly each day if I start to get worried before an exam," she said.

"Any secret words or techniques?" I asked.

"Not really. I just close my eyes, breath deeply, think of some beautiful, peaceful scene, then shift to myself. I imagine studying calmly before the exam, enjoying breaks and walking calmly into the exam room. I go through the details in my mind beforehand. It's really no big deal, but it sure seems to help."

"What are some of those details?" I asked

"Oh, I just see myself sitting there alert but calm, planning my time, carefully reading the instructions, outlining the answers, acting like I'm in charge and confident."

"Don't you feel at all nervous anymore during exams?" I asked.

"Well, a little," she said. "But not like before. It sort of keeps me on my toes."

Here's a list of specific ways to deal with anxiety attacks:

1. TAKE A DEEP, SLOW BREATH. Next slow your rate of breathing and breath more deeply. The trick is to breath like a singer, through the lower part of your lungs. As you fill up with air your abdomen should rise. Breathing more slowly and deeply reduces the level of carbon dioxide in your system, making you feel less dizzy and lightheaded as though you weren't in control. The idea is to return to breathing naturally, instead of the rapid, shallow breathing characteristic of anxiety attack.
2. REPLACE PANIC THOUGHTS WITH POSITIVE THOUGHTS. Say to yourself. "I can handle this situation. I won't let these symptoms get me down. I'll act as if I'm in control."
3. VISUALIZE YOURSELF AS CALM. If you're going into a situation that may make you panicky, in your mind rehearse handling the situation effectively. Go through as many details as possible. This works for many situations such as speaking up in class. You may not get perfect results immediately but you'll do better than you otherwise would. Visualization can also help *during* an anxiety attack.

Here are some ways to help PREVENT anxiety attacks, depression, and the buildup of excessive stress:

1. EXERCISE. Athletic games (tennis, squash, etc.) or aerobic classes give you both social activity and the many health benefits of exercise. *Going for a brisk half-hour to forty-minute walk is one of the best forms of exercising.* Aim to get some exercise every day. The payoffs? Reduced stress, greater energy, and a healthier outlook on life.
2. EAT PROPERLY AND GET ENOUGH SLEEP. A poor diet with inadequate vitamins, minerals, and nutrients can wear you down. Excessive sugar and caffeine can make you jittery, anxious, and less able to cope. Avoid recreational drugs and the excessive use of alcohol.

   Get enough sleep. There are few quicker ways to become depressed and feel stressed out than getting inadequate sleep.

3. **THINK POSITIVELY AND REALISTICALLY.** Deal with inappropriate negative thoughts (see p. 12). Confront issues that require action. List alternatives, get information and advice if necessary, then do what must be done. Putting off problems wastes enormous amounts of emotional energy and may make them worse.

   Avoid categorical (either/or) thinking. Don't blow problems out of proportion or think you must be perfect. If you make a mistake, don't make it a life or death issue.

   Don't expect that things should always go your way, that others should necessarily appreciate you, that life should always be fair. Ease up on yourself and others. Step back and enjoy life. Pursue your goals because they can help you enjoy life. They're not tangible things that should make you miserable.

4. **ENJOY YOURSELF.** Do something for pleasure every day. Build hobbies, recreation, and social activity into your routine.

5. **DEVELOP SOCIAL RELATIONSHIPS.** Probably for most people it's not easy to make friends, but it can be done. Be optimistic and persistent.

6. **SET ASIDE SOME REGULAR QUIET TIME.** Meditation (or prayer if you're religious) each day will help calm you and provide perspective. Here's one simple technique: lie down or sit comfortably in a chair; breath slowly and deeply; see yourself getting progressively more relaxed; and visualize a beautiful scene in all its details; feel yourself in that peaceful scene. Now visualize yourself effectively handling some problem or behaving in some desired way. See as many details as possible.

7. **GET BEYOND YOURSELF AND YOUR OWN PROBLEMS.** Become more oriented toward others. Be concerned about their welfare. Make a contribution. It's true that some people don't think enough of their own needs and subordinate themselves to the needs of others. This can be a prescription for low self-esteem and psychological problems. But being attentive to the needs of others and reaching out beyond ourselves is a great way to give our lives meaning and improve our performance.

EVALUATION AND FEEDBACK

Carefully reviewing your exams when you get them back has a number of payoffs. You may find that your instructor has made a mistake in calculating your grade. Any instructor will be glad to rectify an error in arithmetic. You may discover that an answer to a multiple-choice question was marked incorrect that you feel is right. After checking your text and perhaps with another student to see if you've misunderstood something, see your instructor. Politely explain that you'd like to learn where you went wrong, and describe your reason for your choice.

Occasionally the grader will be willing to accept your reason as legitimate. More often you'll learn where your reasoning wasn't quite on target. This knowledge can help refine your thinking ability and improve your sophistication in taking exams. **THE MAJOR PAYOFF OF REVIEWING YOUR EXAMS IS DOING BETTER ON FUTURE EXAMS.**

The most important step is to carefully read over your instructor's comments or find which objective questions you missed. Try to figure out how you could have done better (even if you got a high grade) or where you went wrong. Did you misread the exam instructions; fail to include certain kinds of material; make mistakes in your writing that led to a lower grade? The more precise you can be in determining where you lost points, the more likely you are to do better next time.

It's also important to think about questions you answered correctly. Why did you perform well on particular questions? How can you broaden these good points to more answers in the future?

If you'll be taking future exams from the same instructor, try to figure out the kinds of questions the instructor likes to ask. Where did the questions come from: lecture, main textbook, current events? Did the instructor emphasize details or main ideas? Although you shouldn't assume that future exams will be the same, knowing the answers to these questions will help you see the kinds of things to give more attention in preparing for the next exam.

One of the most useful steps is to ask your instructor for additional feedback and suggestions, ideally during conference hours. Because instructors are sometimes in a hurry to complete their grading, they may not put as many comments on exams as might be ideal. The idea is to learn how you can improve. You can simply say "I'm trying to develop my thinking skills and my ability to do better on exams, and I'd be very grateful if you could give me a little more feedback on my exam" (which you've already gone over and have brought with you).

Making use of evaluation became one of Linda's major strategies for improving her scores on exams. One day she asked, "Do you realize that my getting evaluation and feedback is no different from a business corporation getting feedback on its marketing operations? I helped my mom set up a new stereo system during spring break. The company had this warranty registration card that asked marketing questions. They wanted to know what kind of store we bought the stereo from, where we heard about it, how old the buyer is, what kind of magazines she reads, how much money she makes a year. They even asked her level of education."

"Do you know why?" Linda continued. "Because then they'll know if they're putting their advertising dollars in the right place and what advertising to emphasize or cut out. I'll bet they also get ideas about production, like what kind of units to build for which markets."

"Right," I said. "But valuable as that information is, it'll be useless unless they actually act on it and make the necessary adjustments."

"Yeah," Linda said, "but can you imagine a business executive dumb enough not to use such information? It's just like gold. The stockholders and directors would hang them if they didn't act on it. Anyway, they'd soon be out of business."

Linda marveled at the fact that she, like most students, had been making precisely this silly error. In fact, she believed that most students didn't actively seek feedback and didn't even consider feedback that was handed to them on a platter, like instructor comments on an exam or report.

Unhappily, I had to agree with Linda. From a common-sense viewpoint it's almost unbelievable that students often fail to follow a simple procedure that is virtually guaranteed to help them make steady and sustained improvement. Maybe it's partly that most students just want to get the job done and over and just forget

Figure 7.1 Asking your instructor for suggestions on improving your performance can help you do better on future exams.

about it. It's like going through a banking transaction and not bothering to fill out a simple form that would let them pick up a $250 refund.

Let me assure you that Linda began to pick up her refunds every time. Like other winning students, she ALWAYS tried to figure out how she could have done better or where she went wrong so she wouldn't make the same mistake next time. I was struck by Linda's enthusiasm over such a simple discovery. And yet many great ideas are surprisingly simple.

SUMMARY

Nothing is more important to success on exams than preparation through regular, paced studying and reviewing. The techniques presented in the three preceding chapters offer the main secrets of doing well on exams.

Beyond the need to study effectively, there are a number of techniques that can help you perform well on exams. Time management during exams will make you more productive and help you avoid foolish mistakes. Taking care of your body will maximize your ability to concentrate and reduce stress and anxiety. Remembering to bring necessary equipment, including a watch, and choosing a good location will prevent needless distractions.

Reading the directions carefully and outlining essay exam questions are basic to effective performance on exams. Many students throw away points because they don't carefully follow instructions. On essay questions it's important to avoid overgeneralizations and consider the key thinking questions (what, how, why, what's the significance, what are the comparisons, classifications, and evaluation) as appropriate.

Stick to the point and use concrete examples when applicable. Use your judgment about the preferences of individual instructors, but most will give considerable credit if students offer appropriate, well-thought-out insights, including insights developed in the readings and in class.

Your performance on multiple-choice exams can improve considerably by following the methods discussed in this chapter. Reading instructions carefully and planning are vital. Looking at the content and structure of questions and possible choices can often provide useful clues.

One of the fundamental mistakes students make in taking exams is failure to use feedback. This alone would prevent a number of repeated mistakes. Successful students often ask for additional feedback from their instructors. The principle of seeking appropriate feedback can help throughout your college years and beyond.

SUCCESS STEPS

STEP ONE: Developing the Habit of Using Feedback

Locate all the exams you've taken so far this term (if it's near the beginning of the term and you have few exams, go back to the preceding term). Carefully read instructor comments, noting suggestions below. Sometimes instructors won't make comments on essay exams or just make cursory observations that aren't helpful, knowing many students won't bother to read their comments anyway. In this case, explain to your instructor that you'd like more feedback so you can improve in the future. Most will be willing to provide you with useful advice. For multiple choice exams, look at all questions you missed and attempt to learn from your mistakes.

Pay special attention to patterns. Are there particular kinds of questions you seem to miss habitually? If you haven't saved questions and answers, make it a practice to do so in the future. Occasionally instructors will collect questions after the exam. If they do, ask if you can look at the questions again, perhaps in the department office, explaining that you're working on exam-taking skills.

For math and other exams with numerical problems, make sure you understand where you went wrong. Work through the problem you missed and do a couple more similar problems so you can handle them in the future.

List common errors and remedies. Don't include the correct answers to questions; you're looking for patterns of response that cause you to make errors, for example over-generalization, failure to choose the *best* answers in multiple choice questions and so on. Don't worry if you have trouble coming up with five error patterns. The important thing about this exercise is that it helps get you in the habit of looking for patterns that can guide you toward future improvement.

1. Error pattern _____

   _____

   Remedy _____

   _____

2. Error pattern _____

   _____

   Remedy _____

   _____

3. Error pattern _____

   _____

   Remedy _____

   _____

4. Error pattern _____

   _____

   Remedy _____

   _____

5. Error pattern _____

   _____

   Remedy _____

   _____

STEP TWO: Rethinking This Chapter

Now review this chapter. Your sole object here is to note specific ideas that seem most likely to help you. Rank techniques that you believe may offer the most benefit.

1. _____

   _____

2. _____

   _____

3. _____

   _____

4. _____

   _____

5. _____

   _____

6. _____

   _____

7. _____

   _____

8. _____

   _____

9. _____

   _____

10. _____

    _____

STEP THREE: Setting Goals

Based on your answers to the questions in Success Steps One and Two, establish five measurable, specific goals for improving your performance on exams. Begin working on these goals immediately. Remove these pages and post or keep where they will serve as a continual reminder.

Goal 1. _____

_____

_____

Action I will take to achieve this goal _____

_____

_____

How I will measure achievement of this goal (Not just higher grades. Example:

number of good suggestions I get from my instructors and others) _____

_____

Goal 2. _____

_____

_____

Action I will take to achieve this goal _____

_____

_____

How I will measure achievement of this goal _____

_____

_____

Goal 3. _____

_____

_____

Action I will take to achieve this goal _____

_____

_____

How I will measure achievement of this goal _____

_____

_____

Goal 4. _____

_____

Action I will take to achieve this goal _____

_____

_____

How I will measure achievement of this goal _____

_____

_____

Goal 5. _____

_____

_____

Action I will take to achieve this goal _____

_____

_____

How I will measure achievement of this goal _____

_____

_____

STEP FOUR: Visualizing Success on Exams

The purpose of this exercise is to begin the process of confidence building. Take your time.

1.   Sit in a comfortable, quiet place.
2.   Relax, close your eyes, breath slowly and deeply.
3.   Visualize a beautiful, quiet outdoor place. Feel the comfort of that place.
4.   Now shift your focus. See yourself studying confidently, following the "repeat" step each time you study, reviewing and rethinking an earlier assignment. See yourself conducting weekly reviews.
5.   See yourself entering examination rooms confident, rested, and calm, but geared for action.
6.   See yourself proceeding step-by-step through your exams, reading directions carefully and following the other steps suggested for taking exams.
7.   Visualize yourself using available feedback, seeking additional feedback when it can be helpful.
8.   Repeat this brief exercise every day until you're satisfied with your level of confidence and success in taking exams.

STEP FIVE: Effective Planning During Exams

1.   Underline, circle, or highlight key words and determine the time available for each question for the following one-hour exam.

Part I   Answer one of the following questions (50 percent of exam grade).

a.   Trace the development of medical research in genetics since 1970, paying special attention to inherited diseases.
b.   Analyze the drug problem in American secondary schools.

Part II   Answer five of the following six questions (10 percent each).

a.   Describe the problems of the Colombian government in its war on drugs.
b.   Identify and explain the significance of Manuel Noriega.
c.   Summarize the current public health policies of the U.S. government with respect to the drug problem.
d.   Critically evaluate the President's current policies on the drug problem.
e.   List five problems confronting specialists in genetic research with respect to ethical and legal questions.
f.   Contrast British and American public health policies dealing with drug abuse.

2.   Reword the following exam question into a positive statement.

Which of the following presidents was not unfavorable toward the use of American military power abroad?

3. Identify the clues or key words in the following questions.
   a. _____ _____ _____ was the author of *Tales of a Wayside Inn*.
   b. No president has ever been impeached.
   c. Which of the following is not a composer from the baroque period:

   1. Bach
   2. Handel
   3. Copeland
   4. Scarlatti

[see pp. 209–210 for answers to planning questions]

ANSWERS TO SUCCESS STEP FIVE QUESTIONS

1. Underline key words and determine the time available for each question for the following one-hour exam.

    30 minutes

    Part I Answer <u>one</u> of the following questions (50 percent of exam grade).

    a. (Trace) the development of medical research in genetics <u>since 1970</u>, paying special attention to <u>inherited</u> <u>diseases</u>.

    b. (Analyze) the <u>drug problem</u> in American <u>secondary</u> <u>schools</u>.

    Part II Answer <u>five</u> of the following six questions (10 percent each).

    6 minutes each

    a. (Describe) the <u>problems</u> of the <u>Colombian</u> government in its <u>war on drugs</u>.

    b. (Identify) and (explain) the <u>significance</u> of <u>Manuel Noriega</u>.

    c. (Summarize) the <u>current</u> <u>public health</u> <u>policies</u> of the <u>U.S.</u> government with respect to the <u>drug</u> <u>problem</u>.

    d. (Critically evaluate) the <u>President's</u> <u>current</u> <u>policies</u> on the <u>drug problem</u>.

    e. (List) **5** <u>five</u> <u>problems</u> confronting specialists in <u>genetic</u> <u>research</u> with respect to <u>ethical</u> <u>and</u> <u>legal</u> questions.

    f. (Contrast) British <u>and</u> American <u>public health</u> <u>policies</u> dealing with <u>drug</u> <u>abuse</u>.

2. Reword the following exam question into a positive statement:

    Which of the following presidents were ~~not~~ ~~unfavorable~~ toward the use of American military power abroad?

3. Identify the clues or key words in the following questions:

    a. ⟨_____ _____ _____⟩ was the author of *Tales of a Wayside Inn*.

    (Henry Wadsworth Longfellow)

b. (No) president has ever been impeached.

c. Which of the following is (not) a composer from the baroque period:

1. Bach

2. Handel

(3. Copeland)

4. Scarlatti

Chapter
8

You Can Write Your Way to College Success

*M*ost students vastly underrate the importance of being able to write well. Much of your grade on essay exams, short identification questions, term papers, and the written portion of scientific and technical reports depends on your ability to write well.

Occasionally students who perform poorly on exams or papers will claim that they really know the material but that they can't communicate their knowledge. This is undoubtedly true at times. But you're graded in college and in life on your ability to communicate and implement the knowledge and ideas in your mind. What a shame to receive less than you should because of an inability to communicate. What an opportunity to give yourself a winning edge by learning to become a good writer. You'll greatly impress your instructors with clear, organized writing that shows you can think.

A number of years ago I drove to work with a man who was a vice-president of a large corporation in the Boston area. We often talked about what makes some people successful and others less so. One morning we turned to the subject of writing. I couldn't shut my friend up. "Why don't you college instructors teach people to write?" he said. "Three-quarters of the graduates we get are nearly illiterate, even from the name schools."

Then he started telling horror stories about written reports he got from subordinates, all college graduates, that showed disorganization, amateurish style, and grammatical errors. He lamented the sloppy thinking demonstrated by such writing. He was embarrassed to read the letters these college graduates wrote to customers, knowing the bad impression they'd make on the company's clients.

"These people won't last long," he said. He identified one young man by his first name, laughing scornfully but not gladly at the "garbage" submitted by this individual during the preceding week. But he also described a couple of rising stars, young people who, among other things, knew how to communicate. I suggested some remedial courses and conferences for the weak employees and assured him that colleges and universities were taking a renewed interest in teaching writing skills.

My point is simple. Your writing is the equivalent of a banner that you carry around above your head. In college and in your career this banner will wave for all to see: "I am intelligent, reliable, competent, literate, and I can think effectively." Or it can proclaim something very different. You cannot rid yourself of this banner, but you can drastically improve its message. The goal of this chapter is to give you a start in developing your writing skills so that you can proclaim all the good things about your knowledge and capabilities.

Set Specific Goals

Becoming a good writer should be a goal of every college student. There are many ways to give this goal precision. You can set specific performance goals such as receiving "A's" on all papers by the time you complete your second year. Taking one or more writing courses beyond the required number is another positive step. Your criteria for choosing courses can include those courses having a significant writing component. When writing papers, you can decide to revise a minimum of three times, to get the writing center's comments and so on. The idea is to set specific long-term and short-term targets aimed at making you a better writer.

Writing Is Thinking

THE MOST IMPORTANT THING TO GRASP ABOUT WRITING IS THAT IT IS A THINKING PROCESS. One of the startling things to many students when they start taking writing seriously is the discovery that much of their thinking is fuzzy. Writing helps you develop new ideas and refine old ones. It's one of the best ways to improve your critical and creative thinking.

When you write down an idea, it's like viewing a football play in slow motion or stop action. In their frozen, written state, you can contemplate ideas and see new relationships, limitations, and insights. Writing lets you organize logically the information you've researched and show its relationship to other ideas and facts. Effective writing enables you to answer the key thinking questions discussed in

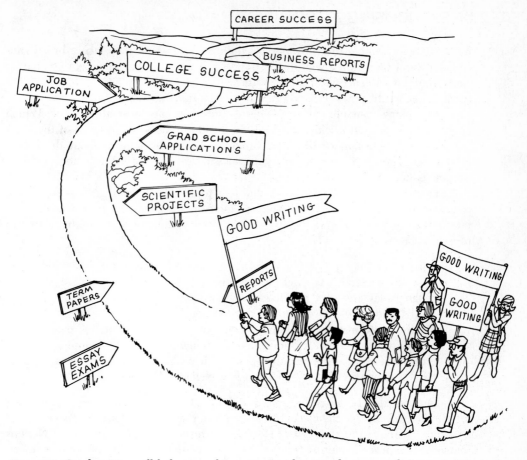

Figure 8.1 Good writing will help you achieve your academic and career goals in many ways.

Chapter 4. It allows you to clarify ideas for yourself and communicate those clear ideas to your instructor.

Do you see the implications for motivation? Writing isn't an exercise in drudgery; it's at the heart of the learning process. It's a key to developing your analytical powers and becoming an effective, independent thinker. Steps that may have seemed mechanical are actually part of effective thinking.

Best of all, your increasing ability to think and communicate is retained from one writing session to the next. It really does get easier, and you really do get better, provided you try. Writing isn't an either/or proposition. Obviously you can write already. But the gap between adequate and very good writing is significant. It takes commitment and a willingness to patiently proceed through the necessary steps such as revision and careful proofreading.

Writing successful term papers and reports requires several steps. For many assignments choosing a topic is a crucial point that trips up many students, but it's actually quite manageable if you follow a few simple guidelines.

STEP ONE: CHOOSING A TOPIC

Most students don't sufficiently narrow their topic. Instead they take a broad subject that can't be handled well in the typical short paper. War may be a fascinating and important subject, but a three- to fifteen-page paper can hardly do more than present generalities. Much better to pin down a narrow, manageable topic.

Try asking yourself, what specifically interests me most about war? Which particular war is most fascinating? Say you decide to focus on weapons of the First World War. Try to narrow the topic further, perhaps by writing about the use of poison gas. Then give your topic significance by developing a thesis about an important issue.

There's no one correct way to choose a topic. The following ideas should be seen only as suggestions. Using your creative imagination can help you develop interesting ideas, but you're usually well advised to subject your creative ideas to some hard tests.

- Are there books, articles, documents, and other material available so you can do research? It might be interesting to do a comparative study of changes in attitudes of Tibetans toward western music, but chances are you'd find little written on the topic.
- Is the topic manageable, given time and page limitations? A comparative study of the role of the world's major religions on family planning and sex roles would be an important topic, but it probably wouldn't be manageable if you only have three weeks and five pages.

You shouldn't be afraid to try researching a topic in which you're really interested. You can always change topics if it doesn't work out. Last semester one of my students wanted to do a paper on an obscure matter regarding United Nations international peace-keeping forces. I explained the difficulty of getting information, but seeing his enthusiasm suggested he proceed with the topic anyway, doing a theoretical analysis if necessary. It turned out to be the best paper in the class.

Here are some key guidelines:

1. Consult with your instructors. They can help you choose a topic, especially if you've formulated several alternative ideas before you meet with them. They can tell you whether they think your project is feasible. And they can direct you to key books and articles, saving you much time.
2. Choose a topic that will contribute significantly to your education. Most students would get more out of doing a term paper on seventeenth-century England than they would studying changing patterns in the stitching on baseballs. On the other hand, many aspects of baseball might be more fruitful such as an analysis of crowd behavior, changes in American culture, equality in American sports, and many others.
3. Select a topic in which you're really interested. This will contribute significantly to your motivation as you do research and writing. If you're major-

ing in physical education, maybe a detailed study of baseball equipment might be useful, especially if you can relate your study to a significant issue such as safety in sports.

4. Consider relating your writing to academic and career goals. If you're a civil engineering student and you're asked to write about some national problem, you might choose an issue like the declining state of the nation's bridges. This could make an interesting report. There have been a number of human tragedies because of collapsed bridges. From a policy standpoint, you could analyze and discuss the tendency of elected officials to avoid expensive long-term maintenance projects because they get no political credit for them. This topic would contribute to your education as an engineer, while developing your knowledge of related public policy issues. You've got motivation and educational relevance going for you with a topic like this.

5. Consider developing greater expertise about a subject by writing about different aspects of it for different courses. *A word of caution:* this should not be done as a means of reducing your work load, but rather to acquire a greater in-depth understanding of a subject. By doing NEW research on related aspects of a subject you also may be able to develop higher levels of research and analytical skills. It's NOT legitimate to turn in the same paper for two different courses unless you're doing a larger scale project that has the knowledge and approval of the instructors involved.

   The idea is to build on a knowledge base. A business major who hopes to work in the oil industry might write papers for different courses on taxation policy, environmental technologies, lobbying practices, and advertising—all focusing on the oil industry. This allows the development of expertise and might be a means of helping to document qualifications when applying for jobs.

   This technique should not be overused. Getting a broad knowledge base can best be achieved by writing on topics in many different subjects.

6. Link your writing to your experiences.

Yesterday one of my friends in the English Department told me about a student named Juan, who dreaded writing his first long paper for the freshman writing course. The instructor advised Juan to try to relate the paper in some way to his experience. Juan had a part-time job working with AIDS patients, and he was greatly moved by the human tragedy of the AIDS epidemic. He identified with the men, women, and children he worked with, and wanted desperately for the government and medical establishment to conquer this terrible disease.

Juan chose to write his paper on the delivery of services to AIDS victims. You can probably figure out what grade he got on the paper; it was an "A." He still had to do research, but by choosing a topic based in part on his experiences, he accomplished several things:

- He was comfortable with the topic, so fear became less of a hindrance to his writing.

- He identified with the topic, so he had a ready source of motivation.
- He already knew something about the subject so he had a jump on his research. His familiarity with the topic helped him put the material he read into perspective.
- He was able to bring his experience and his passion about the subject into his writing. The final product was not only interesting but moving as well.

Juan recognized that usually he'd have to write about things he was not personally familiar with, but writing this paper gave him experience and confidence.

STEP TWO: FINDING GOOD SOURCES

In many ways doing research is like a detective trying to solve a crime. Knowing how to look for clues, choosing the best ones, avoiding blind alleys, and doggedly tracking down leads are keys to success at this game. A healthy concern for efficiency is also crucial. GOOD RESEARCHERS HATE TO WASTE TIME. They don't hesitate to ask the librarian and others for help, and they try to improve their effectiveness and efficiency every time they conduct research.

Last year a student named Chris came to me for advice on some additional reading he wanted to do for my course. Chris was a student in our Honors Progam with a nearly perfect 4.0 grade point average. I asked him the secret of his outstanding academic performance.

Without a moment's hesitation Chris said, "I learned to write well."

"How did that help you?" I asked.

"Simple," he said. "A lot of my grades are based on essay exams and papers, so I have a tremendous advantage. It's almost like my instructors are grateful when I write well. They often comment on my writing when I get my papers back."

"You're right about the way teachers think," I said. "It's a pleasure to read through a clear, well-organized paper or exam essay, instead of struggling through asking yourself, 'What's this student trying to say?' And it's a joy for us teachers to read papers and exams that develop interesting ideas and show that students can think."

"You make it sound like I'm doing instructors a favor," Chris said.

"You bet," I replied. "That's one of the reasons students give themselves such an advantage when they learn to write well. The sad part is the other side of the coin. When instructors get a paper with lots of typographical and other silly errors, or a paper that hasn't been revised, they'll assume the student doesn't care and grade the paper accordingly."

"How did you learn to become a good writer, Chris?" I asked.

"The main thing is I just wanted to write well in my courses, and I practiced."

"That's it?"

"Well, for me that was the most important part. But I've got to do a couple of things consistently. I have to revise my work a few times before it's any good, and I've got to proofread carefully before turning in the final draft. In most subjects you can't write out of thin air, so I also try to do good research. That's what gives my papers their substance."

I asked Chris to identify the steps he'd undertaken in his research for the term paper he wrote for my course. This paper focused on the consequences of participation by American volunteers in the Spanish Civil War of 1935–37. His answer provides a good model for conducting research. I've elaborated on our discussion in order to show you some of the fine points and tricks that can make your research pay off and save you time.

1. First Chris got a general overview from encyclopedias. He read a briefer account of the war in *Colliers Encyclopedia* and then a more detailed analysis in the *Encyclopaedia Britannica*. He didn't take detailed notes at this stage, just a list of key names, dates, and events on a lined sheet of paper. He also jotted down possible major causes and consequences of the conflict as he thought about the articles. He made bibliography cards for promising sources listed at the end of the encyclopedia articles. Reading encyclopedias isn't necessary for all reports, but it's a fast way to get background if you're not familiar with the topic. It also helps you comprehend more detailed sources. There are specialized encyclopedias on many subjects, such as the *Encyclopedia of Philosophy.*

2. Early in the research process Chris began to develop a bibliography. As noted, he wrote bibliography cards on several sources listed in the bibliography included at the end of the encyclopedia articles.

a. He next consulted the *Bibliographic Index* to determine where he could find bibliographies on the subject. The librarian also referred him to two other bibliographies related to his research interest.

b. He looked in the *Subject Guide to Books in Print* in the library reference room to find current books on the topic and consulted the *Cumulative Book Index* for earlier books.

c. Next he consulted the CARD CATALOGUE. He took particular note of the "SEE ALSO" section of the entry cards, and looked up these additional topics. (Some libraries no longer have card catalogues but instead use a computer system. Don't hesitate to get help in learning these systems; they're generally faster and more fun to use than card catalogues.)

d. Many libraries now have indexes and abstracts on CD ROM compact computer disks. Usually several years can be included on one disk, and the material is typically kept current with monthly or quarterly updates. "CD ROM" stands for compact disk, read only memory; in other words it's a computer disk that stores information. You can't write on it or use it for other purposes.

Subject terms can be combined to create a customized list of articles. Using these computer-based materials seems less tedious than other methods, though print sources can be utilized very efficiently.

The key to CD ROM sources is to ask the librarian which indexes and abstracts to use. Using computer-based research material can save you time, but it should be used in conjunction with the steps discussed above, not as a substitute for them. Only selected indexes and abstracts are available in most libraries in this format, and you'll probably miss a majority of available sources if you use these data-bases alone. Chris got a couple of good items from these sources, but most of his data came from the other research steps he took.

3. Next Chris consulted the indexes for *scholarly* articles. THIS IS WHERE MANY STUDENTS LOSE OUT. They fail to track down articles in scholarly journals. Instead they rely on more popular sources such as *Time* and *Newsweek*. These may be adequate as background for a very brief paper in a freshman introduction to whatever course, but they won't give you a major boost to your grade, your learning, or toward the development of your thinking skills.

Even for a brief paper in a freshman course, you can write a much better paper by consulting several scholarly sources. And you're gaining experience that can give you a decisive advantage in more lengthy papers. Like most instructors, I always look for the quality of articles students use in preparing their papers and usually assign higher grades to those who effectively refer to scholarly materials.

There are several ways to tell if a source is a scholarly journal, although none is foolproof: the word "journal" is in its name; it contains little or no advertising; the authors use footnotes, endnotes, or other forms of reference to other work; it is published by a professional society. In some cases it's a judgment call. With practice you'll soon get the hang of recognizing these kinds of journals.

Articles in scholarly journals are written by scholars to be read by other scholars. They usually contain the latest thinking in the field as well as some of the latest references. They show how scholars themselves do research and report their findings and conclusions. There are more articles on most topics than there are books, so you are seriously shortchanging yourself if you fail to use them.

Where did Chris find the titles of scholarly books and articles?

- He got a few from the encyclopedias he'd read.
- Several key sources were listed in the bibliographies the librarian had helped him locate.
- He consulted the *Social Sciences Index* and *Humanities Index,* and for the period prior to 1975 he consulted the earlier versions of these sources entitled the *International Index* and *Social Sciences and Humanities Index.* These listed relevant articles in scholarly journals such as *The American Historical Review* and *The American Political Science Review.*
- He next consulted a specific bibliography for political science JOURNAL articles entitled the *ABC of Political Science.* This kind of reference typically provides more up-to-date information on current sources. *Your instructor and librarian can tell you which ones apply in the field in which you're doing research.*
- He sometimes looked up SUMMARIES of the articles in *Abstracts of Political Science* before tracking down entire articles. By doing this he excluded articles not likely to be relevant. An abstract is a very short sum-

mary of an article, often no longer than a paragraph. The idea is that by consulting abstracts first you can determine if the article is relevant to your research.

Your librarian can tell you which abstracts cover your topic. You can sometimes work more quickly by skipping the abstracts, especially if the scholarly articles and books you're reading tell which sources are most important. On a long paper, it's best to check out the originals of articles for yourself.

Abstracts should be viewed as a time-saving tool—not as a substitute for doing your own research. Having written abstracts for my own scholarly publications, I can assure you that abstracts can only give you a flavor of what's in the original sources. There isn't room to include more. So you're just hurting yourself if you try to use abstracts alone.

- He consulted *book reviews* to help him evaluate books. *Review essays* in which several books are compared and evaluated are particularly helpful. The *Book Review Digest* will give you a start. Again, reviews give one perspective only, and it takes time to look them up. Often you're better advised to check out the book and evaluate it for yourself. Try at first to use book reviews as a means of helping you narrow your sources. You'll soon determine the extent to which reviews can aid you on your project.

One of the smartest and easiest ways to develop your bibliography is to look for discussion of the work of other scholars in the articles and books you read.

MOST SCHOLARLY BOOKS AND ARTICLES DO SOME OF THE BASIC RESEARCH FOR YOU BECAUSE THEY CITE THE MOST IMPORTANT BOOKS AND ARTICLES IN THEIR FOOTNOTES AND BIBLIOGRAPHIES.

MANY SCHOLARLY BOOKS AND ARTICLES BEGIN BY CRITICALLY REVIEWING THE LITERATURE ON THE SUBJECT. AS YOU READ YOU CAN MAKE BIBLIOGRAPHY CARDS ON KEY SOURCES. IN EFFECT YOU'RE ALLOWING LEADING SCHOLARS TO DO SOME OF THE INITIAL RESEARCH WORK FOR YOU. IT'S A PERFECTLY LEGITIMATE AND SENSIBLE THING TO DO, PROVIDED YOU ALSO TRY TO DEVELOP YOUR OWN BIBLIOGRAPHY.

This lets you concentrate your own search in areas less heavily mined and allows you to spend more time on reading and writing. And by reading these scholarly books and articles you develop your thinking abilities and learn how to write for an academic audience. Your instructors will be impressed when they see you make appropriate reference to these articles and when you include them in your bibliography.

4. Chris also wanted to get a feel for the human side of the Spanish Civil War and to find more general background, so he also took a quick look at news magazines from the period. *Time Magazine* and *Life* were good sources, while news accounts from the *New York Times* gave him some human interest reports. Here he used the *New York Times Index* and *The Reader's Guide to Periodical Literature* to find articles in popular magazines. He took few notes at this stage except for some excellent information he found in the *New York Times*.

5. Good fiction often gives a dimension not covered in journalistic and scholarly sources. Chris decided to read *For Whom the Bell Tolls* by Ernest Hemingway, a short novel he'd wanted to read for some time. He told me he'd gotten so interested in the book that he read part of it during his leisure time. Chris only cited the book once in his report, but it gave him additional respect for the human side of the war and helped motivate him to learn more about it. For shorter papers it may be unrealistic to read novels as part of the research process, but short stories, plays, poetry, and films can help enrich your understanding.

6. Chris said, "I especially enjoy going into the stacks to collect books." Here Chris did what all good researchers do: he browsed in the shelves around the books he went to retrieve and found several interesting books that hadn't turned up on his bibliography cards. He took several books at a time back to a desk so he could quickly review them and see which ones would be most helpful. While not all libraries have stacks open to students, some of the libraries you use undoubtedly will. If you have a choice among several libraries, choose the best one. You'll get more useful sources and probably save time.

7. Chris took special note of PRIMARY SOURCES during his research and made a few references to these sources in his paper. PRIMARY SOURCES ARE ORIGINAL WRITINGS SUCH AS NOVELS, POEMS, AND PLAYS AS WELL AS GOVERNMENT REPORTS, DOCUMENTS, STATISTICAL ABSTRACTS, AND SIMILAR ORIGINAL SOURCES. Secondary sources are books and articles that interpret primary and other sources of data. Nonfiction books and articles are usually secondary sources.

Primary documents such as congressional debates, United Nations reports, statistical abstracts, and the like can be found in the Government Documents Room and Reference Rooms of most libraries. Government reports and documents cover many fields and topics. United Nations documents are a great source of data and information on a host of issues such as women's rights and hunger. The Government Document's librarian at your college or university will be glad to assist you in locating relevant reports. You'll find that you return again and again to the rich mine of information available in primary sources.

ONE OF THE HALLMARKS OF GOOD
RESEARCH IS THE EFFECTIVE USE OF
PRIMARY SOURCES. IT SHOWS THAT
STUDENTS SEE THE IMPORTANCE OF
ANALYZING ORIGINAL DOCUMENTS
AND DATA. THE APPROPRIATE USE
OF PRIMARY SOURCES TELLS YOUR
INSTRUCTOR THAT YOU ARE A SERIOUS,
COMPETENT STUDENT AND LENDS YOUR
PAPER MUCH CREDIBILITY.

8. CHRIS NEVER HESITATED TO CONSULT THE LIBRARIAN. For advice on sources and interpretations, he always asked one of the professional librarians, not an aide or work study student. Here's another place most students let themselves down and make unnecessary work for themselves. For some strange reason many students are shy about asking for help. Here, as in much of life, a willingness to be politely assertive gives you a significant advantage. Professional librarians are among the most underrated people in the country. They have university training as well as experience, all designed to help you. Successful students go out of their way to ask the professional librarian for help in finding good sources.

Tip: Most libraries have brochures that explain how they're set up. These can save you hours of time. Even better, many libraries have tours and even brief classes on how to use the library. If you're accustomed to doing research, you'll still probably learn something new. These resources can be tremendous time savers.

9. Chris tried to find experts he might talk to for advice. He discovered that a faculty member in another department had done research on the Spanish Civil War. After doing some preliminary reading, Chris went to see her to discuss the conflict and his paper.

Chris later said that this was the most valuable half hour of his research. She brought up some points he hadn't even considered and lent him some of her own books. Perhaps someone at your school or at a nearby institution or business might be willing to help you. Just make sure you've done the basic reading before you see them, so they will know you're a serious student.

10. CHRIS WON'T TAKE NO FOR AN ANSWER. Chris didn't give up if the book wasn't available. The Circulation Desk told him if the book was on reserve or overdue. If a book was on reserve he read it in the Reserve Room, and if it was overdue he asked the library to recall it if possible. If a book is lost, you may be able to track it down at another library. Some schools are part of a *consortium*, in which colleges and universities pool their resources and allow students to use all the libraries in the group.

The library's *interlibrary loan* service can be a time-saving step. When a book isn't available in the immediate area, Interlibrary Loan can borrow the book from more distant sources. There may be a two- or three-week delay, but you gain access to many more libraries. Sometimes these services are reserved for graduate students and faculty. If you show your instructors that you're serious about your research and have done some good initial work, they may be willing to write a letter enabling you to use consortium libraries and interlibrary loan services.

You may have to condense some of these steps at times. But try to do it right from the very beginning. Be careful to keep a record of what you've done and found so you don't have to repeat steps later. Label photocopies and notes. Be patient, have a sense of humor, and you'll succeed.

Some libraries can do ON-LINE COMPUTER SEARCHES, although they often charge for this service because it costs them to use the external data sources. Ask the librarian supervising these searches if your topic is amenable to such a search and what the approximate cost might be. These on-line computer searches should be a supplement, not a substitute, for the steps suggested above. You'd miss many good sources if you relied on them completely.

STEP THREE: READING YOUR SOURCES AND TAKING GOOD NOTES

Vary Your Reading Techniques to Fit the Source You're Reading

The Remarkable Square Tree method should be modified when you do research. If you're reading an entire book, use the Remarkable Square Tree method on those portions that are central to your research. But use your judgment. If you have ten books and fifteen articles to consider, you'll be better off focusing your special attention on the places that matter.

Here's how to modify the Remarkable Square Tree method when doing research:

• Don't undertake a long review, but a very brief use of the REPEAT step will keep your reading in perspective and help you remember. Simply review your notes quickly from important earlier sources and think about them to see if you can come up with interesting questions as you read the material you want to go over now. It's also a good idea to look at your preliminary outline and thesis statement before you begin reading.

- Next, SCAN the book or article to see if it's relevant. Not all sources are equal. Decide whether the entire book or some portion of the book should be read. Some books and articles will be completely irrelevant. Set these aside and don't include them in your bibliography. If you decide to use the source, check the details of publication with the entry on your bibliography card.
- Always use the QUESTION step. Formulate questions based on *your* research goals. Also, use the headings to develop questions and employ the standard thinking questions.
- Next, READ. But vary your reading speed and the care you take depending on the purpose of the source. If you're looking up one bit of information, scan until you find that section and read it carefully, taking notes as indicated below. If you're just getting background information, proceed through the book or article quickly until you come to a relevant point and read that section carefully. Also read the sections immediately preceding and following that portion so that you have an idea of the context.
- ALWAYS *THINK* about what you read. Continually try to relate the reading to your project. If you haven't yet developed a thesis statement, consider whether the section of material you've just read can help you.
- Use your discretion in the REINFORCE stage. If you don't recite the material back to yourself after each section, you'll forget most of what you read. Don't ignore this step, because one of the purposes of research projects is to help you learn. Vary the amount of time spent on this step depending on the importance of the material. Getting the main points on background reading is enough.
- Take notes as discussed on pp. 224–227.
- After completing a chapter or article, pause to review what you've read; go back to pick up any points not included on your notes. The point is simply to help set the material into your memory and to think of useful ideas. Don't spend more time on this than the material deserves.
- ALWAYS *EVALUATE* the book or article, both as you read and more systematically after you've completed your reading. WRITE A BRIEF ONE- OR TWO-SENTENCE SUMMARY OF YOUR EVALUATION ON THE BIBLIOGRAPHY CARD.

Some books and articles are obviously biased. If you're doing a paper on labor unions and the author is hostile to business or labor, you know the writer is not trying to be objective. The book may still be useful, but you'll have to weigh it against arguments on the other side. Virtually all books are imperfect and few authors command the total truth. Even encyclopedias and other "factual" books may contain errors or articles that are subtly biased.

Part of being an effective critical thinker is to maintain a skeptical attitude. If you read a controversial point or suspect the accuracy of some fact, be sure to

VERIFY THE INFORMATION BY CROSS CHECKING. If an author is criticizing another viewpoint, make sure you read someone that supports that viewpoint so that your judgment isn't one sided.

How to Take Notes

Taking notes is partly science but mostly art. WHEN YOU TAKE NOTES EFFECTIVELY YOU'RE ACTUALLY DOING PART OF YOUR WRITING. An effective system of taking notes can save hours of time and dramatically improve the quality of your writing. The most common tactic is take relatively brief notes on note cards, usually 3 x 5 for your bibliography and either 3 x 5 or 4 x 6 for the actual notes.

Students are sometimes tempted to make many photocopies instead of taking notes. This may just waste time and money, because taking notes really accomplishes part of the writing process. Photocopying should be reserved for long quotes of key material or for copying articles or chapters you must read later. As with all advice, adapt it to your own circumstance. If your schedule doesn't allow you to read in the library, photocopying may be a way to save time. But photocopies should still not be used in place of notes.

The advantage of note cards is their flexibility. You can organize them easily to match the outline of your paper. What you need is the cards, paper clips, rubber bands, and pencil or pen.

Bibliography Cards   The key to bibliography cards is to include all information you may need at a later time. Put the last name of the author first so the cards can be easily alphabetized. Print or neatly write the author's full name, the complete title of the book or article, and details of publication. You should use the same order, form, and punctuation as in the final bibliography so that you don't have to add another step when you're writing the final bibliography. Keep bibliography cards together in alphabetical order.

If in doubt when writing your bibliography cards, include too much rather than too little information. You don't want to have to go back and check the book later. Your goals are accuracy, inclusiveness, and efficiency.

Here's a partial list of things to include; a complete list can be found in one of the major style manuals or in the style guidelines provided by your school or instructor. Remember: It's better to include too much information than too little, so you don't have to backtrack:

Library call number.

Full name(s) of author or authors.

Full title of book or article.

Name of journal.

Place of publication, except for major magazines and newspapers.

Date: year for books; month or season and year for journal; day, month, and year for magazine or newspaper.

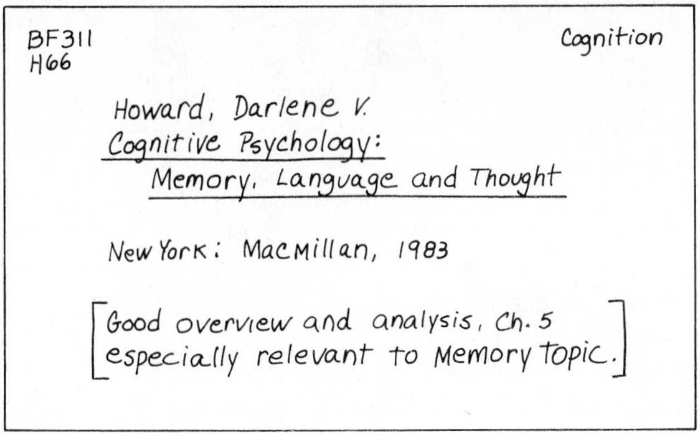

```
BF311                                        Cognition
H66
      Howard, Darlene V.
      Cognitive Psychology:
         Memory, Language and Thought

      New York: MacMillan, 1983

      ⌈Good overview and analysis, Ch. 5 ⌉
      ⌊especially relevant to Memory topic.⌋
```

Figure 8.2 Sample bibliography card.

Edition number of book.

A notation for books that are edited: "Ed." for one editor, "eds." for two or more.

Name of book publisher.

Name of translator(s).

Page numbers for articles or pieces in edited volumes.

Volume and number of journals.

Other publication data as needed.

Your evaluation of the relevance, quality, and content of the book.

Recording Exact Quotes If you're taking exact quotes, write the words down exactly as they are found in the source. Put quotation marks around the quote and write the word "QUOTE" (or "QT") on the top of the card. After you write down the quotation, verify the accuracy of your entry by reading from the document to the card. Make sure you have enough information to identify the source: author's name, short title of book or article, and page numbers. This can be somewhat abbreviated because you will have all of the details on a bibliography card.

Record the page number(s) of the quote at the top of the note card, and indicate where the quote is continued on the next page of the source. You may want to use just part of the quote in your paper and will need to know the exact page(s) on which the quote occurs.

Quotes are best reserved for unusually important points in which you want to give your paper the additional authority of a significant statement by a noted authority or when the style of the author is so distinct that using the exact words adds significantly to the strength of your presentation.

Writing Summaries   One good way to take notes is to write a summary of the article, chapter, or section you've consulted. To write an effective summary you must have understood and thought about what you've read. It should be a brief, accurate presentation in your own words of the author's ideas, reflecting faithfully the meaning intended by the author.

The exact length of the summary will vary, depending on the length and complexity of the material as well as your purpose. Sometimes you may be able to summarize an entire article on the front and back of a 3 x 5 card, or even a couple of sentences. Use the backs of cards as necessary. For longer summaries it may be better to use larger cards or standard note paper.

In your courses, you may be asked to write summaries to be submitted as papers or you may need to summarize a passage or document in your paper to provide the basis for your discussion, so learning to summarize well pays high dividends. If you summarize your textbook chapters as part of note taking when you study, this task should be virtually automatic.

Paraphrasing   A proper paraphrase is an accurate recording of the author's ideas, including significant details, that you record in your own words and style. The goal is to restate the author's message in order, with the same meaning. You record the passage step by step in your own phrasing. Using paraphrases appropriately in papers can give them greater authority or let you discuss in more detail an author's thoughts.

Write paraphrase (or PPH) at the top of the note card. Include enough information to identify the source and location. When you use a paraphrase or part of a paraphrase in your paper you must identify the author and make clear that you are paraphrasing. Here's a very brief paraphrase of comments by Brenda Spatt (see Bibliography) an authority on the subject. Note how I incorporate her material right into the text, clearly identifying it with a reference.

As Brenda Spatt points out, quoting exact words may be desirable if the style is unusually clear, impressive, or if the author's importance gives your discussion greater authority. She adds, however, that most sources aren't that important, and many are written in a tedious or boring style. Not only will you spare your reader by refraining from quoting; you've got an obligation to give them something easier to read, she emphasizes (p. 93).

Recording Facts, Ideas, and Other Information From Sources   MOST OF THE NOTES YOU TAKE SHOULD BE IN YOUR OWN WORDS AFTER YOU'VE THOUGHT ABOUT THE PASSAGE YOU'VE READ. Be very selective in what you write down. Before beginning to read a book or article, go over your goals in your mind. Remember your thesis or focus, and write your notes from that point of view. Don't just change a few words here and there. Really make them your own words in your own appropriate style and you'll have accomplished part of the writing.

Often you'll merely want to jot down an important fact or idea. It's usually best to limit each card to one main piece of information or one main idea, although you can add details, elaborations and brief lists as required. With practice you'll be able to further adapt your note cards to your own needs. Provide enough information at the top left of the card so that you can later identify the source.

Recording Your Critical and Creative Thoughts   Record your own ideas and evaluations on note cards, so that they can be considered when you're writing the paper. These can include comparisons, ways of classifying, points about significance, and ethical implications. You can also note possible thesis statements as well as conclusions about what can be learned from your analysis.

Including Useful Information on Your Note Cards   In the sample note card shown in Figure 8.3, the note taker includes suggestions, in brackets, for writing the paper. Observe also that the probable location to put the quote is indicated in the upper right-hand corner (intro = introduction). The use of abbreviations can help you save space, but don't abbreviate when you're recording quotes.

You can organize your notes in sequence when you get ready to start writing, but you can save yourself time by marking obvious locations or categories when you first write the card. The idea is to include useful instructions and reminders to yourself that can help you when you write your paper.

STEP FOUR: WRITING A SUCCESSFUL PAPER

Develop a Thesis

Often you won't be able to develop a final thesis until you've done much of the research. But you can create one or more tentative theses to guide your research and thinking until you've refined your thoughts. Don't be too rigid at this stage, otherwise you might hamper your creative thinking.

A thesis is a central idea or argument, usually contained in one sentence. A carefully thought out thesis statement at the beginning of your paper can guide your writing and give it significance.

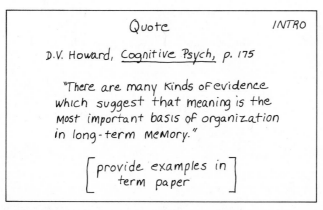

Figure 8.3 Sample note card.

In a course on American literature, you might begin a paper like this: "Richard Dana's enduring popularity as a writer of nonfiction is due primarily to the poetic quality of his work." This kind of thesis presents an argument, which provides instant focus. It is interesting, manageable, and significant. We don't usually think of nonfiction writing as poetic. A number of what's the significance ideas can be developed such as the relative literary merit of fiction versus nonfiction writing.

In college most instructors expect you to do more than merely describe something; they want you instead to write more analytical papers. You might, for example, choose to explain or analyze consequences. Whatever your thesis statement, make it the focus of your writing throughout your paper. Every word, every sentence, and every paragraph should be geared toward supporting your thesis.

In some courses you may be assigned a brief *theme*, which could relate to a personal experience or some other less analytical issue. In literature courses you will be asked to write *critical essays* on literary works. It's equally important to stay focused on your primary topic in this kind of paper. The bottom line? Have a clear target in sight as you write. It will help give your writing coherence, organization, and significance.

Methods of Writing

There are two major approaches to writing advocated in the literature. You should follow the suggestions of your instructor if you're asked to use a particular technique. Otherwise use the method or combination of methods that best suits you.

1. The newer strategy can be termed PROCESS WRITING. The central idea is that writing proceeds on a free-flow basis, with concern for structure, grammar, and other mechanical issues, taking place after the initial draft is done. This approach contains a tremendous psychological advantage. You can begin writing almost immediately, so it's often an effective way of beating writer's block. It can also boost your creative thinking. You may come up with interesting ideas as thoughts flow from your mind to the paper.

Networking is one way to develop creative ideas. Take a clean sheet of unlined paper. Write down a core concept, word, or idea and work out from it. Next, free associate. Simply write down words that come to mind. You can brainstorm, writing down anything that comes to mind, or you can be more directed. Write down key

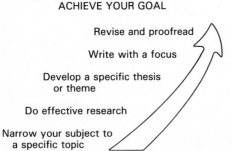

ACHIEVE YOUR GOAL

Revise and proofread

Write with a focus

Develop a specific thesis
or theme

Do effective research

Narrow your subject to
a specific topic

Figure 8.4 Keys to success in writing projects.

concepts, ideas, questions, even feelings about the central word or phrase. This technique also works well with your thesis statement at the center. You can go through your note cards to get ideas, but the goal is to let yourself think freely in an uninhibited way.

The next step is to draw connections as soon as you begin to see patterns and relationships among the entries. The idea here is to perceive as naturally as possible the patterns and organization of your paper.

Figure 8.5 presents a simple example of the networking technique. In this instance it helps provide a way to organize the discussion. The author writes the topic in the center, then quickly jots down thoughts that occur. Connections are made by categorizing similar points. This connecting by concept is a useful way to structure a paper, applying critical judgment about what serves the purpose of your topic sentence.

You may want to add symbols designating the broad structure of an outline. At this point you can begin writing, filling in additional points later. This will help you gain momentum in writing. Or you may prefer first to construct a more complete outline, depending on your purpose and your personal learning style.

2. The **TRADITIONAL METHOD** emphasizes an organized strategy, with attention to the mechanics of writing throughout the process. One of the first steps

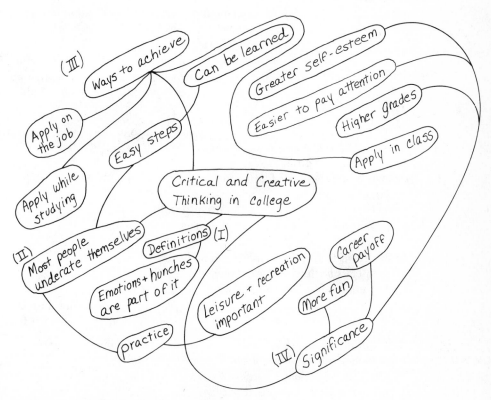

Figure 8.5 Sample of networking technique.

is to develop an outline, which is a step-by-step plan for completing your writing. The main advantage of the traditional approach is that it helps you PLAN the paper. It may also result in a more compact writing style, less likely to leave out important details. It is also a creative thinking process in which you develop new ideas as you proceed.

OUTLINING is an important part of the traditional method. AN OUTLINE IS JUST A TOOL TO HELP YOU WRITE A GOOD PAPER. So use the style that suits you best and avoid letting the outline prevent you from writing. Freely modify it as you go along and get new ideas for the organization of your paper. As you develop your outline, keep in mind the ideas discussed in the chapter on thinking. Pay particular attention to the WHAT, HOW, WHY, COMPARISONS, CLASSIFICATIONS, AND SIGNIFICANCE issues. The following example shows one good way to set up many papers.

> Introduction and thesis statement.
> Definitions and discussion of concepts.
> Background material.
> Systematic discussion of topic and supporting data, with emphasis on causes, significance, classifications, evaluations.
> Comparisons.
> Conclusion: Summary of main points. Significance of paper, what we can learn from it, other important issues.

The simplest kind of outline is a *scratch outline*, which is also useful in process writing. The degree and level of planning can vary greatly. A scratch outline is simply a list of points to be covered that can serve as a direction finder as you write. Here's an example:

> Thesis: U.S. naval superiority was the main cause of the Soviet Union backing down in the Cuban missile crisis.
> Definitions, background.
> Analytical discussion of crisis and factors leading to Soviet withdrawal of missiles.
> > How issues: planning committee, intelligence sources.
> > Why issues: causes of crisis, causes of outcome.
> > Creative ideas (Robert Kennedy's role).
> Comparison to the Soviet blockade of Berlin.
> How to classify the Cuban missile crisis.
> Consequences of crisis: Soviet naval buildup, others.
> Conclusion. Brief restatement of thesis. Evaluation of Soviet and U.S. handling of crisis. Significance of the experience; what can we learn from it.

A *formal outline* gives a detailed plan and is a carefully thought out structure for the paper as a whole. Formal outlines can be done on a sentence or paragraph basis, where the chronological order of each part of the paper is presented. Here's a brief example of part of a formal outline:

   I. Introduction

      A. U.S. naval superiority was the main cause of the Soviet Union's backing down during the Cuban missile crisis

         1. Significance of the Cuban missile crisis

         2. Definition of key terms

            a. Naval quarantine

               (1) Comparison with blockade

               (2) Act of War

                   (a) International law

                   (b) Other cases

            b. Balance of power

      B. Background to the conflict
      (and so on)

Writing the First Draft

The traditional method requires greater care and planning before you begin to write. But WITH EITHER METHOD DON'T EXPECT TOO MUCH OF YOUR FIRST DRAFT. You'll have to revise anyway, and it eases the pressure to know you're just getting your initial ideas down on paper. Whether you use the process or traditional approach, *just get on with it*. Few people write good first drafts, and virtually every good writer has to revise extensively.

Organize your note cards in groups, according to the sections of your outline. If you're following the process method, it's still a good idea to keep your notes handy as a source of ideas. Whatever method you follow, aim for objective writing that shows critical and creative thinking skills. Consider the aids to effective thinking presented in Chapter 4. Ask yourself if there might be multiple consequences and so on. Your instructors will be looking for evidence of effective thinking in the papers they grade.

Because writing represents one of the highest forms of thinking, it often cannot be rushed. Sometimes you'll have to sit for long moments pondering the point you're trying to make. Don't get panicky or frustrated. Patience is a essential. If you get stuck, don't abandon your writing; go on to another easier section.

Documentation and the Pitfalls of Plagiarism

It's important in formal papers and reports to use proper documentation. This shows your instructor that you've done research and understand the requirements of scholarship. In scholarly writing it enables readers to go back and check your sources to determine the validity of your work. It makes it easier for other researchers to pick up where you left off.

Because many students don't take the trouble to use proper documentation, those who do have a decided competitive advantage. The reality is that some form of comparison is invariably used in the grading process. By quoting or citing (making reference to major scholarly works and other sources), you can impress instructors with the quality of your scholarship—provided the sources are employed appropriately and wisely.

When QUOTING word for word, keep these points in mind:

- Don't quote too much. THE BULK OF THE WRITING SHOULD BE YOUR OWN. Unless you are exhaustively analyzing a document or piece of writing, no more than occasional quotations are justified. Students sometimes submit papers that are largely a string of quotations. Usually this is done to avoid writing and gets an appropriately low grade.
- You must always use QUOTATION MARKS when you use someone else's words. You must also put that author's NAME in the text of your paper or in the note.
- You cannot simply change an author's words and submit them as your own. PARAPHRASING is legitimate only when you clearly identify the author and accurately follow his or her thoughts. Its legitimate use is limited to presenting a short selection of an author's writing in which every idea is given in order, using your own words and writing style.

PLAGIARISM is one of the most serious academic offenses. It is the theft of another writer's words or ideas. Intentional plagiarism is one of the dumbest forms of dishonesty because, as Spatt points out, "it is easy for an experienced reader to detect plagiarism" (p. 92). (Note that I've just quoted Spatt; I've used her exact words and put quotation marks around them.)

Frequently plagiarism is caused by not understanding the rules or by careless note taking. How do you know when to document your source? Here are the basic situations that require citations:

When you quote authors word for word. REMEMBER, you can't just alter words and phrases without citation or you are plagiarizing. When quoting word for word you must use quotation marks and identify the author and exact source.

When you are using an original idea from a source.

When you use facts or data from a source.

When you want to show your instructors that you've done good research and have used important sources.

Deciding when to footnote is partly a judgment call. You can't cite everything or you'd bore your readers and never get anything done. It's not necessary to have a citation for something that is common knowledge. Everyone knows that the capital of France is Paris.

A good test of the common knowledge principle is this: if an idea, fact, or piece of data can be found in four or five different sources, there is usually no need for a citation, at least from the standpoint of avoiding plagiarism.

But how can you be sure you haven't unconsciously used someone else's idea or turn of phrase? Every writer, whether consciously or not, is indebted to hundreds of predecessors. Plots of novels, for example, are usually variations on themes used many times by others, though the variation may be highly creative. People can also develop similar ideas independently. So it's possible to worry too much about plagiarism.

You can help protect yourself by clearly identifying quotes and paraphrases in your notes, taking other notes in your own words, and by leaving a gap of time between reading sources and doing the actual writing of your paper. If in doubt, the best policy is to attempt identifying the source.

Use a Standard Form for Documenting and for Your Bibliography

Here's another way to impress your instructors and distinguish yourself from students who don't bother to employ an acceptable form of documentation. Different academic fields use different formats, and you should check with your instructor if they don't tell you which method to employ.

Some colleges or instructors may provide you with a style sheet that shows you how to make reference to your sources, or they will refer you to a specific manual. Often your instructors will tell you to use any suitable, scholarly format. There are a number of manuals available, reflecting different styles.

For a thorough treatment of the traditional footnote or endnote method, consult the book by Kate Turabian listed in the Bibliography. In this system numbers are placed in the text, with an explanatory note at the foot of the page or the end of the paper. Bibliographies are also typically included in papers employing this method.

The styles employed by the Modern Language Association and the American Psychological Association don't require footnotes and are easy to handle. In these systems brief reference to the source is made within the text itself, so that the reader can refer to the bibliography for the full citation. If you have a choice, I recommend the Modern Language Association method used by many English and humanities departments. Available in paperback, the useful book by Joseph Gibaldi and Walter S. Achtert entitled *MLA Handbook for Writers of Research Papers* shows you how to apply this method. An excellent source that provides a more comprehensive discussion of documentation and other aspects of writing papers is James D. Lester, *Writing Research Papers: A Complete Guide (see Bibliography).*

Consider Your Audience

Students often get lower grades because their style is inappropriate. This point was developed in the preceding chapter. Unless you're told to write for some other audience, you should write for your instructor, as if you were also a trained professional in the field. Avoid a too informal or cute style, unless creative writing is encouraged by your instructor.

Avoid Overgeneralization

This problem was also discussed in the preceding chapter. The main point is to write as precisely as you can and to avoid clearly erroneous statements.

"College students are Marxists" is an overgeneralization that any student will recognize. Most college students in North America aren't Marxists, but if even *one* were not the assertion would still be incorrect. In writing research papers students often make similar errors. The remedy is to avoid categorical (either/or) words and acknowledge qualifications. "Many," "some," and "several" are less likely to create overgeneralizations than are statements that use "every," "all," or "none."

Revise

Even the most experienced writers revise their work extensively. It's part of the process by which we refine our thinking and organize our ideas. First drafts are like the first rough cuts of a sculptor into a block of marble. But writers have an advantage over someone working in marble; we can cut our work apart and move it around.

Be patient and take your time as you revise. Usually at least two or three revisions are required before you do the final proofreading for remaining typographical errors. Psychologically it helps to see these revisions for what they are—an absolutely essential step to good writing. Revision is as basic as doing the first draft. Writing is a complex process in which many interconnected thoughts are developed. It's not realistic to expect good results on the first try.

Unless you're working with a word processor that can move blocks of text around, have a large pair of scissors and plenty of invisible tape handy as you revise. If you think one paragraph or section would fit better elsewhere, simply cut and tape.

One of the best ways to pick up grammatical and typographical errors is to READ YOUR DRAFT VERSION ALOUD. Your ear will help you detect grammatical errors and unclear thoughts. The slower pace of reading aloud will let you spot more typographical errors.

Get Outside Advice Before Doing the Final Typing

Students can often get excellent advice on their papers before they turn them in. Some instructors will read your drafts before you hand in the final paper, giving you a chance to improve it. This is a great way to accelerate the process of learning to write. Even if your instructors have no such policy, they may be willing to take a quick look at your paper and offer an initial evaluation. It doesn't take long for an experienced teacher to size up a paper.

USE AVAILABLE RESOURCES SUCH AS THE WRITING ASSISTANCE CENTER AS A MEANS OF IMPROVING YOUR GRADES AND YOUR WRITING. Instructors at some schools will even raise your grade if you show that you've used the Writing Assistance Center (which stamps the original and revised version of papers). Even though most students will not get an automatic grade increase by using these centers, the effect is the same if they use them conscientiously.

The personnel of writing assistance centers can give you advice on many aspects of writing, including how to organize your paper and the appropriate style to follow. Getting their suggestions and including them in your revision will help you obtain a higher grade. Be aware that the quality of advice you get at these centers may vary greatly.

Sometimes students are asked to have other members of the class read their drafts. This feedback can be helpful, but understand that most students are not good writers. If you have a friend or relative who is a writer of proven ability, they may be able to give helpful editorial advice on draft versions of papers and reports. Almost every writer of academic books and articles incorporates the suggestions of reviewers and colleagues in their completed manuscripts. You may not be able to get the advice of professional reviewers, but with effort you can get competent advice and feedback as you develop your paper. The payoff is much faster improvement in your writing performance as well as higher grades.

Occasionally students make the deadly mistake of buying term papers or copying papers of friends. This error has two serious consequences. It's often far easier to get caught than these students may suppose, and there is a lost opportunity to improve writing and thinking skills. Editorial assistance is okay, but it's not ethical to let someone else do the actual writing or even a portion of the writing.

Typing Your Paper

Some instructors require that papers be typed. Even if yours doesn't, it's a good idea because a neatly typed paper is easier to read, makes a good impression, and may give you a slight edge when the grade is assigned. If you can't type, it may be worth paying a typist to do it for you.

You'll probably have to write reports all your life, so learning to type will be a wise investment of time. Consider the hundreds, perhaps thousands of hours you'll save during your professional life. Also, consider the multiple advantages of typing skills, such as much faster use of computers.

Learn to Use the Computer

Millions of students have written "A" papers without computers, so don't get discouraged if you don't have access to one. But tens of thousands of students have discovered that the process of learning to write well and getting better grades on papers can be speeded up greatly by using a word-processing program and a computer.

Your college or university may have computers, word processors (a software program on a disk that you put into a slot on the computer), and printers available for your use. If you plan to buy a computer and word processor, your school may have discount prices available.

Be sure to shop around. You can save hundreds of dollars by getting your computer and word processor at discount. In Tuesday's "Science Times" section of the *New York Times* (check the library), mail order dealers offer excellent prices that can serve as useful comparisons. I purchased my laptop computer this way. Buying from a local discount dealer saves shipping charges and may facilitate getting service if needed, depending on the company. Computers and programs are evaluated by such magazines as *PC*, which should be available in your library.

There's real advantage in getting a word-processing program commonly used on campus: you can get help as you learn. Your school may even offer non-credit or credit courses in its use. Using a computer will save you vast amounts of time, and you'll be able to do multiple revisions easily. There's also a psychological benefit in using computers because the process of writing becomes interactive. The computer is almost like a friend who quickly handles many of the tedious details.

Carefully Read the Comments on Your Paper When the Instructor Hands It Back

Be sure to pick up your paper if it's not handed back, even if you submitted it at the end of the term and the new semester has begun. Getting feedback is one of the keys to college success, as we saw in the preceding chapter.

Some instructors don't put many comments on papers because they're pressed for time or are discouraged that many students don't bother picking up their papers. If you get a paper back with few helpful comments, see the instructor during conference hours, bringing your paper with you. Politely explain that you really want to improve your writing (even if you got an "A") and would greatly appreciate any suggestions. Write these suggestions down and think about them, trying to implement them on your next writing assignment.

Let Journal Writing Ease You Toward Better Writing

Writing between one-half and two pages every day in a personal journal will gradually make you a much better writer. Don't be overly formal and enjoy the process, so you'll have the incentive to keep at it. Choose any topic related to your academic or personal development, and reflect on your progress and means of further development. You might, for example, write about your ability to think more effectively. Alternatively, you could write about some aspect of a course that interests you.

This is a private journal, and you should use any method that will help you most while keeping you at it. A spiral notebook, file folder into which you put numbered pages, or a computer file will work fine.

For journal writing it's better to use the free-flow technique rather than writing outlines first. This doesn't mean you can't think about the subject or use graphic organizers. There's no need to revise, but it's very important to read each entry after you've written it so that you can see where you might have written something better. Also, as you write be conscious of the requirements of good writing, and try to do a good job without unduly slowing yourself down.

Every month or so look back over your journal to see if you can detect patterns of improvement or develop ideas that will help you write better in the future. Make the process of journal writing as enjoyable as possible.

SUMMARY

Developing your writing ability is one of the most important ways to improve your grades. Good writing lets you communicate effectively, while the process of writing helps develop your capacity to think. Efficient research is one key to writing excellent papers and has the added benefit of encouraging creative thought and the development of character traits such as persistence.

This chapter has discussed a number of ways to improve your writing. Among the most important are the development of a thesis statement, writing with a focus, revising and proofreading, getting competent advice, and using feedback in order to improve. Because procrastination is one of the most serious problems for writers, Success Step One at the end of this chapter includes some excellent techniques for overcoming this problem.

SUCCESS STEPS

STEP ONE: Tips for Beating Writer's Block (Procrastination)

For most people there is no greater obstacle to effective research and writing than procrastination. Here are some remedies. You may want to remove these pages and keep them where you can regularly boost your motivation to write.

1. DON'T WAIT FOR A MOOD OF POETIC INSPIRATION. Few writers are ever completely in the mood to write. It's hard work and carries with it psychological uncertainties. You'll never get anything done if you wait till the mood strikes because you probably won't be in the mood most of the time.

   Strangely, your writing will probably be as good when you're not in the mood as when you are. So don't deceive yourself. The time to write is when you've scheduled yourself to do it. Follow the DO IT NOW principle.

2. WRITE THE EASIEST PARTS FIRST. This will be easier to take psychologically and will get you rolling. Taking progressively more difficult sections to write is one way to build up confidence and overcome fear.

3. When you sit down each day to continue your writing, BEGIN BY REVISING WHAT YOU WROTE LAST TIME. At the beginning of each session it's often much easier to revise than to continue writing your first draft. Revising will help you build momentum. You can soon shift to the task of writing new material.

4. USE THE FREE-FLOW TECHNIQUE. If you have a serious block, write about another subject for a few minutes. Some highly successful writers regularly write brief letters before they attempt their main project. I've known some that even write meditations or prayers. Any easy topic will do.

5. SET CLEAR GOALS AS YOU WRITE. Use a schedule, say hourly writing sessions spaced by fifteen-minute breaks. In order to work efficiently, set goals for the amount of material you want to write, perhaps two pages of draft material in the next hour.

   It may help to use an hour timer of the type used for cooking—these are available in many stores. You can put tape over the bell to soften the ring. The timer's clock mechanism can give some people the encouragement they need to complete the writing session.

6. Use the tactics presented in Chapter 3, especially:

   a. Break down the project into segments.
   b. View your writing as a series of decisions.
   c. Start small. Use enabling tasks such as getting notes ready, opening your notebook, calling up a word-processing program or putting paper in the typewriter.

7. AVOID "ONE BEST WAY" THINKING. There are many different ways to write a good paper on any topic. Holding unconsciously the idea that there is one perfect organization of words and ideas is self-defeating. Keep in mind, too, that your first draft is bound to be less than perfect, so relax and get on with it.

8. Recall from Chapter 3 that A KEY TO DEFEATING FEAR IS *ACTION*. Oddly, writing is both a cause of fear and a means of releasing it. As you write, the process becomes more and more manageable. The typical reaction of writers once they break the grip of procrastination is, "What was I afraid of?"

9. DON'T GET DOWN ON YOURSELF WHEN YOU FAIL. If you do fail to keep at it, don't panic, and above all don't get down on yourself. Believe that you can do better next time. Recognize that even the most experienced and successful writers sometimes get writer's block. But try to establish momentum as you write and keep it up. Missing a scheduled writing period makes your task psychologically all the harder.

10. DEVELOP A POSITIVE ATTITUDE. Repeatedly say to yourself (silently) things like:

> "I can handle this project."
> "This is going to be a lot easier than I thought."
> "I'm going to manage this fine by breaking it down into short segments. And I'm just going to take it a little bit at a time."
> "I'm growing to enjoy research and writing." (That's right! This thought will gradually take hold, and you'll begin to enjoy the process more. Sure, maybe you'd rather be at a party or football game, but in time you really will get pleasure out of writing if you follow the advice in this chapter.)
> "It's getting easier every day."

STEP TWO: Easing the Pressure

(For students who are having current difficulties getting started or continuing on a research and writing project.) Take a writing assignment in one of your courses, ideally a long report or term paper (if you have none of these at the moment, then take some other assignment, the longer and more difficult the better). The idea is to gain practice in easing any pressure you may feel.

1. Find a comfortable quiet place. Sit down and get ready to work on the project.
2. Make sure you have specific goals and objectives. What precise grade are you aiming for? Decide what precise benefits you want to get from the project (practice rewriting, increased ability to think analytically, knowledge about a particular subject, greater expertise in your field, mastery of a word-processing program, and so on. Set a schedule with specific deadlines for each part of the project.

3. Close your eyes and breath slowly and deeply, feeling the muscles in your head, shoulders and body relax. Imagine a beautiful scene such as an outdoor view that will help you relax more. Imagine the sounds and smells of this scene as well as the visual image. Take your time.

4. Now shift your thoughts to the paper or project. Continue this relaxed state with your eyes closed. Imagine the finished product completed on time. See an imaginary aura around the paper symbolizing a feeling of pride that you've tried to do a good job, that you've put feeling and caring into the effort and that you've completed it on time. See yourself as touching it, holding it, having a feeling of pleasure. Revive this image each time you work on the project.

5. Continuing in this relaxed state see yourself working on this project, focusing only on the task at hand, forgetting any concern you feel about grades, viewing your specific goal simply as a target that you will eventually achieve.

6. Now begin to work on the project, maintaining a positive frame of mind.

7. Whatever the precise level of success you've achieved at each writing session, see yourself as having done well and doing well in the future. Relax, talk positively to yourself, and generate success feelings that will contribute to your productivity next time. The idea is to always reinforce yourself positively.

STEP THREE: Choosing Good Topics

Below are four topics for term papers. In the space below each topic, improve on the one presented.

1. The Criminal Mind Today

   _____

2. Sexism and Racism in America

   _____

3. Social Norms on Soviet Nuclear Submarines

   _____

4. Social Problems of College Students

   _____

(*Review hint:* topics should be sufficiently narrow and there should be available data.)

STEP FOUR: Let a Journal Lead You Pleasurably to Better Writing

Begin a journal as described in this chapter on p. 236. Choose any subject linked to your academic success. One good subject would be your reflections on how you can become a better writer and what the payoffs are likely to be. If you wish, let this page be the first page of your journal, transferring it later to your new journal notebook.

_____

_____

_____

_____

_____

_____

_____

_____

_____

_____

_____

_____

_____

_____

_____

_____

_____

Chapter
9

Choosing Courses, a Major, and a Career

This chapter discusses many strategies for career success and shows you how to gain a significant career edge while in college. The chapter will be of benefit even if you've already decided on a major and a career or if you're a mid-career student.

*Y*our choice of career is one of the most important decisions you'll ever make. You will derive much of your identity from your career as well as many of your values. Your career will to a great extent determine your lifestyle and will be one source of friendships. Some of your feelings of self-worth will derive from your belief that your job and career are worthwhile.

It's no wonder that students who haven't yet chosen a career get uptight about their supposed lack of direction, especially since they see many students around them who seem to have settled already the decision about what their life's work will be. There's no denying that there are some advantages to knowing what kind of career you want. Perhaps most important is that a career choice helps provide direction and, especially, motivation. If you've got a clear target, your efforts in college may seem more meaningful.

Unfortunately, students often worry needlessly about having no clear career goals. The truth is that more people change jobs several times during their careers and more college graduates make fundamental career shifts along the way. It's definitely advantageous in some fields such as engineering and the sciences to make an early decision about careers because these fields require so much specific technical training. But many engineers and scientists end up in sales, management, and other positions. Besides, a delay of a year or two isn't the end of the world if you later decide to enter a specialized area. Taking the prerequisite math and science courses designed for these majors can help you size up your abilities and the extent of your interest.

Excessive specialization can even be a disadvantage. Technological change is proceeding so quickly that narrow specializations can become outdated. One of the implications of the rapid technological and economic changes the world is undergoing is that EVERYONE MUST MAKE LEARNING A LIFELONG PROCESS IF THEY'RE GOING TO KEEP UP TO DATE IN THEIR FIELD.

The implications for those who haven't yet chosen a career are clear. *There will be uncertainty whether you have a specific career choice or not, and those who have already made a decision should plan for flexibility and consider preparing themselves for possible alternative careers by giving themselves as wide a variety of skills as possible.* Whether you've chosen a career or not, you have every incentive to arm yourself with as many skills, as much knowledge, and as much analytical and problem-solving ability as possible during your college years.

Students sometimes also worry because they're unsure about what subject to choose as a *major.* If you've not yet decided on a major, you may have the feeling that the choice is a life-or-death decision. Unless you're going into a highly technical field, an early choice of major isn't crucial. Even if you get interested in a technical area later you can still decide to enter it.

MANY PEOPLE END UP IN CAREERS NOT DIRECTLY RELATED TO THEIR MAJOR WITH NO HARMFUL CONSEQUENCES. It's common for students to change their majors one or more times. This can be a rational decision process that is part of finding out about different areas and about yourself. An original "wrong" choice isn't really wrong because it can help you to learn about your abilities and interests.

Although there's usually room for flexibility in the choice of major, it's very important to choose courses that build skills and contribute to knowledge. In this chapter I'll discuss course selection, strategies for choosing a major, and, finally, career choice.

CHOOSING COURSES

The flexibility that students have in selecting courses varies greatly. Liberal arts majors may be able to choose the great majority of their courses, while engineering and other students in technical or professional programs may have comparatively little choice. But almost everyone has some choice, and these decisions can have a great impact on the quality of your education and the success you achieve on the job.

I first met Jamie halfway through his sophomore year. Jamie was a likable man who told me, "I just want a college sheepskin (diploma) so I can get a good job. I'm not interested in knowledge and a lot of intellectual stuff."

As we began to discuss possible course selections I asked him how he decided on the courses he'd written down on his course selection form. I admired his honesty. "To tell you the truth," he said, "I've heard these are gut courses. Not much work and the profs are easy graders."

"How do you think these will help your career?" I asked.

"Well, I'll get my degree and help my grade point average at the same time."

"Jamie, you can take what you like as long as you meet the basic requirements for your degree, but you may be cutting your own throat."

"How's that?" he asked.

I explained the importance of having a strategic plan in choosing courses. We talked for a short while, and Jamie decided to substitute microeconomics and a core course in his major for two he had on the list. We met several times over the course of the next year, and I outlined the following strategies that have made winners out of tens of thousands of college students.

Take Quality Courses

The most important criteria in choosing courses and instructors are the contribution to your education and the quality of the course and the teaching. Taking courses just because they're easy doesn't make sense. Sure, your grade point average matters, and it's wise to consider possible impact on your grade point average as *one* of many factors to weigh in making selections. Occasionally you'll run into instructors who think they're the official guardians of cosmic quality—people who refuse ever to award an "A" or who like to give lots of "D's" and "F's" without good reason. Unless you're required to take that person's course or there's some other compelling reason to take it, you may have good reason to consider an alternative.

You shouldn't avoid taking a course that can benefit you all your life just because you may end up with a "C" or because you've got to do some tedious problem solving. These courses can often turn out to be more interesting than you thought if you keep an open mind. And they may be crucial to your career success.

Take Courses That Will Develop Your Thinking and Analytical Ability

You already know from Chapter 4 the crucial importance of thinking and analytical ability. The capacity to plan and to understand and solve problems is one of the keys to career success, and making this one of your criteria in course selection will have many career benefits. These courses will also help you perform better in college.

ONE OF THE BEST COURSES FOR DEVELOPING YOUR CRITICAL THINKING ABILITY IS LOGIC. Don't be frightened by the title. You should be able to handle a basic introduction to logic course fine, though if you're a freshman you may want to wait until your sophomore year. Advanced courses are also helpful. Often overlooked are philosophy courses in ethics. The thinking skills developed in this area have applicability in a wide variety of career fields well beyond consideration of ethical issues.

"Philosophy of Science" courses are among the most useful. They deal with scientific methodology, and these principles have applicability in almost any field. Courses in the methodology of a particular subject can be enormously beneficial. They cover methods of thinking and analysis in depth. Titles vary, but courses such as "Scope and Methods of Sociology" illustrate this type of course. Before signing up, make sure you have the prerequisites; it's also a good idea to find out from the instructor whether the course is designed for majors in the field and requires a lot of technical knowledge. You'll be able to handle many courses on methods, scope and methods, and the like just fine. Some methods courses provide an excellent introduction to statistics.

Here's a list of courses that are especially helpful in developing your capacity to think and analyze:

Logic (usually offered by the Department of Philosophy).

Statistics.

Philosphy of science and related courses.

Courses in the *methodology* of a discipline or field.

Writing courses (because writing is a thinking process).

Psychology courses.

Any social science courses that emphasize reading, writing, and analysis.

Humanities courses that emphasize reading, writing, and analysis.

Courses in the sciences.

Other courses that emphasize thinking and analysis.

The fact that a course is offered in the social sciences, humanities, or sciences is no guarantee that a particular course will emphasize thinking and analysis. You should investigate each course in these areas before signing up. Many courses in other fields will also be helpful in contributing to your thinking ability. Look for a focus on analysis and thinking, challenging reading and writing assignments, and outside projects and exams that focus on analysis (causes, evaluation, etc.) rather than description.

Take Courses That Will Contribute to Your Understanding and Appreciation of the Historical and Philosophical Roots of Human Society

One of the hallmarks of an educated person is the knowledge and appreciation of the philosophical and historical roots of human society. There are both intellectual and practical reasons for acquiring a background in this area. One of the most important benefits is perspective, which contributes to more effective reasoning and judgment.

History courses in Western and Eastern Civilization, American or Canadian History, or other countries and areas are ideal. Basic introductory courses such as Western Civilization often provide a good overview. Philosophy courses are also important. Again, basic introductory courses can offer a good background, and you can specialize later if you wish. Because introductory courses typically have a wide cross section of students, they are often a good choice if you feel you lack sufficient background to take a more advanced course at this point.

Don't forget that an understanding of the third-world areas of Asia, Africa, and Latin America constitutes a fundamental part of understanding the roots of human society and ideas. The Third World is also becoming increasingly important economically and politically, so there are also practical benefits to be acquired from gaining knowledge in this area.

Don't Lose Out on An Important Career Skill Because of a Misguided Fear of Statistics and Mathematics

Most college graduates do not have the statistical and mathematical skills that they should to perform most effectively on the job. Many problems can be better understood and many decisions made more effectively by using basic mathematical techniques and statistical analysis. MATHEMATICAL AND STATISTICAL THINKING CAN SIGNIFICANTLY IMPROVE YOUR CAPACITY TO UNDERSTAND AND SOLVE PROBLEMS ON THE JOB AND THEREFORE CONTRIBUTE TO YOUR CAREER SUCCESS. In our computer age the ability to understand and use statistics is especially important.

I know what some of you are thinking: "You just don't understand. I'm really awful at math, and it bores me silly." You have my sympathy because I felt that way myself during my first year in college. Women especially sometimes underrate their own abilities in math and statistics, while they often underrate the importance of these subjects for their careers. This is largely the result of biases still remaining in the educational system.

What everyone needs to keep in mind (unless you take an advanced class designed for engineers or science majors) is that MOST OTHER STUDENTS IN CLASS PROBABLY BELIEVE THE SAME THING ABOUT THEMSELVES. In other words, you have nothing to fear from the standpoint of competition. Simply check in advance to see if the course is for math, science, or engineering majors or for students who aren't specializing in technical fields. Naturally, if you're specializing in a technical area you'll want to take all the advanced math and statistics courses you can to help prepare you for your field.

Many students seriously underestimate their capacity to learn and use mathematics and statistics. All college students can learn statistical and mathematical skills that will be of great help to them in their careers.

It's largely a matter of being systematic, neat, and making sure you understand as you go along. Statistics is really a matter of learning and applying some basic techniques that virtually anyone can handle. It's good to understand the reasoning behind the statistical principles, but *the minimum goal is to become statistically and mathematically literate.*

You need to be able to understand statistical arguments and reports and use basic techniques for a variety of computations and problems. As one illustration, nearly everyone has to submit and defend budgets at numerous points in their career. Statistical knowledge and thinking will enable you to present a much more effective case, so you can get more financial support for your projects and people and thus be more effective on the job.

You can probably get a much higher grade than you think by getting help from fellow students, the instructor, and the Math Assistance Center, if one's available at your school. Looking at long-term implications of decisions is one sign of good thinking, and deciding whether or not to take math and statistics is a classic opportunity to choose wisely. I'll bet you find many interesting aspects of these subjects. You'll also be rightly proud of yourself for having the courage and wisdom to have taken courses in these fields.

Take Courses That Will Develop Your Writing Ability

In the last chapter I discussed the importance of learning to write well, so I'll be brief here. One of the best strategies for developing this skill is to TAKE MORE WRITING COURSES THAN YOUR COLLEGE REQUIRES if your major gives you this flexibility. You should also consider a course's writing requirements as one measure of its ability to help prepare you for future courses and for your career. Term papers are a plus, giving you the chance to work on this ability and increase your thinking skills.

Take Good Courses in the Sciences

Many students are afraid of physics, chemistry, biology, and other courses that are basic to an understanding of the sciences. It's true that some courses do require an advanced background in mathematics, but the basic courses are usually quite manageable for most students. Like math, these courses can be conquered by approaching them systematically, keeping up, and getting assistance if needed.

If you have doubts about your abilities to successfully complete a course, talk to the instructor. Students sometimes find that they not only have the ability but the inclination to make one of the sciences a major and a career. There are few areas where the need for qualified people is so critical to society. If a particular science interests you, follow the steps in "Choosing a Major and a Career" below to find out about job and career opportunities.

Take Courses That Will Develop Your International Understanding

One of the hallmarks of educated people is the understanding and appreciation of countries and cultures other than their own. In large and powerful countries there's a danger that its citizens and leaders will be so oblivious to the strengths and virtues of other cultures that they draw erroneous conclusions and make faulty business and government decisions.

The world is growing more interdependent every day. In business and government alike, the most effective people are aware of the viewpoints of experts in other countries and are willing to learn from them. No country or age has a monopoly on virtue and competence. Again, don't forget the important third-world areas of Africa, Asia, and Latin America in selecting courses.

Taking courses that deal with foreign areas and countries will not only help your understanding of the world, it will make the world a more interesting place to you and make you a more interesting person. Aside from the obvious social advantages, COURSES THAT INCREASE YOUR UNDERSTANDING OF FOREIGN COUNTRIES CAN HAVE IMPORTANT CAREER BENEFITS. Modern companies as well as government agencies increasingly deal with foreign countries, and they often employ many people from abroad. Many citizens themselves have foreign roots, so a knowledge of diverse cultures increases the capacity to deal with people on the job. Learning about foreign lands and cultures increases your understanding of your own country and its people and perhaps your own roots.

Becoming proficient in a foreign *language* makes you more employable for many companies. Spanish is an increasingly useful language within the United States, while German, French, Russian, Chinese, and Japanese have many business and government applications. Even if you don't take enough language courses to become fluent, you will still gain substantial knowledge of another culture through language courses and provide yourself with the framework to learn greater fluency later.

In addition to modern languages, here are other important areas that will give you increased understanding of the world. Look in the course catalogue for specific quality courses that cover foreign countries and issues:

History

Political Science

Sociology

Economics

Literature

Anthropology

Area studies (such as Latin America, Europe, Africa, etc.)

International Business

Religions of the world

Courses in other fields covering international subjects

Consider "study abroad" for a year or a semester. Many colleges and universities have programs abroad that welcome students from other colleges and give academic credit applicable at your own institution. Your library and international office on campus should be able to provide you with information. Many of these programs are surprisingly affordable. It's important to learn as much about the culture as possible before you go. Doing so will make it one of the great experiences of your lifetime.

You may have to wait until after you graduate to travel in foreign countries, but your background of international courses will make the experience far more interesting than it otherwise would be.

Take Courses That Will Develop Your Background in Literature and the Arts

Students often underrate the importance of courses in literature, music, and art. These courses contribute substantially to your knowledge base, helping you to better understand history, society, and many other fields. One reason for this is that cultural issues are often mentioned or discussed in the texts and other books you read. Your knowledge makes it easier to understand these references. Literature courses are also good at helping you to develop critical thinking skills and provide an interesting way of learning to better understand human behavior.

An appreciation of literature, music, art, the theater, and related areas will greatly enrich your life. The more deeply you get into these areas the more satisfaction you'll derive from them. I'm not suggesting that you abandon popular music or give up popular magazines and novels—merely that the greater the breadth and depth of your cultural awareness, the more things in life you'll have to enjoy. Obviously THIS KIND OF KNOWLEDGE CAN GREATLY ENHANCE YOUR SOCIAL LIFE BECAUSE YOU'LL HAVE SO MUCH MORE TO TALK ABOUT AND DO.

There are significant career benefits in being conversant in literature and the arts. The top people in most fields as well as many members of the public with whom you may deal have a good background in literature and the arts. Your knowledge of these areas may give you an edge in communication and establishing rapport with your superiors and colleagues in the field. Courses in these areas are an important part of developing a broad educational background that can pay career as well as personal dividends.

Take Courses That Will Develop Your Ability to Speak in Public

This is one of the skills students are most likely to ignore. Whatever your career choice, the ability to speak effectively in public will be an advantage. The capacity to influence others is essential in accomplishing most jobs. You will probably attend many meetings where an ability to express yourself well will give you a significant advantage. Even occupations that might seem somewhat solitary often have far more interaction with the public and opportunities for presenting material to groups than you might suppose.

Sometimes students resist developing their speaking ability because of shyness. The fascinating thing is that shy people often make superb public speakers, not to mention actors and other professionals who address large groups of people. Maybe it's because we see speaking ability as a method of compensating for our shyness. Most students drastically underestimate their ability to become good speakers.

How do you develop speaking ability? The answer is training and practice. Take a course or two in public speaking. If you can't fit a course into your schedule, at least you can read books on public speaking in spare five- and ten-minute snatches.

There are other options. If you have the time and the inclination, the debating club or debating team can be a way of increasing your speaking as well as sharpening your analytical skills. That this experience can be invaluable for the future lawyer or teacher is obvious.

Speak up in class. You needn't be afraid of your fellow students or your instructors. Plan questions you might raise in advance. Listen to the discussion and lecture rather than worrying about yourself.

Often class participation will motivate an instructor to raise your course grade, especially if your mark is on the borderline. Another benefit of practicing your public speaking is the boost it gives to your sense of personal poise. It won't transform you into an extrovert if you're not already one, but it sure can help ease the tension you feel in social situations.

Be Willing to Experiment and Take Some Courses Just Because They Pique Your Interest

One of the joys of college education is the chance to learn about things just because you're interested in them. If you've always thought you might like to learn about Chinese history or French literature, sign up for a course in the subject. Maybe there's a technical subject that interests you but you're not sure about your qualifications to take the course. Talk to the instructor and explain your interest.

Find out if there's a system of PASS/FAIL GRADES at your school. Instead of being assigned a letter grade you receive a "pass" or "satisfactory" instead of an "A," "B," "C," or "D" grade. This means that you can take courses without damaging your grade point average. There are usually limits to the number of pass/fail courses you can take, and required courses or courses in your major are usually excluded. Check in the appropriate school catalogue and with your adviser. The pass/fail system was designed primarily to make it easier and less risky for students to experiment, so you might as well take advantage of the system if it exists at your school.

Take Courses That Will Help Develop Your People, Political, and Organizational Skills

One of the most important components of career success is the ability to work well with people. Much of your effectiveness in accomplishing results on the job will depend on your ability to understand and motivate others. This is an ability that can be developed through education as well as experience.

You can develop much insight through a variety of courses. Sociology provides an understanding of human behavior in groups. Literature courses are an often underrated source of insight into human behavior. PSYCHOLOGY COURSES ARE PARTICULARLY HELPFUL IN DEVELOPING PEOPLE SKILLS. All of the subjects have a number of other benefits as well, such as increasing your understanding of how the world functions.

A crucial related skill is the capacity to understand how organizations work and to effectively wield influence in achieving your goals. We live in an administrative age, and most college graduates will work in organizations. To perform effectively you've got to understand how bureaucracies operate and be able to use the system in meeting your responsibilities.

Courses that can help you in this area may be located in several different departments (psychology, management, sociology, political science, public or business administration). They go by such names as "organization theory," "organizational psychology," and "organizational behavior."

Take Courses That Will Make You More Marketable and Give You More Career Flexibility

Liberal arts students may be wise to take several courses in the business school if permitted, such as accounting and marketing. This will give you additional skills and demonstrate interest in business should you seek employment in the private sector. Sometimes students have such limited choice that it's reasonable to take several of their options just for the pleasure and intellectual break it gives them from their technical criteria. Although engineering students might be wise to take writing, and other high-payoff courses, they deserve an occasional break. Go ahead and take that History of Japan course if you can fit it into your schedule.

Make Your Course Selections According to Specific Criteria Based on Your Academic and Career Goals

Jamie gradually developed into a very good student, who has begun a career of government service and is targeted for an interesting, successful career. Among the most important things he did in college was to carefully select his courses. With the above broad strategies in mind, he implemented these specific steps, which have been followed by tens of thousands of successful students:

- He read carefully the college catalogue and department instructions concerning the requirements for his major and his degree.

- He met regularly with his adviser to discuss his selections and his progress.
- He read course descriptions carefully before signing up.
- For elective courses, he often asked the instructor in advance for a copy of the course syllabus and asked about course goals and requirements.
- He asked instructors in many of his courses for their recommendations about what other courses to take.
- He asked other students for their recommendations, making sure that quality remained one of his main criteria for course selection.
- He planned ahead. Asking his adviser how often required courses were offered, he plotted out a schedule for taking all required courses, making sure they were completed well prior to his senior year in case conflicts or problems arose.
- He developed a list of possible elective courses he could take so that he could more quickly make course selections each semester.
- He anticipated deadlines and always registered for courses as soon as possible. This kept him from being needlessly closed out and saved time.

Plan Ahead for Course Selections

Take the time to plan a year or two in advance. You can't always be certain which courses will be offered, but you can develop a list of options based on careful thought and consultation with others.

MAKE SURE YOU UNDERSTAND COURSE REQUIREMENTS FOR YOUR MAJOR AND YOUR DEGREE. Read the appropriate catalogue, and go over these requirements with a competent adviser. *Don't wait until the last minute to take required courses.* They may not be offered or their times may conflict with other required courses. You may have to delay graduating as a result. If your major doesn't map out a program that includes telling you when to take required courses, plan to take them in a paced, logical sequence. Consult with your adviser to see if your plan is sound.

For electives, the first step is to get the data. Obtain catalogue and course description books as well as department handouts. Where possible, get a copy of the syllabus for courses that interest you. Ask instructors in advance about their courses if you're uncertain about them.

Faculty advisers can usually give you good advice. They'll often steer you toward courses that are well taught as well as having intellectual quality. Few instructors will tell you who the bad teachers are, but it's enormously helpful to have the professional's viewpoint on where the quality lies.

The worksheet in Figure 9.1 can assist you in choosing electives. Simply fill in the courses that interest you most, taking into account the criteria at the top of the worksheet. Checking the appropriate boxes beside each course can help you decide which ones you should take first.

Don't forget the teachers of the courses you're taking now. Say you're taking an introductory course in economics and are thinking of signing up for an advanced course in a year or two. Go to your instructor during conference hours, explain your goals and interests, and ask for suggestions. Consult the course bulletin before you

Write possible choices on the left, putting check marks beside each entry as appropriate. Don't simply add up check marks in deciding courses. Weigh each course in your mind and make a qualitative judgment based on your goals. Rank your choices. Sometimes the hour and day a course is offered may be crucial, but don't miss out on a good course just to sleep an hour later.

Remember the importance of taking *required* courses in a paced, orderly way, without waiting until you're near graduation, unless that is part of the program guidelines. Consult with your adviser each semester.

Figure 9.1 Worksheet for choosing *elective* courses.

go so that you can ask specific questions. Just realize that faculty members are human and have their own biases, understandably in the direction of the usefulness and importance of their own fields. You need to maintain your independent critical judgment with faculty advice.

Fellow students are a good source of information on points such as course requirements and the interest level generated by the instructor. Published reports of student evaluations of teachers can be very helpful. Be aware that many students may base their assessments on lecture style. This can make the courses more fun and help you learn but is not always directly correlated with course quality. It's often difficult for students to judge the competence of course content except in extreme cases, though students with good critical thinking skills will usually make pretty good assessments.

If your degree program prevents your taking a wide range of courses, your understanding of the importance of the above areas can still lead to much broader understanding of the world. Your pleasure reading, television selections, and courses you take after you graduate are among the best ways of continuing to develop your knowledge and appreciation of these areas.

Tip: If a course is really important to you and it's closed, you can sometimes gain admittance by asking the instructor for permission to register. If a student has a good reason, which may be something no more profound than a clear interest in the subject matter, instructors will sometimes agree. Don't take it personally if they ask you to wait until a later semester; you're gaining good experience in courteous and appropriate assertiveness.

CHOOSING A MAJOR

What to Consider in Choosing a Major

Ideally your choice of a major will be closely linked to your career interests, and in many cases the choice of major is dictated by the decision to enter a particular career. Somebody planning to be an electrical engineer must major in electrical engineering.

Often, though, there's no need to make a final choice of a major immediately. Remember, many college students end up in careers unrelated to their majors. Marketing majors may find they prefer working in finance; English majors may go into law or even accounting; sociology majors may decide to pursue a career in business. Often people don't know what they really want to do until they've had some work experience (the next chapter deals in part with this important subject).

Many major fields provide a good background for going into business. Students majoring in business will take many courses that help prepare them for work in the private sector. Their task is to broaden their background and skills by taking lots of writing courses as well as the other subjects discussed earlier.

A number of fields in the liberal arts also provide a good background for business because they develop analytical and thinking skills so well. But liberal arts students who are considering the possibility of going into the business sector are well advised take statistics, economics, and similar courses as electives. They may also be able to take a few business courses such as accounting as electives at some schools. Job recruiters will see these kinds of courses as evidence of skill development as well as commitment.

If you're undecided about what major to choose, take courses in the areas that interest you. Begin career planning as suggested later in the chapter, and link your ultimate choice of major to your career goals. If you can't define precisely your career field at this point in your life, a general degree with solid courses is still a fine investment.

Here are some specific ways you can help yourself find a good major:

Try to determine your career interests and aptitudes by enrolling in programs at the career development office if your school has one.

Consult books on choosing careers.

Undertake the career planning measures discussed in the next section of this chapter and in the Success Steps at the end of the chapter.

Investigate the major fields available to you at your school. Obtain the appropriate catalogues and information sheets from departments or divisions.

Talk to faculty members, especially those in administrative positions (chairperson, executive officer, etc.) about requirements, opportunities, and so on. Visit them in their conference hours or make an appointment. Ask them about the pro's and con's of the major, expectations of students, and career opportunities.

Talk to students majoring in areas that interest you, especially those near the end of their program. Ask about the quality of courses and instructors as well as advising. Learn their feelings about requirements and attitudes toward students.

Take courses required of majors in fields that you find interesting. This will help you determine your interest and abilities in these fields.

Consider taking double majors if allowed or taking a minor in one of the fields that interests you.

Give your chosen major a reasonable chance. Discuss possible changes in major with faculty members in the departments concerned and with advisers in the appropriate dean's office. But don't be afraid to change majors if you find your real interests lie elsewhere.

Consider keeping your career options open if the major you decide on allows flexibility in course selection, for example, by taking a few courses in business administration, statistics, and so on, if you're majoring in philosophy.

Try to relax and realize that you're just as important as students who have already chosen a major and a career. Many of these students will themselves change majors and career goals.

Throughout your college career, try to take good courses according to the principles discussed earlier; realize that every course you take can help you in your career.

CHOOSING A CAREER

It's both reasonable and intelligent to consider financial benefits and levels of security in planning for a career. But they shouldn't be your only consideration. Students often have the mistaken impression that there are professions that will offer guaranteed security. In our era of rapid technological change and an uncertain, unsteady world economy few, if any, careers or organizations guarantee a secure future.

Ultimately your security depends on your skills, abilities, and performance as well as your success in developing the resources you need to advance your career. This simply means that employment security is something that lies within yourself. It also means that COLLEGE PROVIDES A TREMENDOUS OPPORTUNITY TO ARM YOURSELF WITH MANY SKILLS AND ABILITIES THAT WILL BENEFIT YOU DURING YOUR ENTIRE CAREER.

The most important thing to understand is that *your career choice is a decision you must make for yourself.* Having a career forced on you by well-intentioned parents or others is a recipe for unhappiness and conflict. This doesn't mean you shouldn't go into the same field as one of your parents. There's often considerable advantage in the background and insights you will have acquired from a parent, not to mention the connections you'd have and other forms of assistance. But any decision to enter a parent's career must be your own, based on your interest in the field.

Most of us have to create our own connections, and we may not have the same advantages as people with influential family. It's our job to turn the lack of connections to our advantage by making an extra effort in career-building. Most constructive achievement in the world has required getting the help and support of others, and building a successful career usually demands a similar effort.

If you decided on a career in high school or earlier, it's a good idea to analyze your decision in light of your more mature perspective. Maybe your career choice is sound, but it can't hurt to consider seriously the implications of your decision. At the least, careful consideration of the costs, benefits, and alternatives of a particular career will make you more informed and better able manage your own career development. It a good idea for all students to consider their career goals at regular intervals.

Never Underrate the Importance of Enjoying Your Work

If you're fascinated by your field and enjoy the work, you're much more likely to succeed. Going into a field solely because of the money, family pressure, or other external reasons is unlikely to give you a sense of satisfaction and fulfillment in your life. If a particular career interest is inconsistent with your abilities, say biomedical engineering, you might consider a related career, perhaps as a manager in a biomedical corporation.

Pay and other criteria are important in considering possible careers. But if you choose to follow a career path you don't really value, you may end up with a sense of emptiness and futility—and maybe a feeling that you've wasted your life. So it's wise to choose a career carefully and be willing to change if new values, goals, and opportunities make this a desirable and realistic option.

Reasons for Career Indecision

There are many reasons for career indecision. Sometimes students just need more time to adapt to the world and learn more about their own interests and abilities. Often career indecision is the result of lack of information about careers or about your own intersts and abilities. Here the Career Development counselers can assist you. Should you be at a school where there is no career counseling program, the books listed in the Bibliography will be of great help.

Consult the Career Planning Office

This office may be combined with Counseling and Testing or it may be a separate entity. It may be called Career Placement or some similar title. AT MANY COLLEGES THE CAREER DEVELOPMENT PROFESSIONALS OFFER FREE COURSES AND SEMINARS THAT CAN BE OF CONSIDERABLE BENEFIT. Typically these courses are not for credit and may be briefer than the entire semester. They help you identify your interests, personality traits, and values and discuss careers in relationship to these personal characteristics.

I strongly recommend these courses if you haven't yet chosen a career. Even if you have, they can help you if you're unsure you've made the right choice or if you want to learn more about alternatives and career success strategies. The Career Development Office may have a library that will contain books and references like the ones listed in the Bibliography.

Consider the Possibility of Taking Standardized Tests

A number of standardized tests can help you identify your values, interests, skills, abilities, and personality characteristics. These can then be linked with particular occupations so that you can see the correlations between yourself and possible career fields. Many career development and counseling and testing offices can administer these tests. Often you have to request that you be allowed to take them.

Probably the benefits of these tests are somewhat overrated. Quantitative information about your traits along some particular dimension may provide an overview that's useful, but it can't effectively measure motivation, political sensitivity, and many intangible qualitative feelings that ultimately are crucial in determining which careers may be right for you. While testing can be a helpful PART of a career development plan, it can't make your career decisions for you.

Sometimes the more general type of tests are more effective in putting you in touch with your feelings. One of the best is *PATH: A Career Workbook for Liberal Arts Students* by Howard Figler. This book is useful for any undecided students, whether or not you're enrolled in a liberal arts program. For a more detailed analysis of possible occupational choices the sources discussed by John Holland and the Holland book itself (see Bibliography) may also be helpful.

Interview Experienced and Entry-Level People in the Field

One of the best ways to learn about careers is from people already in the fields you're thinking about. If possible, tap into family and friends or acquaintances, including acquaintances of your parents and other relatives. If they're in careers you're considering, interview them about their work. If they just know people in these fields, ask for an introduction or for permission to use their names.

Sometimes you'll just have to approach people cold. But use some creative thinking. Usually there are friends of a friend or some connection you can use. Maybe an attorney your uncle employed to do some work would be willing to speak with you.

When you call to make an appointment you might say to the secretary, "One of Ms. Brown's acquaintances, Michael Shannon, suggested I call to speak with her about my career plans. I'd estimate the meeting will take only fifteen to twenty minutes, and I'll be happy to come at her convenience." Most people are glad to talk about their jobs and may even feel flattered to be asked, so don't be afraid to call even if you have no personal connection.

Nine times out of ten Ms. Brown will be glad to speak with you, though as a busy professional she may have to schedule you in. Naturally you'll want to be prompt and stay no longer than the amount of time you've been scheduled for, unless you're specifically asked to stay longer. Be well groomed and dress neatly. Bring a notebook and pen and take notes as appropriate. Think about the interview in advance.

Do some advanced reading about the field if possible. The last part of *The New York Times Career Planner* by Elizabeth Fowler, listed in the Bibliography, provides good, though brief introductions to a variety of fields. Be courteous. That same day write a short, neat, grammatically correct, handwritten thank-you note on appropriate personal stationery.

Some of the questions you should ask include how people in the field spend their time, what are the most and least desirable aspects of the work, and what are the opportunities of gaining responsibility and advancement. It's also helpful to inquire how best to get into the field and what skills and attributes are required for success.

Use Professional Associations

There's another easy way to talk with people in the field that will also help you develop career skills—attend local, regional, or even national meetings of professional associations.

People who achieve great success in their careers are usually adept at creating their own opportunities. They do this in part by establishing contacts with many people who can help them. Professional associations can be a good way of accomplishing this. Professional organizations can also help you stay current on the latest techniques and concepts in their fields. These associations often produce journals that keep their readers on the cutting edge of the discipline.

Like anything else, you can spend so much time being involved in professional associations that your work suffers, so you have to make a cost/benefit decision about how much time to allocate. For college students who have not yet chosen a career, attending conferences and association meetings of several different professions can be quite revealing and lead to insights and even job opportunities. It's also generally fun attending these meetings. You can speak to established people in the field at receptions and other functions.

Just go up to someone you've identified from the program or otherwise know to be in the field and say:

"Hello, my name is Sally Smith. I'm a student at Westfield State College and am interested in a career in _____ . May I ask you a couple of questions about the field?"

Usually you'll get a positive response; if you don't, ask someone else.

How do you find out the names of relevant professional associations? Any instructor in the field can tell you the names of the organizations and probably give you information about meetings and conferences. Don't be afraid to ask them, even if you haven't taken courses with them. The professional librarian at the library can also help you find the names and addresses of associations. And local phone books may help you locate organizations in your area if you live in a large or medium-sized city.

At national conference meetings there's usually a registration fee. But student fees and membership rates are often available. While it's not proper to attend an entire conference without registering, few would object to a student visitor making discrete inquiries. Local meetings usually don't charge membership fees for visitors, though there may be a cost for a meal. If you can't afford to attend the dinner and the talk, you might find it useful to go just for the social hour. If you can speak to an instructor or someone who's a member, they'll be able to clue you in, help you gain admission, and maybe even offer to introduce you to people.

Get Work Experience in Fields You're Considering

Students often find that the actual experience of working in a career field is different from their expectations. If you can get a part-time job, internship, or cooperative education assignment in fields you're considering, you greatly increase your chances of making good career decisions. This experience can tell you if you really like a career area and are suited to it.

SUMMARY

Your choice of courses will have a major bearing on your career success. Arming yourself with specific skills, knowledge, and abilities will make you more employable and help you once you're in your career field. Quality courses in the areas discussed above can also contribute to your social life and make life more interesting. They can make you a truly educated person. If you're in a field that limits your ability to take some of these courses, you can try to read during summers, attend lectures and cultural events on campus, and take courses later in your life. But if you have a chance while in college, you will benefit yourself in many ways by following the principles of course selection developed in this chapter.

Choosing a major and a career are very important decisions. But they are not life-and-death choices—you can usually change your mind with comparatively little damage. There are often good reasons for changing your mind in college. Your values, interests, and abilities usually become clearer. You may develop new interests and values as you proceed, and you should certainly acquire new skills. Even failure to perform well in a particular area or the recognition that you really don't like the subject can be a positive thing. It can help you change directions to an area you're more suited to.

Still, you should begin to explore possible careers as soon as possible. Unless you're interested in a highly technical field, it's usually not important to make a final early decision on a major. Even for technical fields, there's no great harm in losing a little time if you later decide to enter one of these areas. It's much more important to make rational and intelligent choices.

Several ways of learning about possible majors and careers have been discussed in this chapter. The essential thing is to realize that career development is a lifelong process that requires conscious thought, planning, and effort. There are many resources on campus and beyond that can help. The next chapter discusses, among other things, part-time employment. You will see that this can be an excellent vehicle for learning about your interests and abilities as well as helping you develop skills that will make you successful in your career. Before going on, complete the following Success Steps so that you can maximize the help this present chapter can give you.

SUCCESS STEPS

STEP ONE: Beginning the Self-Assessment Process

This exercise is designed to help you begin the process of identifying your career-related values, interests, and abilities. Also consult Success Step One on pp. 45–46.

A. What are my major talents, skills, and abilities that I've identified so far? (Include your own judgments as well as those made by family, friends, teachers, employers, and others.)

1. _____

2. _____

3. _____

4. _____

5. _____

6. _____

7. _____

B. What four occupations and jobs do *I* value most? Which ones do I thnk are the most praiseworthy and contribute most to society?

1. _____

2. _____

3. _____

4. _____

C. What activities and fields interest me most? What would give me, or might give me, deep satisfaction?

1. _____

2. _____

3. _____

4. _____

5. _____

6. _____

D. How do the activities, occupations, jobs, and fields I've identified above relate to my other values such as family time, good income, or whatever may be important to me?

1. _____

2. _____

3. _____

4. _____

5. _____

6. _____

E. In what areas may I be needlessly selling myself short? (For example, many students think they're no good in math, statistics, or science simply because they haven't done well in the past. It may be that they've experienced uninspiring teachers or simply haven't tried. Be generous to yourself in answering this question.)

1. _____

2. _____

3. _____

4. _____

5. _____

F. How can I find out whether I may really have ability in these areas? Are there courses I can take, cooperative education or part-time jobs I can seek, or extracurricular activities I can undertake?

1. _____

2. _____

3. _____

4. _____

5. _____

STEP TWO: Course and Career Planning

The purpose of this Success Step is to help you set goals. Rate yourself on the following questions. Give yourself 1 to 5 points for each question; the more positive your response, the higher the number you should assign (1 = strongly disagree, 5 = strongly agree). If the question doesn't apply to you, write "N. A." for not applicable. Remember that the purpose of the exercise is to help you set new goals and chart your progress as you proceed through college. There are no passing or failing grades.

Evaluate yourself now and at the beginning of each semester. Make these pages a part of your permanent career journal as described in Success Step Four. (Jot down the date beside the points you assign, for example: 2 (10/3/92) 3 (10/17/92) 5 (1/93).

Choosing Courses   (Even if you have little choice of courses in your program, these questions can help you identify areas of focus for the future).

1. Is taking quality courses with good instructors one of my top priorities in choos-

   ing courses?_____

   _____

2. In choosing courses do I consider their potential contribution to my thinking

   and analytical ability?_____

   _____

3. Do I let a fear of math or statistics keep me from taking suitable courses that can benefit my future career? Do I realize that there are many sources of help

   and ways I can succeed in these courses?_____

   _____

4. Do I allow unreasonable fear to keep me from taking suitable, good courses in

the sciences?_____

_____

5. In choosing courses do I consider the potential contribution toward my ability

to write well (term paper assignments, etc.)?_____

_____

6. Do I recognize that knowledge of foreign cultures and nations is an important
part of education, and do I consider international understanding as one factor in

planning my course selections?_____

_____

7. Do I realize that courses in literature and the arts are important in many ways
and offer real educational, personal, and career benefits. Have I considered

these courses in planning my course selections?_____

_____

8. Do I recognize that public speaking ability is an important asset, and do I
plan to include training and practice in my course selection criteria as time

allows?_____

_____

9. Recognizing that an ability to deal with people and an understanding of organizational behavior are a significant part of career success, do I consider
courses dealing with these issues in making my course selections?

_____

_____

10. Have I considered developing marketable skills as an important component of
my college education and realize that even if I'm a liberal arts student I can

still arm myself with many useful skills that will help me get a job and succeed in my career? Do I include skill development as one of my goals in college?

_____

_____

11. Have I read and understood the course requirements for my major and degree and discussed these with my adviser? Do I plan to take my required courses before I near graduation, so that I don't run into such problems as required

courses not being available?_____

_____

12. Do I plan ahead in choosing courses, checking out instructors and courses in the ways discussed in this chapter (my adviser, student evaluations and

suggestions, reading course outlines in advance, etc.)?_____

_____

13. Do I register for courses on time?_____

_____

14. Have I completed the elective course identification form provided on p. 254?

_____

Establishing a Plan for Career Development

1. Have I established a plan for acquiring necessary information about myself and

possible careers so that I can make an informed decision once I'm ready?____

_____

2. If I've already decided on a major and a career, have I taken steps to learn about different career paths in my field, and begun systematically to learn success strategies from people who have done well in my field?_____

_____

Implementing a Plan for Career Development

1. Have I found out which office(s) on campus engage in career counseling, and determined their location(s)?_____

   _____

2. Have I learned whether career development courses or seminars are offered on campus?_____

   _____

3. Have I made an appointment with a career counselor?_____

   _____

4. If I've discovered that career development help on my campus is quite limited, have I made plans to work on career development on my own, reading the books noted in this chapter and in the Bibliography?_____

   _____

5. Have I met with relevant instructors to discuss the pros and cons of different majors and careers?_____

   _____

6. Have I set up appointments with professionals in majors and careers in which I'm interested? If I don't know these professionals personally, have I contacted family members or acquaintances to see if they might know of people I can speak with?_____

   _____

7. Have I learned the names of associations in career fields I'm interested in, and have I made plans to attend meetings or conferences?_____

   _____

8. Have I begun my own library of career development and quality personal success books (the Bibliography includes several good choices)?_____

_____

For Community College Students

1. Have I considered continuing my education after earning my degree by seeking a bachelor's degree at a regular four-year college or university?_____

_____

2. Have I talked to counselors at my college and at four-year schools I might attend about the pros and cons of continuing my education?_____

_____

3. Recognizing the possible benefits of a bachelor's degree as well as the fact that a bachelor-level education is not for everyone, have I made an informed decision to attend or not to attend a four-year institution based on my personal career and life goals?_____

_____

Qualitative Measures

1. Do I believe that career development is something I must work at?_____

_____

2. If I haven't yet decided on a major or career, do I understand that this is usually no cause for alarm and that many successful people delay making a decision until they have the necessary information and are psychologically ready to decide?_____

_____

3. Do I realize that career development throughout a person's life requires flexibility concerning changing circumstances, interests, and values? Do I under-

stand that many people change their careers and that most people change jobs

several times after they graduate?_____

_____

4. Do I understand that career development information is readily available on most campuses as well as in books such as those listed in the Bibliography?

_____

_____

5. Do I feel that I can acquire all the information and help I need to make informed choices, even though it may take some effort?_____

_____

6. Do I believe that conscious attention to career development throughout one's working life is a necessary part of most successful careers?_____

_____

7. Do I understand that continual attention to career development will give me a significant edge in my career life?_____

_____

8. Do I have a positive attitude about choosing a major and a career?_____

_____

STEP THREE: Setting New Goals

A. Based on your responses to the above questions, establish specific, measurable goals that you can begin to implement soon. These might include finding out the name and location of the career counseling office, setting up an appointment with a counselor, looking over some of the literature and books in the office, etc. Work them into your schedule rather than taking time from other important activities. Remove these pages and post or keep where they will serve as a reminder.

Goal 1. _____

_____

_____

Action I will take to achieve this goal _____

_____

_____

How I will measure achievement on this goal _____

_____

_____

Goal 2. _____

_____

_____

Action I will take to achieve this goal _____

_____

_____

How I will measure achievement of this goal _____

_____

_____

Goal 3. _____

_____

_____

Action I will take to achieve this goal _____

_____

_____

How I will measure achievement of this goal _____

_____

_____

Goal 4. _____

_____

_____

Action I will take to achieve this goal _____

_____

_____

How I will measure achievement of this goal _____

_____

_____

Goal 5. _____

_____

_____

Action I will take to achieve this goal _____

_____

_____

How I will measure achievement of this goal _____

_____

_____

STEP FOUR: Beginning a Career Development Journal

This is a journal you'll use and value all your life. Choose a quality loose-leaf notebook so that you can move to a larger size notebook later or begin another career journal. Adapt the journal to your own needs. Here are some suggestions:

1. List your career development goals, beginning with the ones you've established above. Over the years try to state your goals in precise, measurable form. Establish short-range, medium-range, and long-term goals.
2. Measure your progress at regular intervals—each semester, every year, and every time you make a major career move or decision. These decisions include your choice of major, key courses, deciding to attend professional meetings, turning up your own interviews as well as the ones sponsored by the placement office, choice of jobs, etc.
3. Include your feelings as well as your objective analysis. For example, if a choice of major or job doesn't work out, note your feelings, including negative ones. But also include your objective analysis, where you try to provide perspective. Note the positive aspects of change. Include suggestions made by counselors and advisers.
4. Have a section for recording ideas from instructors and other college personnel, career development books, colleagues and superiors on the job, and books in your professional field. Note the title and author as well as date and publisher (so that you can later refer your colleagues and subordinates to the book if you wish). Keep it simple. You may begin your journal entry below and transfer this journal entry to another notebook later.

_____

_____

_____

_____

_____

_____

_____

_____

_____

_____

_____

_____

_____

_____

_____

_____

_____

_____

_____

_____

_____

Chapter
10

Managing Your Finances

*A*lmost everyone has money problems, and students usually have some of the most severe financial difficulties. But there are steps you can take to drastically improve your financial circumstances. This chapter discusses financial aid, money management, part-time employment, and internships. With determination and the right strategies, you can make the task of funding your education far more manageable.

GETTING FINANCIAL AID

If you're committed to getting a college education, there's almost always a way to get the necessary financing. But financial assistance is seldom given automatically. You must actively initiate your requests by filing applications that must be submitted on time. You must usually reapply each year. The key to handling this important matter effectively is to plan ahead, seek advice, and follow through in a timely fashion.

The Most Important Source of Financial Assistance Is the Financial Aid Office

To plan effectively you must do some research and investigate all realistic possible sources of funding. The counselors in the Office of Financial Aid will help you decide what these programs are and their application procedures. They'll also give you literature that you should read carefully. Also consult the books available in the Financial Aid Office. The more you understand about the financial aid process and specific programs, the more likely you are to get the assistance you need.

Other campus offices can also give you help. Veterans will find assistance at the Veterans Affairs offices available on many campuses. Members of minority groups will find valuable advice and assistance in university offices dealing with minority affairs. Offices of handicapped services can be of great help, not only for advice on assistance programs, but also for arranging a variety of services, such as providing sign-language interpreters for your courses.

PLANNING AHEAD IS ESSENTIAL IN FINANCING YOUR WAY THROUGH COLLEGE. SEE A FINANCIAL AID COUNSELOR EARLY AND ANTICIPATE APPLICATION DEADLINES. THE TRICK IS TO BUILD FINANCIAL PLANNING INTO YOUR SCHEDULE AND APPROACH THE APPLICATION PROCESS IN A MEANINGFUL, METHODICAL WAY.

The first step is to fill out the FAF and other necessary forms, which are generally available in the Financial Aid Office. MAKE SURE YOU KNOW THE DEADLINES for all forms and applications. Allow plenty of lead time to get the necessary tax and other information, and submit these forms as early as possible.

Next, speak with a counselor in the financial aid office. The activity of these offices runs in cycles, with the most hectic times being at the beginning of each term. So try to anticipate your need for advice and see a counselor during the middle of the semester if possible. Work out a plan with them and then follow through.

Counselors in the financial aid office will help you decide which loans, grants, or scholarships are most suitable. Loans have to be paid back. Grants *give* you money that doesn't have to be paid back. Scholarships also give you funding that doesn't have to be repaid; generally they are awarded at least in part on the basis of academic achievement.

If you and your parents haven't already filed the appropriate Financial Aid Form to determine need, your Financial Aid Office will supply you with the proper form. While the instructions on the forms are self-explanatory, the Financial Aid Office can answer any questions you might have.

Numerous government-backed loan programs exist: The Stafford Loan, PLUS, TERI, and many others. Some are based on parental income limitations and some (e.g., PLUS and TERI) are not. Some are granted to parents, some to students, and some to both. Financial need is determined by the difference between educational costs and your and your family's capacity to pay these costs. Because costs at more expensive institutions are higher you may be eligible for more grants as well as higher loans at these schools.

With a few exceptions such as specific provisions for students who enter the military, LOANS MUST BE PAID BACK. They are a serious financial and legal undertaking. Is it worth putting yourself in debt to continue your college education? The typical college graduate will earn hundreds of thousands of dollars more in the average career than a non-college graduate. From a financial viewpoint, for most students it's definitely worth borrowing to stay in school. There are many other benefits of a college degree—educational, social, and others that make the investment well worthwhile.

Still, indebtedness of thousands of dollars when you graduate does represent a real burden. THE SECRET IS TO BORROW ONLY WHAT YOU REALLY NEED AND BE REASONABLY SURE YOU CAN PAY IT BACK. If you borrow too little, you may burden yourself so heavily with part-time jobs and worry that your grades suffer and your success in college becomes jeopardized. If you borrow more than you need, you may be robbing yourself in the years after you graduate. Your Financial Aid Office has forms and pamphlets that will let you calculate the amount you can reasonably borrow.

If you think you might be eligible for a loan or grant program, APPLY FOR IT. Many students falsely assume that they may not be eligible for financial aid because of their parents' income or some other consideration. Talk with a financial aid counselor. If there's at least a possibility, GO FOR IT.

IF YOU FACE A FINANCIAL CRISIS DURING THE SEMESTER, BE SURE TO TELL THE FINANCIAL AID OFFICE. Don't be shy about letting them know about your problems. Sometimes money available to the school will be freed up partway through the semester, so it may be smart to check back at various points to see if additional money has become available. Many schools also have short-term Emergency Loan Funds. Ask your counselor in the Financial Aid Office whether you may be eligible for additional funding.

Special Programs May Pay Part or All of Your Tuition Costs

The military services have ROTC programs that will pay not only for tuition, fees, and books but will give a generous stipend per month ($100 per month at this writing). You must meet academic requirements, attend special classes and sessions, and serve four years on active duty after graduation, though shorter plans are available. If you have positive feelings about military service and are willing to commit yourself to the demands on your present and future time, ROTC can be a viable option in financing your education. Your financial aid counselor can tell you about other programs that may be of interest.

The Bursar Can Often Help

Frequently colleges and universities have a budget plan that allows for payment in steps, so be sure to find out about payment options. Sometimes students who don't pay get blocked, meaning they can't register for courses until they've made arrangements to pay their tuition. Graduation may also be held up, and the registrar may refuse to send transcripts until bills are paid. These measures seem harsh, but the schools are just trying to survive.

Despite the pressure students sometimes feel in dealing with the Bursar's Office, it's really true that most of these officials care about students. They want students to remain in school, and they understand the real difficulties students face. They're often more flexible than many students might suppose, so be sure to seek their help when necessary.

If you simply can't come up with the money to pay your bill and you face having to drop out of school, talk to the associate or assistant bursar about working out an arrangement. Go in with a portion of the money owed to show good faith and responsibility. Be prepared to demonstrate how you plan to pay the remainder. There's no guarantee they'll be accommodating, but it's worth a try. Also tell your academic dean or associate academic dean about your problem. Be persistent. Visit your financial aid counselor and others several times if your circumstances are desperate and you've done all you can to help yourself.

Rick's financial problems first came to my attention as we discussed his course selections for the next term. As we talked it became apparent that he'd become nearly incapacitated because of money problems. He worked forty hours a week, mostly at night, and could hardly stay awake in class. He was so consumed by money worries that he couldn't concentrate on his courses when he did find time to study. Despite his worried and agitated state, it was obvious that Rick was a dedicated student. By sheer force of will he was determined to make it through school and get his degree, which he correctly believed could open many opportunities.

Rick knew that grades were important. He hoped someday to go to graduate school, and was concerned that he might not get in. "I feel like I'm just spinning my wheels," Rick said.

I suggested that Rick see counselors in the Counseling and Testing Center and the Financial Aid Office as well as the Associate Dean of Arts and Sciences. When I saw Rick toward the end of the next semester I asked how he was doing. "It's not exactly easy now, but I feel like a new man," he said.

I inquired about his grades. "Got a 2.3 last semester, but I'm doing lots better now." Here's what Rick did to improve his financial and academic circumstances:

- The day we'd had our first conversation, Rick made an appointment with a counselor in the Financial Aid Office. He asked what material he should bring and made sure he had the appropriate information when the appointment arrived.
- Prior to the appointment he read the literature offered by the Financial Aid Office, and consulted some of the books that office made available to students. (Some of the best books are listed in the Bibliography.)
- He found that he might be eligible for a larger loan on easier terms.
- He took particular note of application deadlines and made sure that he applied in plenty of time.
- He went to the Bursar's Office to make specific arrangements for getting caught up.
- He began to manage his money effectively. He wrote down everything he spent so he could see patterns of waste. And he developed a budget to guide his spending.
- Every month he allotted time for financial planning, including balancing his checkbook, paying his bills, and planning for the next month and semester.
- He gave up some expensive habits that he described as "bad and self-destructive."
- He began to play basketball Tuesdays and Thursdays at the gym.
- He built some pleasure into each day and undertook a program of stress management.
- He began to think positively about his ability to plan financially and manage his money.
- He worked hard on study skills so he could make better use of the time he spent studying. "I had no idea how much time I was wasting when I studied," he said.
- Rick began to THINK about his studies and consult with his instructors. He found that seeking advice and using the math and writing centers actually saved time.
- These steps enabled him to cut back on the number of hours he worked each week.

"I didn't get any grant money, but they gave me a bigger loan," Rick said. "And I don't have to pay it back until I've finished school." He seemed much more upbeat and optimistic; in fact he seemed happy. "I've got a new job, fewer hours, and better conditions. My boss says he wants to make me a supervisor, but I'll have to think about it."

Rick went on to complete his degree with a good record. Last I heard he had a job with a fine company and was going for his Master of Business Administration degree in an evening program. I've known many students like Rick. They're among the most admirable people I've ever met. Against difficult obstacles they set a goal, and with courage, determination, and stamina go after it. They create their own opportunity, making the money necessary to supplement their loans or grants. These same people are typically successful in their careers in part because of the determination and persistence they acquired in getting their degree.

But sometimes they put more stress on themselves than is really necessary. They may not take advantage of the financial resources available to them, and they sometimes neglect to consider long-term consequences of their financial and employment decisions. This is understandable given the pressures they face. But like Rick, they can often improve their financial circumstances considerably by paying a little more attention to planning and financial management. They may still have to work, but in a way that won't destroy their academic goals or enjoyment of school.

MANAGING YOUR MONEY

There is one basic principle of money management that can alter your life. This principle, eloquently stated by John Wilbur, simply states:

HOW YOU MANAGE YOUR MONEY IS MORE IMPORTANT THAN HOW MUCH MONEY YOU HAVE TO MANAGE

Sure, it matters how much money you have. There's no denying that most students undergo considerable stress because of money problems. But these problems can be eased considerably by relatively simple techniques of money management.

Don't Fritter Away Money on Trivia

The first step is to find out where your money is going. Many students discover that they are spending five dollars or more a day on things that are totally unnecessary or for which there are much cheaper substitutes. This highlights one of the central points of good financial management, shown in Figure 10.1.

Think in mathematical terms. Look for
the long term consequences of spending,
saving and investing.

$3.00 a day = $1,095.00 in one year
$5.00 a day = $1,825.00 in one year
$7.50 a day = $2,737.50 in one year

Figure 10.1 This figure shows the importance of watching daily expenditures as
well as the power of regular saving.

The trick to gaining control of these expenses is to RECORD THE MONEY
YOU SPEND ON A DAILY BASIS. Use a separate, small notebook, sheet of paper,
or simply jot down everything you spend on your action list or weekly schedule.
When you know where your money goes, you can control it by substituting, cut-
ting, or moderating what you pay. THE MERE ACT OF WRITING IT DOWN
WILL SERVE AS AN INSTRUMENT OF CONTROL.

Each day glance over your expenditures and circle unnecessary items or items
where there is a less expensive alternative. THINK CREATIVELY ABOUT POS-
SIBLE ALTERNATIVES TO THIS WASTED MONEY. Sometimes people buy soft
drinks and eat just because they're thirsty. Just drinking more water will often cut
back the craving for food and drink. Consider the negative consequences of that
snack. A candy bar will give you a quick boost in energy, but you'll be more tired
than ever when your blood sugar plummets after forty-five minutes or so. A walk or
a more nutritious snack will do a much better and longer job of restoring your
energy. You can come up with many ideas that will save you money.

Set a *few* goals for altering your spending behavior. Don't try to change everything at once, and don't expect to become a machine. Continue to allow yourself
pleasures you really enjoy, only do it more consciously. If you set up unrealistic,
herculean goals you're less likely to be successful.

Don't Buy Consumer Items on Credit

Everywhere in our culture someone's trying to sell you something. It may be flat-
tering when you're first out on your own to realize that local jewelry stores will
offer you credit. You may even have access to a credit card of your own or your
parents. If you're in mid-career, you probably have several credit cards. Advertisements try to stimulate buying with sex, fame, and other appeals to desires unrelated to our real material needs.

Don't be seduced by credit cards. For most
students they're best used only for major expenses
you've *planned* in advance or for emergencies.
Writing a check and, especially, paying by cash can
make you a more conservative spender.

SEMESTER BUDGET

INCOME	EXPENSES
Grants/scholarships _____	Rent, room fee or mortgage _____
Loans _____	Food _____
Salary _____	Tuition _____
Money from parents or spouse _____	Books, supplies, college fees _____
Refunds _____	Transportation _____
Sale of items no longer needed _____	Clothes _____
Own business or services _____	Entertainment _____
Other _____	Personal items _____
_____	Charitable contributions _____
_____	Insurance _____
_____	Telephone _____
_____	Child care _____
	Medical _____
	Gifts _____
	Other _____

TOTAL INCOME _____   TOTAL EXPENSES _____

Figure 10.2 Semester budget and planning guide.

Naturally, borrowing sometimes makes sense. Financing your education is necessary for most students. Getting a loan to buy textbooks may be essential. These are sound investments in your future. Tightly managed business corporations borrow all the time to invest in equipment, buildings, or other items that will help them make money. And you may really need to buy a car on credit, although automobile expenses (payments, repairs, insurance, gasoline and oil, registration, excise tax, sales tax, etc.) can contribute to poverty as quickly as anything.

Use a Budget as the Key to Financial Management

A budget allows you to plan and make rational financial decisions. You don't have to be a slave to your budget. If you're too strict, your budget will be self-defeating; you probably won't follow it. So it's good to allow yourself some flexibility. Figure 10.2 depicts a good system, but don't hesitate to modify it to meet your own needs.

Include financial planning in your time schedule.
Set aside a block of time every month to go over
your finances. Balance your checking account and
pay your bills at these sessions, plan your budget
for the next month and review your semester
budget, making alterations if needed.

Figure 10.2 is a worksheet for a semester budget. It can serve as a basis for compiling a weekly or monthly budget. Begin by filling out the worksheet. A weekly or monthly budget form is provided in Success Step Four on pp. 302–303.

Using pencil, the first step is to list all sources of income and cash on hand. Write this total at the bottom of the section marked "Income." Next list your expenses, making realistic estimates where necessary. If you're like most students, you'll find that expenses exceed income. But even if they don't, proceed to the next two steps for revising your expenses.

First, go over each expense and ask yourself two questions: (1) Do I really need this? If not, cut or reduce it. But don't cut out everything for entertainment and pleasure. (2) Is there a less expensive alternative (for transportation, living quarters, etc.)? Next, prioritize your expenses, noting which ones are vital and which ones are less essential. It may help to use a numbering system.

Then shift to the income side of the equation and ask yourself how you can supplement your income without sacrificing your academic and important personal goals. A number of ideas are presented below both for reducing expenses and supplementing income. If your total income is less than your total expenses, go back over your expense and income lists to see if you can make cuts, reductions, postponements, or add new income sources, keeping in mind your academic and other goals.

After you've finished this chapter and have done the Success Steps on pp. 302–303, come back to the semester budget and see if you can make further revisions.

Think Creatively, and Look for Alternatives

Rick eventually cut back drastically on his educational expenses by making changes that would save him big bucks. During his third year of school he decided to become a resident assistant in one of the dormitories. Not only did this provide him with free room and board; it gave him a small stipend as well.

The job of resident assistant is not for everyone. It takes a fair amount of time advising students, supervising and mediating disputes, and otherwise helping to create a positive living environment for students. In Rick's case the experience tied in directly with his career plans where he would be working with people and trying to create a cooperative environment.

Here are some alternatives for saving money:

a. Buy used clothing. Many thrift stores and outlets for used clothes offer tremendous savings. Especially good selections of women's clothes can often be found.

b. Learn the rate system for long-distance calls. Try to call when special rates are in effect. Plan your calls ahead. Write instead of calling when possible.

c. Take advantage of the free entertainment offered by your college and other institutions in the area. Most colleges and universities sponsor a variety of concerts, plays, dance groups, and other activities that you can attend free or at nominal cost. Not only are these activities a great source of entertainment, they can also contribute substantially to your social life and cultural education. Don't forget visiting speakers. You can hear the talk and get together with friends afterwards to discuss the speaker's ideas.

Students often create a false equation between money and fun. Thinking back on their lives, most people find little relationship between the best times or the best dates and the amount of money spent. Going for a walk can be one of the most pleasurable and romantic activities.

---

d. Living at home can cut down considerably on college expenses. But consider the competing benefits of living on campus, such as easier access to study groups, libraries, and cultural activities. Weigh the costs and benefits. Living at home may be a satisfactory alternative.

e. Be a smart shopper. The first rule is DON'T BUY IT UNLESS YOU REALLY NEED IT. If you need something that affects your performance in your classes or your health, it should receive top priority. But many purchases can be deferred.

Check a consumer magazine such as *Consumer Reports*. You'll save money and get better quality. Hair dryers, typewriters, computers, software, and most consumer products are evaluated by these magazines. After finding what you want, COMPARE PRICES at different stores including discount stores, using the telephone to save time and travel expenses. Use coupons and manufacturers' rebates as appropriate. You can save substantially by comparing the costs of different banks for their checking accounts or credit cards.

f. Bring your lunch so you can save money and have healthier food. Try to use leftovers from dinner. Otherwise eat cheap, nutritious foods you enjoy. Try to make the meal as attractive as possible.

Shop at larger grocery stores and stock up on sales. Try to avoid shopping for groceries at convenience stores, which are usually much more expensive. Bringing your lunch instead of using the cafeteria or a restaurant will not only save you money, it will save you time waiting in line and allow you to have more quiet time for relaxation and study.

g. Save on transportation costs by planning ahead. Use special rates on air fares even if it means traveling at odd hours or changing planes. Consider using a bus or train for long-distance travel. One of my students just traveled to Virginia (via Washington, D.C.) from Boston by train for Thanksgiving break. He told me that he did the third draft of his paper for my course and also got much of his reviewing for finals completed on the train.

h. Save on commuting costs by sharing rides with other students who drive. Consider public transportation alternatives. Remember that quiet bus and train lines offer a tremendous opportunity for study. There are few temptations, so travel time becomes a chance for regular study, a terrific form of time management.

i. If you have children, consider sharing babysitting responsibilities with trust-worthy neighbors or classmates.

j. If you cook for yourself or family, consider cooking in bulk, freezing enough for two or three future meals (or more if you have a large freezer). This will allow you to purchase perishable foods less expensively in greater bulk. You'll also save preparation time later.

k. Don't feel pressured to buy expensive gifts or feel that you must spend a lot of money entertaining your friends, dates, or spouse. While it's important to spend time with family and friends, seldom does this require putting a harsh financial burden on ourselves. You may find that the recipient treasures a three-dollar creatively chosen gift far more than an expensive radio.

Make Yourself Available for Scholarships and Other Opportunities for Financial Help

Sometimes students who might be eligible for scholarships or paid trips to academic conferences fail to get aid because no one knows that they might be qualified. Faculty and administrators sometimes get bogged down in other administrative work and don't take the time to search for eligible students. If you've got a grade point average above 3.0, make yourself and your qualifications known to your instructors, department chair in your major, and associate academic deans. Even if your grades have not yet reached these levels, there may be awards and opportunities for which you might qualify. You're much more likely to be nominated for a financial award if people who are asked for nominations know you.

PART-TIME JOBS

The First Principle of Working Is to Link Work Directly to Your Goals

It's true that many students have to work part-time jobs while attending school full-time. But it's also true that students sometimes work for the wrong reasons or at jobs that are wrong for them.

If you're working to support your car, stereo, or desire for a trip to Florida during Spring break, ask yourself: what is the impact of my job or proposed job on my grades and future career? Carefully assess the costs and benefits.

For freshmen it's particularly important not to work more than necessary. Your major goal should be to get the highest grades possible. While it may be necessary to work, you should try to minimize the number of hours you work each week so that you can devote more time to your studies. Be sure that you have obtained available assistance from the Financial Aid Office. Don't be discouraged if you have to work—there are benefits to be gained. Working can help structure your time, decrease stress, and help you reward yourself. The trick is to keep your eye on your studies and avoid overdoing it.

Job opportunities are often posted near the Financial Aid Office. The Personnel or Human Resources Management Office at your institution may have job listings for positions on campus. Some colleges and universities have programs called cooperative education, which means you alternate periods of study with full-time work on jobs arranged by the school.

Most schools have federally funded WORK-STUDY programs in which part-time employment on campus is supported by the federal government. The Financial Aid Office will tell you about these programs. Work-study jobs may fit into your schedule more easily than outside employment because you can work between classes. They may provide other benefits such as letting you work in an area of academic interest.

Many students arrange for their own employment through aggressive searching for good jobs. IT'S GOOD PRACTICE TO GET IN THE HABIT OF RELYING PRIMARILY ON YOURSELF TO GENERATE JOB OPPORTUNITIES. Checking the local newspapers and contacting companies directly are basic steps. The books listed in the Bibliography will give you additional ideas. Most people change jobs several times during their careers, and learning how to go after job opportunities is an important skill in career development.

Always Do a Good Job

Students may not see the importance of being reliable and doing a good job even in seemingly menial positions. I've known dozens of students who turned what seemed like dead-end jobs into stepping-stones for great career success.

There's a grain of truth to the old saying that good people are hard to find. The problem is not really that there are few good people; it's that many people are unwilling to perform well because they see their jobs as less than ideal. Students who show initiative and responsibility may well find themselves tapped for supervisory or even higher management positions. Often the transfer or resignation of someone higher up the chain of command will create vacancies that effective workers will be asked to fill. The problem then becomes deciding whether to accept or reject the promotion, depending on whether it helps or hinders your academic career goals.

Another important benefit of doing a good job is the effect it has on building your resume. Showing work experience is sometimes important in finding permanent employment after graduation. Even more important is being able to document that you've been a good employee. Superior letters of recommendation and other evidence of excellence can give you a significant edge in applying for full-time positions. Most important, you're building good work habits that will make later career success come much easier.

Students who work conscientiously in their part-time, work study, and cooperative education jobs benefit themselves in many ways. Never underestimate the importance of doing good work, even if the job isn't permanent.

There will be limits on the kind of job you're willing to take, depending on your personal background and outlook. Some students, for example, may be unwilling to take drug tests because of personal sensitivities. The point is to think consciously about your own values and goals and not needlessly limit your potential ability to earn money.

Some limits, however, should be set. It's wise to AVOID NEEDLESSLY DANGEROUS WORK. A position requiring contact with dangerous pesticides is an example of a job best passed by.

Use Good Ethical Thinking

It's an unfortunate fact that many people try to exploit college students, who are often financially vulnerable and inexperienced. Over the years I've heard and read about students who became drug dealers or prostitutes as a means of making money, with the inevitable outcomes of destroyed health, imprisonment, and other tragedies. Once I saw an advertisement in a newspaper that had been distributed on campus. The ad was by an "escort" service that sought college men and women for a business that was clearly engaged in prostitution (it appeared on a page of sex ads, which also spell trouble). You may have seen newspaper accounts of terrible rackets that exploited students. It is not just at large universities where such horror stories occur.

Naturally the overwhelming majority of students have the good sense to avoid these extremes. But less horrendous shady operations also prey on students. Sometimes students will be asked to invest money before they can sell a product, generally an indication that the job may be a rip-off. Some jobs that pay by commission only also exploit the inexperience of students.

Unscrupulous companies may try to cheat the public through illegal schemes such as marketing fraudulent stocks and securities. THE BOTTOM LINE IS TO BE SURE OF WHAT YOU'RE SELLING AND, FOR ANY JOB, KNOW THE

REPUTATION OF THE COMPANY OFFERING THE POSITION. Don't misunderstand—selling is an honorable profession. Countless students, including myself, have gotten excellent experience from selling. Even some commission-only jobs provide good experience, though I would generally advise against them, except for ambitious students with some business savvy, who first carefully check out the operation.

As a student Jim took a job with a company that bred show dogs. He soon found that it was a shady operation. Against regulations, the ears of some dogs were slit with a razor and small lead weights inserted prior to showing the dogs. These made the dogs' ears conform more perfectly to established show standards. Sometimes the markings of the dogs were darkened with shoe polish to make them fit show criteria more closely. Clients were thus induced to pay for stud services that they otherwise would have bypassed.

When I asked Jim how he handled the problem he said, "Simple, I quit." Today Jim is a senior administrator in a large organization. Part of his success is attributable to his reputation among his colleagues as a "straight shooter." If it sometimes cost him in the short run, sound ethical judgment served to promote career success in the long term.

Students occasionally tell an employer, "I've quit school and am looking for full-time employment," knowing full well that they plan to quit the job and go back to school in a few months. This sours employers on other applicants from the student's school. And it hurts their career chances later on. How can they list the job on their resume? If they include it, prospective future employers may telephone to see how the applicant performed. You can imagine that the recommendation will be less than glowing.

Never compromise your integrity because of financial desperation. There's always a legitimate way to obtain money. If you're in really serious financial shape and don't know how you're going to make it, talk it over with a counselor in the Financial Aid Office, the associate or assistant bursar, your academic dean or associate dean, the dean of students, and others in a position to help you. Then follow through on their advice.

Consider Cooperative Education Jobs If Your Institution Offers This Program

Cooperative education is a program in which academic course work is alternated with paid full-time employment arranged by the college or university. Most students at these schools have the option of being in the cooperative education program or attending college full time.

Even if money is no object, cooperative education can provide vital job experience and strengthen your resume. This may result in better job offers after you finish school. At my university, one-third of the students are offered permanent employment by their cooperative education employers on graduation. Like other kinds of temporary jobs, these positions can help you discover a career interest that will give you satisfaction and success throughout your life. They can also help you eliminate career fields you find don't find really interest you after all.

Consider Marketing Your Skills or Starting Your Own Business

Babysitting, or even house sitting, can provide income. People may even want a sitter to wait for the washing repair person or automobile mechanic. These jobs usually allow you to hit two targets with one shot—make money while studying. (Some security jobs have the same advantage, but use your judgment in avoiding positions that may be dangerous.)

If you have mechanical skills, you can advertise yourself as a "fix-it" person who can do simple repairs around the house or fix bikes or whatever. Some students manage to establish quite profitable businesses while in school. Use your imagination and think creatively. You may be able to develop a source of income that will complement your career development.

Practice Your Skills at Applying for Jobs and Interviewing When You Apply for a Position

Present yourself well when you apply for the job. Look neat, be courteous, and submit a good resume if one is required (consult one of the books in the Bibliography for advice on resume writing; any good book store has effective books on getting a job, as does the library). BESIDES IMPROVING YOUR CHANCES OF GETTING THE JOB, YOU'RE GAINING VALUABLE EXPERIENCE IN AN IMPORTANT CAREER SKILL THAT WILL BENEFIT YOU IN LATER YEARS. Be sure to follow these steps:

1. Do a little homework. Find out as much about the organization and its business as you can before the interview. This will make you look good and help make the interview more useful for both you and the employer.
2. Practice the interview beforehand. Imagine the questions being asked and practice answering them. Visualize yourself as relaxed and poised. See yourself as answering questions effectively, without unduly rushing.
3. Be appropriately and neatly dressed.
4. Be courteous and businesslike. Don't sit down until asked.
5. Don't hesitate to inquire about details of the job. Diplomatically check out everything you need to know to ensure it's the kind of organization you want to work for.
6. Remember that you're ultimately in charge, so don't be intimidated or accept conditions inconsistent with your basic goals and values.
7. Take a notebook and pen so that you can write notes as appropriate. You will appear professional in doing so.
8. If you want the job, find out when you'll receive notification that you've been selected.
9. If you're offered the job but aren't sure you want it, thank the interviewer and ask for a deadline by which you must notify the employer of your decision.
10. Whatever the outcome of the interview, thank the interviewer as you leave.

11. The bottom line is to BE AS PROFESSIONAL AS POSSIBLE AT THE INTERVIEW AND ON THE JOB.

Develop Your People Skills and Political Savvy While on the Job

Many abilities help determine the degree of a person's career success. We've seen that one of the most important of these is political sensitivity and the capacity to work well with people.

Understanding who's influential; recognizing the reasons people are promoted; and following organizational protocol all determine the ability of people to get things done and make a good impression on their superiors. Of course you must think and evaluate independently and not simply go along with something just because you're told to do it. You wouldn't follow a directive that meant breaking the law. Sometimes you have to stand up to authority or to competitors, but knowing when and how to fight your organizational battles is vital. Making needless enemies isn't smart.

While employed in your part-time job, keep your eyes and ears open. Observe how the system works. Practice dealing with people in a professional way. The more knowledgeable and effective you become in these areas the more career success you're likely to see.

INTERNSHIPS

Internships are training positions of a specific duration, say for a semester or for three months during the summer. Although salaries are sometimes paid to interns, these positions are frequently voluntary with no pay. Typically these jobs are with government or nonprofit institutions. Many of my own students have worked at the state legislature, federal, state, and local government agencies and even on political campaigns. Your school may have a specific office that handles internships. Some academic programs such as public administration and nursing will probably manage their own internship programs.

The value of an internship depends on your goals and the nature of the specific internship position. You should weigh the benefits and costs of an internship against your academic and career goals. A student who wants to get into politics is obviously well advised to work in political campaigns and in the offices of elected officials. Many internships provide valuable experience that future employers will recognize. Internships listed on your resume help document that you have practical experience.

The key to a successful internship experience is to investigate the position as carefully as possible before you apply. Ask the internship director at your school about the job. Determine if it's routinely evaluated by a faculty member or administrator. Where positions are not evaluated, call or visit the organization and ask to speak with one of the interns. You may also be able to speak with the internship manager there. The following questions are basic.

What kinds of tasks would you perform? Be on the lookout for "GOPHER" jobs, where you just run meaningless errands, being asked to "go for" supplies or coffee. These are positions you'll usually want to avoid, though some errand running may be acceptable.

What are the working conditions? Look for interaction with officials, integration of students into significant activities, and interesting work that will provide useful experience. You shouldn't expect to be making major government policy decisions. If the job is directly related to your chosen career, the contacts you make and the familiarity with the working environment may still make the experience worthwhile, even if the actual work often seems menial. Students are sometimes exploited on these jobs, so investigation is essential.

You can often earn academic credit for internships. In these cases a faculty member works with the organizations offering the internships to ensure that the job and service are worthy of academic credit. Sometimes students will have to write papers or complete other projects to be graded by faculty members. Depending on your career direction and the nature of the internship position, internships may be a useful part of your education.

SUMMARY

Financial worries are one of the most common concerns college students face. But you can do several things to ease the burden. Consulting with the Financial Aid Office and completing all necessary applications on time are essential. If you don't know whether you're qualified, be sure to check with a counselor in the Financial Aid Office.

Many students are already in full-time jobs, and the majority work part-time or in summers. Relating work to goals and allowing sufficient time for your studies is an important part of college success. Choosing jobs and internships carefully as well as doing good work will pay off in many ways.

Financial planning and money management are two of the most important ways to minimize financial stress. The Success Steps at the end of this chapter can be of great benefit in starting this process, which may be less difficult than you might think. You'll help get a grip on your finances and at the same time encourage habits that will serve you well all your life.

SUCCESS STEPS

STEP ONE: Establishing a Baseline

Rate yourself on the following questions. Give yourself 1 to 5 points for each question; the more positive your response, the higher the number you should assign (1 = strongly disagree, 5 = strongly agree). If the question doesn't apply to you, write "N.A." for not applicable. Remember that the purpose of the exercise is to help you set new goals and measure your progress as you proceed through college. There are no passing or failing grades.

Establishing a Plan for Financial Aid

1. Have I filled out the necessary forms (e.g., FAF) available at the Financial Aid Office? Do I know the deadline for filing these forms, and have I allowed sufficient lead time to get the necessary information from my own, my spouse's, or

   my parent's records?_____

2. If I'm a part-time student with a full-time job, have I determined whether my employer has a policy of providing assistance for my college education?

   _____

3. Have I met with a counselor in the Financial Aid Office to set up a plan for

   financial aid for next year?_____

4. If not, have I set up an appointment with a counselor to discuss financial aid for

   next year?_____

5. Have I set dates for filling out forms and submitting applications for the aid

   programs designated by my plan?_____

6. Have I considered the various GRANT programs for which I may be eligible such as special programs for veterans, minority students, and others?

   _____

7. If I'm so pressed that I just can't pay my college bills, have I talked it over with

   a counselor in the financial aid office and the bursar?_____

8. If stress is becoming an obstacle to my performance, am I dealing with stress as discussed in Chapter 7, pp. 195–196. (The Counseling Center can provide assistance in the case of severe stress.) _____

Making and Implementing an Effective Job Strategy

1. If I'm a full-time student who must work during my freshman year, do I avoid working unnecessarily long hours or under conditions that undermine my ability to study?_____

2. If I'm attending part-time and have a full-time job, have I considered the possibility of finding another position that will benefit me financially and better serve my career goals?_____

3. Especially if I'm a mid-career student or will soon graduate, have I considered taking a short-course in personal financial management and begun to investigate available books?_____

4. If a full-time student, have I linked my need for a job to academic and career goals rather than the desire for more spending money?_____

5. If I need a job, have I mounted an effective job search, including consulting with the Financial Aid Office?_____

6. Have I considered my capacity to do the job?_____

7. Have I ruled out unnecessarily dangerous or ethically questionable positions?

    _____

8. Have I considered the long-term career implications of choosing the right job and performing it in a responsible and effective way? (These are possible promotions, resume entries, letters of recommendation, recruitment by employers impressed with my performance, developing winning work habits.)

    _____

9. Have I considered the career benefits of internships or cooperative education and weighed these benefits against my academic and career goals, coming up with a decision that's right for me?_____

10. Am I using the job application and interview process as a training ground for my future career development activities?_____

11. While on the job am I trying to develop my people skills and political savvy about how the organization works and how to influence people positively?

_____

Developing and Implementing a Money Management System

1. Have I made effective money management an important goal that I really work at? Do I remind myself that this will help me develop skills that contribute significantly to my personal success in life?_____

2. Do I know where my money goes? Do I write down the things I spend money on so that I can avoid frittering it away on trivia or things unconnected with my goals?_____

3. Do I have a budget that I use to determine how I spend my money (with a reasonable amount allowed for discretionary spending so that I don't lose motivation to stay within my budget)?_____

4. Do I use all my financial resources effectively, especially the Financial Aid Office?_____

Qualitative Measures of Success

After beginning to implement the financial management steps in this chapter, wait one week and answer the following questions using the same scale as above.

1. Do I feel that I'm beginning to get a grip on my finances?_____

2. Has my implementation of financial planning and money management made me feel more in control of my life?_____

3. Is my thinking about money positive? Do I consider all of my financial advantages such as access to medical care and adequate food, and the chance to get a college education that will benefit me financially and in many other ways as well?_____

4. Am I beginning to realize that there are many ways I can improve my financial

    situation?_____

5. Am I philosophical about money problems, recognizing that it's often part of
    the territory of being a student? Do I feel that learning to handle money is an

    opportunity to develop a useful skill?_____

6. Can I think positively about grants and loans? Do I avoid the mistake of turning

    myself down?_____

7. Do I take increasing pride in my growing ability to handle money, without set-

    ting unrealistic expectations?_____

STEP TWO: Finding Where Your Money Goes

Over a five-day period write down everything you spend money on: purchases, phone calls, anything. Use the space below or write directly onto your action list or weekly schedule if there is room.

At the end of each day circle items that you decide are unnecessary or for which less expensive substitutes are readily available. This Success Step is merely to help you set new goals. Remember that it can be counterproductive not to include some allowance for pleasure and recreation.

DAY 1	DAY 2	DAY 3	DAY 4	DAY 5

TOTALS

STEP THREE: Setting New Goals

Based on your answers to the above Success Steps, establish measureable, specific goals to help you manage your money and overcome or minimize financial problems. Begin working on these goals during the next week. Post or keep these pages where they will serve as a continual reminder.

Goal 1. _____

_____

_____

Action I will take to achieve this goal _____

_____

_____

How I will measure achievement of this goal _____

_____

_____

Goal 2. _____

_____

_____

Action I will take to achieve this goal _____

_____

_____

How I will measure achievement of this goal _____

_____

_____

Goal 3. _____

_____

_____

Action I will take to achieve this goal _____

_____

_____

How I will measure achievement of this goal _____

_____

_____

Goal 4. _____

_____

_____

Action I will take to achieve this goal_____

_____

_____

How I will measure achievement of this goal _____

_____

_____

Goal 5. _____

_____

_____

Action I will take to achieve this goal _____

_____

_____

How I will measure achievement of this goal _____

_____

_____

STEP FOUR: Creating a Weekly or Monthly Budget

A budget is the most important financial planning tool available to most students. A monthly budget is more efficient from the standpoint of planning time, but a weekly budget may at first enable you to more quickly make progress in managing your finances effectively.

The following form is one of many useful ways to construct a budget. To simplify the process, it is identical to the semester budget format presented on p. 284. Allow some money for recreation and pleasure or you'll feel so restrained that you might ignore your budget guidelines. The idea is to THINK critically and creatively about ways to save money on the expenditure side and increase available money on the income side.

Creating a budget is essentially a decision-making process that helps you to make more rational decisions about where you spend your money and maximize the benefit of available income. Don't be too rigid, and keep it simple so you're more likely to stick to it. Refer to your answers in the above Success Steps as well as the semester budget on p. 284 as you develop this budget.

Remember to go over each expense and ask yourself two questions: (1) Do I really need this? (But don't cut out everything for entertainment and pleasure.) (2) Is there a less expensive alternative (for transportation, living quarters, etc.)? Next, prioritize your expenses, using a numbering system to rank items if you find this helpful. On the income side of the equation, ask yourself how you can supplement your income without sacrificing your academic and important personal goals.

If your total income is less than your total expenses, review your expense and income lists to make necessary cuts, reductions, postponements, or to add new income sources, keeping in mind your academic and other goals.

WEEKLY OR MONTHLY BUDGET

INCOME

EXPENSES

Grants/scholarships _____

Rent, room fee or mortgage _____

Loans _____

Food _____

Salary _____

Tuition _____

Money from parents or spouse _____

Books, supplies, college fees _____

Refunds _____

Transportation _____

Sale of items no longer needed _____

Clothes _____

Own business or services _____

Entertainment _____

Other _____

Personal items _____

_____

Charitable contributions _____

_____

Insurance _____

_____

Telephone _____

_____

Child care _____

Medical _____

Gifts _____

Other _____

_____

TOTAL INCOME _____

TOTAL EXPENSES _____

Chapter
11

Putting It All Together: The Winning Edge

*T*his book has provided you with many top-notch techniques for maximizing your success in college. Adapting these methods to your own individual needs and using them regularly can give you a decisive winning edge in meeting the challenges of college successfully. Whether you're a full-time or part-time student, whether you're continuing right out of high school or returning in mid-career, whether you're attending a two-year community college or a four-year institution, the consistent application of these techniques will make your education a far more successful and enjoyable process.

One of the underlying themes of this book has been the importance of attitude. Applying the various learning and study methods presented here will go a long way toward building self-confidence and motivation. But most of us need sometimes to work consciously on our attitude, and a number of steps have been suggested for developing a perspective that supports the effort to succeed academically. The attitudes and predispositions discussed throughout this book can be summarized by the term "character."

THE CENTRAL ROLE OF CHARACTER

Character refers to the manner in which a person typically reacts to the stresses and crises of life. It's character more than anything else that determines success in college and in life. A person of character typically reacts to problems and obstacles

305

with determination, tempered by ethical values. Character enables us to succeed in the face of fear, frustration, and temptation. It encourages us to consider the needs of others and hold values beyond ourselves. It contributes to a healthy self-respect and makes us patient with ourselves as we work toward our goals and live our lives. The following character traits are particularly important for success in college: courage, industriousness, persistence, ethical sensitivity, concern for others as well as things beyond ourselves, and patience.

Courage

Courage is simply the desire and ability to stand up to fear. Of course fear can be a useful emotion that alerts us to real danger. But most of us are sometimes afraid of things that could benefit us. To a significant degree courage can be developed by recognizing when fear is holding us back and deciding to stand up to it.

We can turn fear on its head and use it as a source of constructive motivation. ("If I'm worried about next month's exam, I'd better keep up with my assignments. And I'd better make room for an hour review session each week.") Often just acting as if we were already courageous will do the trick, and it gets easier with practice. Deciding to face that tough chemistry assignment and meet other challenges head on not only assists us in completing the work; it helps build an attribute of character that can dramatically increase our level of success.

Industriousness

Success in college requires effort. You've got to be willing to do the work. This doesn't necessitate that you be a slave to your studies, but it does mean that you recognize the importance of working toward your goals. You must see yourself as being in college for more than just a good time (though pleasure is also an important part of college success).

We've seen many techniques for encouraging ourselves to work. Time management strategies, good study location, working with friends, using rewards, and focusing on the immediate task at hand are among the many ways of helping ourselves do the necessary work. We free ourselves of much uncertainty and indecisiveness when we believe that work is a necessary part of successful living, that it adds to the richness and enjoyment of life, and that we are fully capable of doing it well. Developing the habit of doing necessary work is one of the easiest ways to help guarantee our success.

Persistence

Persistence refers to our willingness to keep trying despite real obstacles and despite our own mistakes and imperfections. In college and in life we face obstacles and problems all the time. Courses may be closed, books may be unavailable, and assignments may seem long and difficult. Knowing that there's a way over, or sometimes around, virtually every obstacle helps us keep at it. The trick is to stay positive about ourselves and stick with it until we overcome the difficulty, using our critical and creative thinking ability to help us solve the problem.

We need to be flexible and willing to change goals sometimes, but we also need the determination not to quit. Like courage, persistence can become a habit by recognizing its central role in determining our success and using the techniques in this book that help us keep at our goals. Time management, action, using college resources, and the systematic, regular use of thinking and study skills help us stick to the task at hand.

Ethical Sensitivity

We've seen that sensitivity to questions of quality, right and wrong, as well as good and bad are a crucial part of effective thinking that helps us in our studies, writing, exams, career decisions, and personal lives. It aids us to see the significance of events and evaluate things for ourselves. Ethical sensitivity is a core part of being able to think for ourselves.

In their personal lives, truly successful people recognize that getting to the top by any means, whether in college or on the job, is an unacceptable compromise. So they achieve their goals within the context of broader values. They recognize that this gives them greater self-confidence and self-esteem, which provides them with a powerful source of motivation and achievement.

Ethical sensitivity makes us better decision-makers. It can greatly reduce trouble in our lives, make us feel more positive about ourselves, and provide a strong underpinning to academic and career success. Applying the techniques of thinking and studying discussed in this book is one way of refining our ethical sensitivity and thus our ability to think effectively.

Concern for Others and for Ideals Beyond Ourselves

Successful students look beyond themselves. They concern themselves with the needs of others and take time to cultivate relationships with friends and family. We've seen that having the support of family, acquaintances, and friends is an important part of doing well in college. Concern for others makes it easier to establish and sustain these relationships.

Fulfilled people seek not merely to take from the world but also to give something back. Whatever form it may take in their lives, they know that trying to make a contribution and reaching out beyond themselves will greatly enrich their own existence. College courses can be an important means of helping us refine the ideals and values to which we orient our lives.

Patience

Students sometimes make the mistake of assuming that grades, getting a degree, or other external measures of success reflect their true worth. As we've seen, such attitudes create terrific pressure and are self-defeating.

Successful students try to be patient with themselves. They don't run themselves down when they fail to measure up, but rather have faith in themselves and their long-term progress. They recognize that successful achievement of long-term goals requires a long-range perspective.

They try to become comfortable with themselves, attempting to modify any self-destructive behavior while accepting personal imperfections that cannot be changed. They recognize that nobody is perfect and that they don't have to be first in their class or most-popular-person-on-campus to be fully worthwhile human beings. Often the greatest accomplishments are achieved by those who seem for the moment not to be members of some abstract and arbitrary elite group.

Effective students see that most successful accomplishments are achieved in little bits, so they concentrate on the task at hand rather than creating a mountain of responsibility in their minds. They're not afraid to set realistic high goals for themselves, but they keep their perspective, recognizing that success is as much a process as an outcome. And they never give up on themselves.

THE IMPORTANCE OF FEELING AND EMOTION

If we used only our will power and our thinking ability, we'd be robots, not human beings. We've seen the importance of emotions and feelings in motivation, evaluation, studying, writing, choosing a major and a career, and every facet of college life. It is feeling and emotion, enriched and restrained by critical thinking and evaluation that provide the underpinning to human achievement. They contribute to our moral sensitivity. But they serve us best when subjected to critical thinking.

THE POWER OF GOOD THINKING

Our ability to think is also basic to our humanity. We've seen that developing thinking skills is a key that can unlock academic potential and make you far more successful in your career. It may be the most important thing you get out of college. Learning to think effectively is far easier than most students suppose. Developing this capacity is relatively straightforward, and requires at the outset habitually asking a few basic questions, being open-minded, trying to evaluate for yourself, and encouraging your creative potential.

Thinking about your subjects makes it easier to understand and remember. Trying to think makes learning much less tedious and a lot more interesting. The decision to apply the basic thinking techniques discussed in Chapter 4 is one of the most important things you can do to give yourself a decisive winning edge. As subsequent chapters demonstrated, thinking is basic to effective study, success on exams, and good writing.

THE IMPORTANCE OF LEISURE AND RECREATION

Truly successful students enjoy life and have fun. They work hard toward their goals, but they see life as a process rather than as an outcome, so they don't put off happiness until they get their degree or become established in their careers. Sure,

SUCCESS IN COLLEGE AND BEYOND

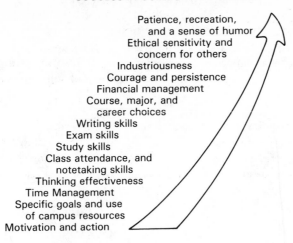

Patience, recreation,
and a sense of humor
Ethical sensitivity and
concern for others
Industriousness
Courage and persistence
Financial management
Course, major, and
career choices
Writing skills
Exam skills
Study skills
Class attendance, and
notetaking skills
Thinking effectiveness
Time Management
Specific goals and use
of campus resources
Motivation and action

Figure 11.1 The winning edge.

it's necessary to defer some pleasure in order to achieve anything worthwhile, but it's still important try to get pleasure from life as we go along.

A sense of humor can ease stress and help release creative ideas. Attending plays, concerts, and other college-sponsored events is fun, contributes to your cultural education, and can help you to meet people, develop valuable skills, and contribute to your career success. However busy you may be, building leisure and recreation into your schedule is an essential part of performing well in college.

Some of the basic principles of this book and this concluding chapter are presented in Figure 11.1. They're shown in the order discussed in the book, though they should be seen as an integrated whole that can help immeasurably in your efforts to be successful in college.

You will find books for additional reading listed in the Selected Bibliography beginning on p. 329. Books especially recommended for reading and purchase have asterisks beside them. Many are available in paperback editions or can be obtained through your library.

CONCLUDING THOUGHTS

I'm really interested in how you apply the principles in this book, and your suggestions for revised editions would be greatly appreciated. You can write to me care of Northeastern University, Boston, MA 02115. If you're ever in the area, stop by to say hello. Because I use the time management and study strategies discussed in the book, please call first (617) 437-2796 just to make sure that I'm not someplace else doing research, writing, or relaxing. I always try to keep my conference hours and appointments, and our secretary will be glad to set up a convenient time. It would be a pleasure to meet you.

THIS BOOK CAN HELP YOU THROUGHOUT YOUR COLLEGE CA-
REER, SO KEEP IT HANDY IN THE YEARS AHEAD. It should have a prominent place in your personal library. Pick it up and browse through it occasionally. If
you have a problem with procrastination, are worried about an upcoming exam, are
beginning to work on a term paper or whatever, turn to the appropriate pages to
find winning techniques and to help regenerate the hope and self-confidence that
lie within you.

You have more potential than you may ever have realized. Your unique combination of experience, abilities, and personality is exactly matched by no one else
on earth. Whatever your circumstances, the techniques discussed in this book can
greatly improve your performance and the pleasure you get out of college. Adapting
these ideas to your own needs and circumstances can pay great dividends in college
and in your career.

So hang in there.

And enjoy.

Appendix
A

Building a Better Vocabulary by Learning Prefixes and Suffixes

You can often figure out the meaning of words from the context of the sentence and paragraph in which they occur. Looking up words you don't know when you come across them is also important. Be sure to write down the meaning on a 3 x 5 card, and try to use the word several times over several days until it's fixed in your memory.

One of the best ways to build your vocabulary rapidly is through learning the prefixes and suffixes of words. Become familiar with these words segments by spending ten minutes each day with this list until you're comfortable with them. (*Source:* Excerpts from *Reference Guide to English: A Handbook of English as a Second Language* by Alice Maclin, copyright 1981 by Holt, Rinehart and Winston, Inc., pp. 378–83, reprinted by permission of the publisher.)

PREFIXES

Prefixes are one- or two-syllable additions at the beginning of a word that change its meaning but do not change its part of speech. In this list nouns are indicated by an article in front of them, *a* or *an* for a countable noun and *the* for an uncountable noun. Verbs are indicated by *to*. All other words in the list are adjectives.

311

Today most prefixes are not followed by a hyphen, but always look in a dictionary if you are not sure whether to use one or not.

Notice the large number of prefixes that are negative: *a-, counter-, dis-, in-, non-,* and *un-.* Different negative forms on the same base word can have different connotations and meanings.

Prefix	Meaning	Example
a-	not	*a*moral
		an *a*theist
ante-	before	to *ante*date
anti-	against	an *anti*body
		the *anti*freeze
arch-	highest	an *arch*bishop
auto-	self	an *auto*biography
bi-	two	a *bi*cycle
		to *bi*sect
		a *bi*centennial
co-	with	to *co*ordinate
		a *co*pilot
counter-	against,	*counter*clockwise
	opposite to	a *counter*revolution
de-	reverse action	to *de*frost
dis-	not	*dis*loyal
	reverse action	to *dis*connect
ex-	former	an *ex*-president
	out of	an *ex*patriate
exo-	outside	an *exo*-skeleton
fore-	before	to *fore*tell
hyper-	too much	*hyper*sensitive
in- (il-, im-, ir-,)	not	*in*sensitive
		*il*logical
		*im*moral
		*ir*religious
inter-	between, among	*inter*national
mal-	bad, badly	*mal*formed
maxi-	most, large	a *maxi*skirt
mini-	least, small	a *mini*skirt
mis-	wrong, wrongly	a *mis*print
		to *mis*print
mono-	one	a *mono*rail
multi-	many	*multi*racial
neo-	new, revived	*neo*colonialism
non-	not, without	*non*stop
out-	to do something to	to *out*do
	a greater degree	
	away from	an *out*patient

Prefix	Meaning	Example
over-	too much	to *over*eat
	above	an *over*pass
para-	alongside	a *para*phrase
	resembling	
post-	after	*post*war
pre-	before	*pre*war
pro-	on the side of,	*pro*-communist
	in favor of	
proto-	first, original	a *proto*type
pseudo-	false, imitation	*pseudo*-classic
quad-	four	a *quad*rangle
re-	again, renew	to *re*start
semi-	half, partly	*semi*private
		a *semi*circle
sub-	beneath, less,	a *sub*way
	lower than	*sub*normal
trans-	from one place to	to *trans*port
	another, across	*trans*atlantic
tri-	three	a *tri*cycle
ultra-	extremely, beyond	*ultra*nationalism
		*ultra*sonic
un-	reverse action	to *un*cover
	not	*un*broken
under-	too little	to *under*expose
uni-	one	(a) *uni*form
vice-	deputy, one who	a *vice*-president
	acts in place of	

Note: A few prefixes change their spelling before roots beginning with certain consonants. An example of a prefix that does this in the table above is *in,* which becomes *il-* before a root beginning with *l, im-* before a root beginning with *m,* and *ir-* before a root beginning with *r.*

SUFFIXES

A suffix is an ending added to a word, which usually changes the part of speech of the word and may also change the meaning of the word. Look up forms that are new to you in a dictionary, as not all suffixes can be added to all words. In some cases, more than one suffix can be added to the same word: nation, nation*al,* nation*ality,* nation*alism.*

The endings *-s* and *-ed* on regular verbs and *-s* and *-es* on nouns do not change the part of speech.

Adjectives

The following suffixes change other words into adjectives.

Suffix	Meaning	Example
-able, -ible	able to be, having the quality of	teach, teach*able* reduce, reduc*ible*
-al	having the quality of, related to	nation, nation*al* person, person*al*
-ant	having the quality to	tolerate, toler*ant* dominate, domin*ant*
-arian	having the quality of	authority, authorit*arian*
-ative	connected with	argument, argumen*tative*
-ed	adjective form of nouns and verbs (see Participles)	wall, wall*ed* please, pleas*ed*
-ese	showing national origin	Lebanon, Leban*ese* China, Chin*ese*
-esque	in the style of	picture, pictur*esque* Roman, Roman*esque*
-ful	having, full of	meaning, meaning*ful* thank, thank*ful*
-ic	having the quality of	democracy, democra*tic*
-ical	having the quality of	theory, theore*tical*
-ish	belonging to (national origin)	Swede, Swed*ish* Ireland, Ir*ish*
-ish	somewhat, approximately	red, redd*ish* young, young*ish*
-ive	having the quality of	explode, explo*sive* collect, collec*tive*
-less	without, lacking in	child, child*less*
-like	having the quality of	child, child*like*
-ous, -eous, -ious	having the quality of	virtue, virtu*ous* courtesy, court*eous* ambition, ambit*ious*
-some	full of	burden, burden*some* bother, bother*some*
-worthy	deserving	praise, praise*worthy*
-y	full of, covered with, having the quality of	hair, hair*y* sand, sand*y* brain, brain*y*

Nouns

The following suffixes change other words into nouns.

NOUNS REFERRING TO PEOPLE

Suffix	Meaning	Example
-an	member of, belonging to, favoring	Atlanta, Atlant*an* republic, republic*an*

NOUNS REFERRING TO PEOPLE

Suffix	Meaning	Example
-ant, -ent	agent, a person who does, makes	inhabit, inhabit*ant* correspond, correspond*ent*
-arian	belonging to a group, favoring	vegetables, veget*arian* authority, authorit*arian*
-crat	a person connected with	democracy, demo*crat* bureaucracy, bureau*crat*
-ee	variation of -*er*, a person	absent, absent*ee* employ, employ*ee*
-eer	a person who does, makes, operates	auction, auction*eer* engine, engin*eer*
-er	a person who does, makes	bake, bak*er* dream, dream*er*
-ese	national origin	Portugal, Portugu*ese* China, Chin*ese*
-ess	feminine form	waiter, waitr*ess*
-ian	connected with	Paris, Paris*ian*
-ite	member of a group	social, social*ite*
-let	small, unimportant	star, star*let*
-ling	unimportant (derogatory)	weak, weak*ling*
-or	variation of -*er*, a person who . . .	survive, surviv*or*
-ster	a person making or doing something, a member of	trick, trick*ster* gang, gang*ster*
-y	familiar form (usually used in family, with children)	dad, dad*dy* Bill, Bil*ly*

IMPERSONAL NOUNS

Suffix	Meaning	Example
-age	extent, amount	drain, drain*age* sink, sink*age*
-ant	agent, personal or impersonal: the thing that . . . the person who . . .	lubricate, lubric*ant* inform, inform*ant*
-ation, -ition	institution, condition of being done	organize, organiz*ation* educate, educ*ation* nourish, nutr*ition* note, not*ation*
-er	agent, the thing that . . . , something having	silence, silenc*er* two wheels, two-wheel*er*
-ery	place of activity	refine, refin*ery* surgeon, surg*ery*

IMPERSONAL NOUNS

Suffix	Meaning	Example
-ery	collective, uncountable	machine, machin*ery*
		baskets, basket*ry*
-ette	small, compact	kitchen, kitchen*ette*
		room, room*ette*
	imitation	leather, leather*ette*
-ful	the amount contained	mouth, mouth*ful*
		cup, cup*ful*
-ing	turns countable nouns into	pipe, pip*ing*
	uncountable nouns	wire, wir*ing*
	indicating material	panel, panell*ing*
	activity from action of the verb	walk, walk*ing*
-let	small, unimportant	pig, pig*let*
-or	thing that . . .	conduct, conduct*or*
-y (sometimes -ie)	familiar	nightgown, night*ie*
		dog, dog*gy*
		bird, bird*ie*

ABSTRACT NOUNS

Suffix	Meaning	Example
-age	act of, extent	marry, marri*age*
		cover, cover*age*
		shrink, shrink*age*
-ance, -ence	activity, condition	guide, guid*ance*
		attend, attend*ance*
		independent, independ*ence*
-ancy, -ency	activity, condition of being	constant, const*ancy*
-ation	state of doing something	dominate, domin*ation*
		communicate, communic*ation*
-ery	domain, condition	brave, brav*ery*
		slave, slav*ery*
-hood	status	false, false*hood*
		mother, mother*hood*
-ion	act of doing something	confess, confess*ion*
-ism	doctrine, belief, condition	commun*ism*, absentee*ism*
-ity	state, quality	complex, complex*ity*
		curious, curios*ity*
		sane, san*ity*

Appendix
B

Reading Selections: Applying the Remarkable Square Tree Method

Here's a quick review of the Remarkable Square Tree method of study:

1. Repeat (a brief review and rethinking of the previous lesson).
2. Scan (looking over the material to get an idea of the contents and organization).
3. Question (setting questions in your mind, including thinking questions, such as how, why, what's the significance, comparison, etc.).
4. Read.
5. Think (including criticisms, creative ideas, comparisons, evaluations, etc.).
6. Reinforce (to help lock the material in memory; also to remind you to reward yourself in some way as you study).

The following brief selections are from introductory textbooks in logic, geology, and sociology. They'll give you a practice run with the Remarkable Square Tree method. You won't be able to apply the Repeat step in the first reading. Instead, wait until after you've done all three selections, then go back and apply the Repeat technique.

After completing all three sections, list three ways you could make your use of the Remarkable Square Tree method more efficient and effective when you apply it to your textbooks.

1. _____

   _____

2. _____

   _____

3. _____

   _____

READING SELECTION ONE

This selection has no subheadings. For the Scan step simply skim the material to get an idea of what's in the text. As you do this, formulate questions. At the Reinforce step write notes as explained on pp. 161–184. Both the outline method and visual organizers (e.g., a tree, star, or chart) are suitable. You might wish, for example, to chart the similarities and differences between psychology and the study of logic.

What Is Logic?*

Logic is the study of the methods and principles used to distinguish good (correct) from bad (incorrect) reasoning. This definition must not be taken to imply that only the student of logic can reason well or correctly. To say so would be as mistaken as to say that to run well requires studying the physics and physiology involved in that activity. Some excellent athletes are quite ignorant of the complex processes that go on inside their bodies when they perform. And, needless to say, the somewhat elderly professors who know most about such things would perform very poorly were they to risk their dignity on the athletic field. Even given the same basic muscular and nervous apparatus, the person who knows might not surpass the "natural athlete."

But given the same native intelligence, a person who has studied logic is more likely to reason correctly than is one who has never thought about the general principles involved in that activity. There are several reasons for this. First, the proper study of logic will approach it as an art as well as a science, and the student will do exercises in all parts of the theory being learned. Here, as anywhere else, practice will help to make perfect. Second, a tradi-

---

*Reprinted with permission of Macmillan Publishing Company from *Introduction to Logic*, 8th ed., by Irving M. Copi and Carl Cohen, pp. 3–5. Copyright © 1987 by Macmillan Publishing Company.

tional part of the study of logic has been the examination and analysis of fallacies, which are common and often quite "natural" mistakes in reasoning. Not only does this part of the subject give increased insight into the principles of reasoning in general, but an acquaintance with these pitfalls helps to keep us from stumbling into them. Finally, the study of logic will give students techniques and methods for testing the correctness of many different kinds of reasoning, including their own; and when errors are easily detected, they are less likely to be allowed to stand.

We are often moved by appeals to emotion. But an appeal to reason can be tested and appraised by criteria that define correct argument. If these criteria are not known, then they cannot be employed. It is the purpose of logic to discover and make available those criteria that can be used to test arguments for correctness.

Logic has frequently been defined as the science of the laws of thought. But this definition, although it gives a clue to the nature of logic, is not accurate. In the first place, thinking is studied by psychologists. Logic cannot be "the" science of the laws of thought, because psychology is also a science that deals with laws of thought (among other things). And logic is not a branch of psychology; it is a separate and distinct field of study.

In the second place, if "thought" refers to *any* process that occurs in people's minds, not all thought is an object of study for the logician. All reasoning is thinking, but not all thinking is reasoning. Thus one may "think" of a number between one and ten, as in a parlor game, without doing any "reasoning" about it. There are many mental processes or kinds of thought that are different from reasoning. One may remember something, or imagine it, or regret it, without doing any reasoning about it. Or one may let one's thoughts "drift along" in a daydream or reverie, building castles in the air or following what psychologists call free association, in which one image is replaced by another in an order that is anything but logical. There is often great significance to the sequence of thoughts in such free association, and some psychiatric techniques make use of it. One need not be a psychiatrist, of course, to gain insight into people's characters by observing the flow of their streams of consciousness. It is the basis of a very effective literary technique pioneered by James Joyce in his novel *Ulysses*. Conversely, if a person's character is sufficiently well known beforehand, the flow of that person's stream of consciousness can be traced or even anticipated. We all remember how Sherlock Holmes used to break in on his friend Watson's silences, to answer the very question to which Dr. Watson had been "led" in his musings. There seem to be certain laws governing reverie, but they are studied by psychologists rather than by logicians. The laws that describe the movements of the mind in reverie are psychological laws rather than logical principles. To define "logic" as the science of the laws of thought is to make it include too much.

Another common definition of logic calls it the science of reasoning. This definition is better, but it still will not do. Reasoning is a special kind of thinking in which problems are solved, in which inference takes place, that is, in which conclusions are drawn from premises. It is still a kind of thinking, however, and therefore still part of the psychologist's subject matter. As psychologists examine the reasoning process, they find it to be extremely complex, highly emotional, consisting of awkward trial-and-error procedures illuminated by sudden—and sometimes apparently irrelevant—flashes of insight. These are all of importance to psychology.

The logician, however, is concerned primarily with the correctness of the completed process of reasoning. The logician asks: Does the problem get solved? Does the conclusion reached follow from the premises used or assumed? Do the premises provide good reasons for accepting the conclusion? If the problem gets solved, if the premises provide adequate grounds for affirming the conclusion, if asserting the premises to be true warrants asserting the conclusion to be true also, then the reasoning is correct. Otherwise, it is incorrect.

The distinction between correct and incorrect reasoning is the central problem with which logic deals. The logician's methods and techniques have been developed primarily for the purpose of making this distinction clear. The logician is interested in all reasoning, regardless of its subject matter, but only from this special point of view.

READING SELECTION TWO

The idea of continental drift is generally accepted today. The newer, more complete theory of plate tectonics is a major theory in the field of geology. At one time, the argument that continents had been joined together was not generally accepted. The following selection from a geology textbook traces the ideas of Alfred Wegener, who began discussing the idea of continental drift in 1912. This selection is useful not only as a practice reading in science but also because of Wegener's contribution as a creative thinker. Figures are not essential for comprehension so are not included.

As you read this selection, underline and write in the book as explained on pp. 159–163.

Continental Drift: An Idea Before Its Time*

The idea that continents, particularly South America and Africa, fit together like pieces of a jigsaw puzzle originated with improved world maps. However, little significance was given this idea until 1915, when Alfred Wegener,† a

---

*Reprinted with permission of Merrill, an imprint of Macmillan Publishing Company from *Earth Science*, 5th ed., by Edward J. Tarbuck and Frederick K. Lutgens, pp. 156–162. Copyright 1988 by Merrill Publishing.

†Wegener's ideas were actually preceded by those of an American geologist, F. B. Taylor, who in 1910 published a paper on continental drift. Taylor's paper provided little supporting evidence for

German climatologist and geophysicist, published an expanded version of a 1912 lecture in his book *The Origin of Continents and Oceans.* In this monograph, Wegener set forth the basic outline of his radical hypothesis of **continental drift.** One of his major tenets suggested that a supercontinent he called **Pangaea** (meaning "all land") once existed (Figure 6.1.) He further hypothesized that about 200 million years ago this supercontinent began breaking into smaller continents, which then "drifted" to their present positions. Wegener and others who advocated this position collected substantial evidence to support these claims. The fit of South America and Africa, ancient climatic similarities, fossil evidence, and rock structures all seemed to support the idea that these now-separate landmasses were once joined.

Fit of the Continents

Like a few others before him, Wegener first suspected that the continents might have been joined when he noticed the remarkable similarity between the coastlines on opposite sides of the South Atlantic. However, his use of present-day shorelines to make a fit of the continents was challenged immediately by other earth scientists. These opponents correctly argued that shorelines are continually modified by erosional processes and even if continental displacement had taken place, a good fit today would be unlikely. Wegener appeared to be aware of this problem, and, in fact, his original jigsaw fit of the continents was only very crude.

A much better approximation of the outer boundary of the continents is the seaward margin of the continental shelf. Today the continental shelf's edge lies several hundred meters below sea level. In the early 1960s, Sir Edward Bullard and two associates produced a map with the aid of computers that attempted to fit the continents at a depth of 900 meters. The remarkable fit that was obtained is shown in Figure 6.2 on page 158. Although the continents overlap in a few places, these are regions where streams have deposited large quantities of sediment, thus enlarging the continents. The overall fit obtained by Bullard and his associates was better than even the supporters of the continental drift theory suspected it would be.

Fossil Evidence

Although Wegener was intrigued by the remarkable similarities of the shorelines on opposite sides of the Atlantic, he at first thought the idea of a mobile earth improbable. Not until he came across an article citing fossil evidence for the existence of a land bridge connecting South America and Africa did he begin to take his own idea seriously. Through a search of the literature

---

continental drift, which may have been the reason that it had a relatively small impact on the geologic community.

Wegener learned that most paleontologists were in agreement that some type of land connection was needed to explain the existence of identical fossils on the widely separated landmasses.

To add credibility to his argument for the existence of the supercontinent of Pangaea, Wegener cited documented cases of several fossil organisms that had been found on different landmasses but which could not have crossed the vast oceans presently separating the continents. Of particular interest were organisms that were restricted in geographical distribution but which nevertheless appeared in two or more areas that are presently separated by major barriers. The classic example is *Mesosaurus*, a presumably aquatic, snaggle-toothed reptile whose fossil remains are known to be limited to eastern South America and southern Africa (Figure 6.3). If *Mesosaurus* had been able to swim well enough to cross a vast ocean, its remains should be widely distributed. Since this was not the case, Wegener argued that South America and Africa must have been joined.

Wegener also cited the distribution of the fossil fern *Glossopteris* as evidence for Pangaea's existence, because this plant was known to be widely dispersed among Africa, Australia, India, and South America during the late Paleozoic era. Later, fossil remains of *Glossopteris* were discovered in Antarctica as well. Wegener knew that these seed ferns and associated flora grew only in a subpolar climate; therefore, he concluded that these landmasses must have been joined, since they presently include climatic regions that are too diverse to support such flora. For Wegener, fossils proved without question that a supercontinent had existed.

How could these fossil flora and fauna be so similar in places separated by thousands of kilometers of open ocean? The idea of land bridges (isthmian links) was the most widely accepted solution to the problem of migration (Figure 6.4). We know for example that during the recent glacial period the lowering of sea level allowed animals to cross the narrow Bering Straits between Asia and North America. Was it possible then that land bridges once connected Africa and South America? We are now quite certain that land bridges of this magnitude did not exist, for their remnants should still lie below sea level, but are nowhere to be found.

Rock Type and Structural Similarities

Anyone who has worked a picture puzzle knows that in addition to the pieces fitting together, the picture must be continuous as well. The "picture" that must match in the "Continental Drift Puzzle" is represented by the rock types and mountain belts found on the continents. If the continents were once together, the rocks found in a particular region on one continent should closely match in age and type with those found in adjacent positions on the matching continent.

Such evidence has been found in the form of several mountain belts which appear to terminate at one coastline only to reappear on a landmass across the ocean. For instance, the mountain belt that includes the Appalachians trends northeastward through the eastern United States and disappears off the coast of Newfoundland. Mountains of comparable age and structure are found in Greenland and Northern Europe. When these landmasses are reassembled, the mountain chains form a nearly continuous belt.

Wegener was very satisfied that the similarities in rock structure on both sides of the Atlantic linked these landmasses. In fact, he was too zealous with this evidence and incorrectly suggested that glacial moraines in North America matched up with those of Northern Europe. In his own words, "It is just as if we were to refit the torn pieces of a newspaper by matching their edges and then check whether the lines of print run smoothly across. If they do, there is nothing left but to conclude that the pieces were in fact joined in this way."*

Paleoclimatic Evidence

Since Alfred Wegener was a climatologist by training, he was keenly interested in obtaining paleoclimatic (ancient climatic) data in support of continental drift. His efforts were rewarded when he found evidence for apparently dramatic climatic changes. For instance, glacial deposits indicate that near the end of the Paleozoic era (between 220 and 300 million years ago), ice sheets covered extensive areas of the Southern Hemisphere. Layers of glacial till were found in southern Africa and South America, as well as in India and Australia. Below these beds of glacial debris lay striated and grooved bedrock. In some locations the striations and grooves indicated the ice had moved from the sea onto land (Figure 6.5). Much of the land area containing evidence of this late Paleozoic glaciation presently lies within 30 degrees of the equator in a subtropical or tropical climate.

Could the earth have gone through a period sufficiently cold to have generated extensive continental glaciers in what is presently a tropical region? Wegener rejected this explanation because during the late Paleozoic, large swamps existed in the Northern Hemisphere. These swamps with their lush vegetation eventually became the major coal fields of the eastern United States, Europe, and Siberia.

Fossils from these coal fields indicate that the tree ferns which produced the coal deposits were indigenous to the tropics, because their fronds were large and their trunks lacked growth rings. Wegener believed that a better explanation for these paleoclimatic regimes is provided when the landmasses are fitted together as a supercontinent with South Africa centered over the South Pole. This would account for the conditions necessary to generate extensive expanses of glacial ice over much of the Southern Hemisphere. At the

---

*Alfred Wegener, *The Origin of Continents and Oceans*. Translated from the 4th revised German edition of 1929 by J. Birman (London: Methuen, 1966).

same time, this geography would place the northern landmasses nearer the tropics and account for their vast coal deposits. Wegener was so convinced that his explanation was correct that he wrote, "This evidence is so compelling that by comparison all other criteria must take a back seat."*

How does a glacier develop in hot, arid Australia. How do land animals migrate across wide expanses of open water? As compelling as this evidence may have been, fifty years passed before most of the scientific community would accept it and the logical conclusions to which it led.

The Great Debate

Wegener's proposal did not attract much open criticism until 1924 when his book was translated into English. From this time on, until his death in 1930, his drift hypothesis encountered a great deal of hostile criticism. To quote the respected American geologist R. T. Chamberlin, "Wegener's hypothesis in general is of the foot-loose type, in that it takes considerable liberty with our globe, and is less bound by restrictions or tied down by awkward, ugly facts than most of its rival theories. Its appeal seems to lie in the fact that it plays a game in which there are few restrictive rules and no sharply drawn code of conduct."

One of the main objections to Wegener's hypothesis stemmed from his inability to provide a mechanism for continental drift. Wegener proposed two possible energy sources for drift. One of these, the tidal influence of the moon, was presumed by Wegener to be strong enough to give the continents a westward motion. However, the prominent physicist Harold Jeffreys quickly countered with the argument that tidal friction of the magnitude needed to displace the continents would bring the earth's rotation to a halt in a matter of a few years. Further, Wegener proposed that the larger and sturdier continents broke through the oceanic crust, much like ice breakers cut through ice. However, no evidence existed to suggest that the ocean floor was weak enough to permit passage of the continents without themselves being appreciably deformed in the process. By 1929 criticisms of Wegener's ideas were pouring in from all areas of the scientific community. Despite these attacks, Wegener wrote the fourth and final edition of his book, maintaining his basic hypothesis and adding supporting evidence.

Although most of Wegener's contemporaries opposed his views, even to the point of openly ridiculing them, a few considered his ideas plausible. For these few geologists who continued the search, the concept of continents in motion evidently provided enough excitement to hold their interest. Others undoubtedly viewed continental drift as a solution to previously unexplainable observations.

------

*Ibid.

READING SELECTION THREE

Understanding how scholars think and do research is one of the best ways to develop your own thinking abilities. The following selection from an introductory sociology text will give you practice applying the Remarkable Square Tree method while at the same time providing additional ways to think more effectively.

As you read this selection, underline and write in the book as explained on pp. 159–163.

Doing Sociology: The Methods of Research*

Sociological research offers the challenge of going as a "stranger" into the familiar world, often to find one's assumptions shattered by the facts that one discovers. Research in sociology is really a form of detective work—it poses the same early puzzles and suspicions, the same moments of routine sifting through the evidence and inspired guessing, the same disappointments over false leads and facts that do not fit, and, perhaps, the same triumph when the pieces finally fall into place and an answer emerges. Research in sociology is where the real action takes place. It is in the field, far more than in the lecture room, that the sociologist comes to grips with the subject.

There are two sides to the sociological enterprise: theory and research. Both are essential, and each thrives on the other. Facts without theory are utterly meaningless, for they lack a framework in which they can be understood. Theories without facts are unproved speculations of little practical use, because there is no way to tell whether they are correct. Theory and research are thus parts of a constant cycle. A theory inspires research that can be used to verify or disprove it, and the findings of research are used to confirm, reject, or modify the theory, or even to provide the basis of new theories. The process recurs endlessly, and the accumulation of sociological knowledge is the result.

Guesswork, intuition, and common sense all have an important part to play in sociological research, but on their own they cannot produce reliable evidence: that requires a reliable research methodology. A **methodology** is a system of rules, principles, and procedures that guides scientific investigation. The sociologist is interested in discovering what happens in the social world and why it happens. Research methodology provides guidelines for collecting evidence about what takes place, for explaining why it takes place, and for doing so in such a way that the findings can be checked by other researchers. It is vital that the sociologist use appropriate methodology, for an invalid method can produce only flawed results.

Source: Ian Robertson, *Sociology.* 3rd ed. New York: Worth, 1987, pp. 29–31.

The methods of sociology can be applied only to questions that can be answered by reference to observable, verifiable facts. The sociologist cannot tell us if God exists, because there is no scientific way to test theories on the subject. But the sociologist can tell us what percentage of a population claims to believe in God, or what reasons they have for believing in God, because these facts can be established by using appropriate methods.

The Logic of Cause and Effect

To explain any aspect of society or social behavior, the sociologist must understand relationships of cause and effect. One basic assumption of science is that all events have causes—whether the event is a ball rolling down a hill, a nuclear bomb exploding, an economy improving, a political party losing support, or a student passing an examination. A second basic assumption is that under the identical circumstances, the same cause will repeatedly produce the same effect. If we did not make these assumptions, the world would be utterly unpredictable and therefore unintelligible to us. The problem facing the sociologist is to sort out cause from effect in the complexities of social life, and to determine which of several possible causes, or which combination of causes, is producing a particular effect.

Variables   Like all scientists, the sociologist analyzes cause and effect in terms of the influence of variables on one another. A **variable** is any characteristic that can change or differ—for example, from time to time, from place to place, or from one individual or group to another. Differences in age, sex, race, and social class are variables. So are the rates of homicide, divorce, and narcotics addiction. So are differences in intelligence, nationality, income, and sense of humor. Causation occurs when one variable, such as the quantity of alcohol a driver consumes, influences another variable, such as the likelihood of the driver being involved in a traffic accident. A theory simply attempts to generalize about the influence of one variable on another "Drunken driving contributes to traffic accidents." "Malnutrition causes children to perform poorly in schoolwork." Such statements serve to link variables in a cause-and-effect relationship.

An **independent variable** is one that influences another variable—in other words, it acts as a cause. A **dependent variable** is one that is influenced by another variable—in other words, it is affected. Thus, degree of drunkenness is one independent variable (though not necessarily the only one) that can produce the dependent variable of a traffic accident. Similarly, childhood nutrition is an independent variable (though, again, not necessarily the only one) that can affect the dependent variable of school performance.

Recurrent relationships among particular variables allow us to make generalizations about the links between them. Such a statement applies to the general category of variables that is being considered, not to any specific case within it. Thus, medical scientists can tell us the characteristics of the people most likely to suffer a heart attack at some time in their lives, but they cannot tell us precisely which individuals will be affected. In the same way, a sociologist can tell us about the general characteristics of the marriages most likely to end in divorce, but cannot predict the fate of specific marriages. All generalizations in science are statements of *probability*—not certainty—for the entire category of variables under consideration.

Correlations   Determining cause and effect, then, involves tracing the effect of variables upon one another. But how does the sociologist do this?

The basic method is to establish whether there is a **correlation**—that is, a relationship between variables that occurs regularly. By analyzing the statistics, the sociologist can easily establish whether there is a correlation between drunk driving and traffic accidents and between malnutrition and poor school performance. In both cases, the evidence shows that the correlation is very high. In fact, not only are drunk driving and traffic accidents closely associated, but the more alcohol drivers consume, the more likely they are to have traffic accidents. Similarly, malnutrition is associated with poor school performance, and the more malnourished children are, the worse their school performance is likely to be. This seems to prove the case. But does it?

Logically, no. The fact that two variables are highly correlated does not prove that one caused the other, or even that they are related in any way at all. Consider another example: in North America there is a high correlation between the sale of ice cream and the incidence of rape. The more ice cream that is sold, the more likely it is that rapes will occur. If a high correlation between two variables were sufficient to prove a causal connection, we would have to conclude that eating ice cream causes rape or, alternatively, that rape causes people to eat huge amounts of ice cream. Clearly, neither of these theories is acceptable, they fail to link the facts in a meaningful way. But what explains the correlation? A moment's thought suggests the answer, in the form of a third variable that influences the other two: the heat of summer. People eat more ice cream when it is hot than when it is cold. Rapes are far more likely to occur in the summer than in the winter, partly because people are more likely to venture out of their homes at night and partly because the nature of rape is such that the act is not easily performed outdoors in freezing weather. The rape–ice cream association exists, but it is a **spurious correlation**—one that is merely coincidental and does not imply any causal relationship whatever. Spurious correlations present a constant trap for the careless researcher.

Selected Bibliography

The primary purpose of this bibliography is to provide you with good sources for further reading. Although most of the entries deal with topics discussed in individual chapters, a few of the better general study skills books are included for your additional reference. I particularly recommend the volumes indicated by asterisks.

*Adams, James L. *Conceptual Blockbusting: A Guide to Better Ideas*. 2d ed. Reading, MA: Addison-Wesley, 1990.

American Psychological Association. *Publication Manual*. Washington, D.C.: American Psychological Association, 1983.

Barnet, Sylvan, and Marcia Stubbs. *Practical Guide to Writing*. Rev. ed. Boston: Little Brown, 1977.

Baron, Joan Boykoff and Robert J. Sternberg, eds. *Teaching Thinking Skills: Theory and Practice*. New York: W. H. Freeman, 1987.

Bartholomae, David, and Anthony Petrosky. *Facts, Artifacts, and Counterfacts: Theory and Method for a Reading and Writing Course*. Upper Montclair, NJ: Boynton/Cook, 1986.

Bartholomae, David, and Anthony Petrosky, eds. *Ways of Reading: An Anthology for Writers*. New York: St. Martin's, 1987.

Barzun, Jacques, and Henry F. Graff. *The Modern Researcher*. 3d ed. New York: Harcourt Brace Jovanovich, 1977.

Beck, R. *Motivation: Theories and Principles*. 2nd ed. Englewood Cliffs, NJ: Prentice-Hall, 1983.

Bolles, Richard Nelson. *What Color is Your Parachute? A Practical Manual for Job-Hunters & Career Changers*. Berkeley: Ten Speed Press, 1988.

*de Bono, Edward. *Lateral Thinking: Creativity Step by Step.* New York: Harper & Row, 1970.

*Burns, David D. *Feeling Good: The New Mood Therapy.* New York: Penguin, 1981.

Charlesworth, Edward A., and Ronald G. Nathan. *Stress Management: A Comprehensive Guide to Wellness.* New York: Ballantine, 1985.

Crypton, Dr. *Timid Virgins Make Dull Company, and Other Puzzles, Pitfalls, and Paradoxes.* New York: Penguin Books, 1985.

Crystal, John C., and Richard N. Bolles. *Where Do I Go From Here with My Life?* Berkeley: Ten Speed Press, 1974.

Dennis, Marguerite J. *Keys to Financing a College Education.* New York: Barron's Educational Series, 1990.

Duffy, James P. *Cutting College Costs.* New York: Barnes & Noble, 1988.

Ennis, Robert H. "A Concept of Critical Thinking." *Harvard Educational Review.* Vol. 32, No. 1 (Winter, 1962), 82–111.

Falvey, Jack. *What's Next? Career Strategies After 35.* Charlotte, VT: Williamson Publishing, 1987.

*Feder, Bernard. *The Complete Guide to Taking Tests.* Englewood Cliffs, NJ: Prentice-Hall, 1979.

*Figler, Howard E. *Path: A Career Workbook for Liberal Arts Students.* Cranston, RI: The Carroll Press, 1979.

Fowler, Elizabeth M. *The New York Times Career Planner: A Guide to Choosing the Perfect Job from the 101 Best Opportunities of Tomorrow.* New York: Times Books, 1987.

Franken, R. E. *Human Motivation.* Monterey, CA: Brookes/Cole, 1982.

Gardner, Howard. *Art, Mind, and Brain: A Cognitive Approach to Creativity.* New York: Basic Books, 1982.

*Gibaldi, Joseph, and Walter S. Achtert. *MLA Handbook for Writers of Research Papers.* 3d ed. New York: Modern Language Association, 1988.

Gordon, Virginia N. *The Undecided College Student: An Academic and Career Advising Challenge.* Springfield, IL: Charles C Thomas, 1984.

Hanks, Kurt, and Jay A. Parry. *Wake Up Your Creative Genius.* Los Altos, CA: William Kaufmann, 1983.

Higbee, Kenneth L. *Your Memory: How It Works and How to Improve It.* Englewood Cliffs, NJ: Prentice-Hall, 1977.

Hoffman, Elizabeth, and Nancy H. Stafford. *Financial Aid for College Through Scholarships and Loans.* 5th ed. Wellesley Hills, MA: Richards House, 1989.

Holland, John L. *Making Vocational Choices: A Theory of Vocational Personalities and Work Environments.* 2d ed. Englewood Cliffs, NJ: Prentice-Hall, 1985.

Hook, J. N. *How to Take Examinations in College.* New York: Barnes & Noble, 1958.

Houston, J. P. *Motivation.* New York: Macmillan, 1985.

Howard, Darlene V. *Cognitive Psychology: Memory, Language and Thought.* New York: Macmillan, 1983.

Johnson, Linda Lee, "Learning Across the Curriculum with Creative Graphing," *Journal of Reading* (March, 1989), pp. 509–19.

Kesselman-Turkel, Judi and Franklynn Peterson. *Test Taking Strategies*. Chicago: Contemporary Books, 1981.

*Lakein, Alan. *How to Get Control of Your Time and Your Life*. New York: New American Library/Signet, 1973.

*Lester, James D. *Writing Research Papers: A Complete Guide*. 5th ed. Glenview, IL: Scott, Foresman, 1987.

Loehr, James E., and Peter J. McLaughlin. *Mentally Tough: The Principles of Winning at Sports Applied to Winning in Business*. New York: M. Evans, 1986.

Lorayne, Harry, and Jerry Lucas. *The Memory Book*. New York: Ballantine, 1974.

McCay, James T. *The Management of Time*. Englewood Cliffs, NJ: Prentice-Hall, 1959.

McKim, Robert H. *Thinking Visually: A Strategy for Problem Solving*. Belmont: Liftime Learning, 1980.

McWhorter, Kathleen T. 3d ed. *College Reading and Study Skills*. Boston: Little, Brown, 1986.

*Millman, Jason and Walter Pauk. *How to Take Tests*. New York: Mcgraw-Hill, 1969.

Pauk, Walter. *How to Study in College*. 4th ed. Boston: Houghton Mifflin, 1988.

*Perkins, D. N. *The Mind's Best Work*. Cambridge: Harvard University Press, 1981.

*Phifer, Paul. *College Majors and Careers: A Resource Guide for Effective Life Planning*. Garrett Park, MD: Garrett Park Press 1987.

*Polya, George. *Mathematical Discovery: On Understanding, Learning and Teaching Problem Solving*. Combined edition. New York: Wiley, 1981.

Porter, Sylvia. *Your Own Money: Earning It, Spending It, Saving It, and Living on It in Your First Independent Years*. New York: Avon, 1983.

Randolph, W. Alan, and Barry Z. Posner. *Effective Project Planning and Management: Getting the Job Done*. Englewood Cliffs, NJ: Prentice-Hall, 1988.

Rivers, William L., and Susan L. Harrington. *Finding Facts: Writing Across the Curriculum*. 2d ed. Englewood Cliffs, NJ: Prentice-Hall, 1988.

Robinson, Francis P. *Effective Study*. New York: Harper & Bros., 1946.

Sheehan, David V. *The Anxiety Disease*. New York: Bantam, 1983.

Spatt, Brenda. *Writing from Sources*. 2nd ed. New York: St. Martin's, 1987.

Spence, J. T. Ed. *Achievement and Achievement Motives*. New York: Freeman, 1983.

Sternberg, Robert. *The Triarchic Mind: A New Theory of Intelligence*. New York: Penguin, 1988.

*Strunk, William Jr., and E. B. White, *The Elements of Style*. 3d ed. New York: Macmillan, 1979.

Turabian, Kate L. *Student's Guide for Writing College Papers*. 5th ed. Chicago: Chicago University Press, 1987.

van Leunen, Mary-Claire. *A Handbook for Scholars*. New York: Knopf, 1978.

White, Jan V. *Using Charts and Graphs: 1000 Ideas for Visual Persuasion*. New York: R. R. Bowker, 1984.

Wilson, Reid R. *Don't Panic: Taking Control of Anxiety Attacks*. New York: Harper & Row, 1986.

*Zimbardo, Philip G. *Shyness*. New York: Jove, 1978.

Index